Halloween Horror Nights Unofficial: Around the Globe

Christopher Ripley

ISBN: 978-0-9955362-6-5

Author contact: hhnunofficial@gmail.com

To my amazing wife Emily

CONTENTS

"...just think what this would mean, to see the inner workings of the biggest moving picture plant in the wide, wide world. A whole city where everyone is engaged in the making of motion pictures, a fairyland where the craziest things in the world happen. A place to think about and talk about for the rest of your days! See how we blow up bridges, burn down houses, wreck automobiles...see how buildings have to be erected just for a few scenes of one picture and then have to be torn down to make room for something else. See how we have to use the brains God gave us in every conceivable way in order to make the people laugh, cry or sit on the edge of their chairs the world over!"

Carl Laemmle, March 15th, 1915

ACKNOWLEDGMENTS

The Author would like to thank his colleagues for their assistance in producing this book, plus the following:

John Murdy, Patrick Moloney, Michael Burnett, Isaac Cruz, Lisa M DeHaven, Ann Keo, Suzu Trigoi, and Scott Yuken.

Edited by Janet Davies

Assistant Researcher: Drew Baker

HHN Hollywood

Creating the DNA of Horror...

Universal had been the crowned home of horror since the 1920s, when Lon Chaney Snr delighted audiences with *The Hunchback of Notre Dame* and, more successfully, *The Phantom of the Opera* (The set still remained intact on Soundstage 28 on the backlot up until 2015, when it was demolished to make way for park expansion. Most of the surviving set pieces were retained for storage in the studios' expansive prop storage warehouse.) Building on Chaney's success, the mantel was passed to British (by patronage) Boris Karloff and Hungarian-born Bela Lugosi, who terrified audiences with *Frankenstein's Monster, The Mummy* and *Dracula* movies with all sorts of permutations and sequels. Lon Chaney Jnr joined the franchise in the 1940s with *The Wolf Man*, using detailed makeup, like his father before him, to both delight and terrify audiences in equal measures. This legacy of horror continued well into the 1960s when the ever-increasing series of self-reverential comedy parodies (*Abbott and Costello meet the...* series etc.) eventually resulted in the regular succession of hits coming to a slow end. It was the renewed interest of the *Monster Kids* of the late 1960s and the current 1980s generation, who had not grown up with attending the cinema to see these classic monster hits, that allowed for a whole new plethora of monster-related serials, merchandise, books and comics to feed into popular culture, once again putting the Universal Monsters center stage in the cultural lexicon.

Halloween Horror Nights in its current form of mazes, scarezones and shows first appeared in Hollywood in 1986, but the true story of how this event came to be goes back much further. We'll come to the story of that eventful year a little later on but first we must dive into their archive to go back even further. What many people are not aware of is the fact that Universal Studios Hollywood had thrown a variety of Halloween parties many times before 1986, with varying levels of publicity. We won't try to look at every party they have held at Universal

Hollywood, but we will take a peek at the best ones. One of the earliest and most widely publicized Halloween events occurred on October 30th, 1953. Organized by cowboy actor Bob Steele, it was a celebration of Universal's success in shooting six major motion pictures simultaneously on the backlot in the same year. The event was hosted on the backlot and all the cast and crew from these respective movies, along with many of the Studio's long-time crew members, were invited.

Following Alfred Hitchcock's move to Universal in the early 1960s, his legendary persona would be extended to offering a series of Halloween parties, each one more dramatic and macabre than the last. Hitch would stay at Universal until he retired shortly before he died in 1980. During this tenure he occupied Bungalow 5195 (he was also knighted there). The Bungalow was his center of operations where he would plan all of his thrilling showpieces and tirelessly ponder over every last detail of his forthcoming pictures. But he wasn't just planning movies and TV shows; he also used this space to plan his Halloween parties.

Not much is known about his parties. A great deal of hearsay and speculation circled the Lot regarding what went on, but one of his parties in the early 1970s hit the headlines. Maude Chasen, owner of the former Chasen's restaurant in West Hollywood, recounted in 1979 to the *LA Times* that she planned and hosted one of his most memorable Halloween parties in the late 1950s. In unmistakable Hitchcock fashion, the event took over the entire restaurant. There was a select guest list and the event was packed with drama. The party had an organ and as guests entered the dimly lit venue, lugubrious and haunting music was played. Fog machines were placed in the corner and the party's cocktail was 'black water': an unknown combination of spirits served from a coffin. All of this was embellished by a tightly-choreographed fight in the kitchen between actors portraying the waiting staff and the Head Chef. The meal was interrupted with this 'unprofessional' screaming argument bellowing from the kitchen followed by silence; seconds later a bloodied chef with a faux kitchen knife in his back was dragged out into the dining room. The party was so popular that Hitch subsequently relocated most of his parties to the Chasen's venue. Hitch, along with Frank Sinatra, James Stewart, Walt Disney and Groucho Marx would all have their own booths at the restaurant, which was mightily popular with Hollywood's elite. Sadly, the venue closed in 1995 and is now demolished.

Another popular Halloween party that Hitchcock threw was a fully-fledged haunted house. He planned it during the pre-production phase of one of cinema's greatest movies, *Vertigo*. Hitchcock rented a large house in the center of New York and dressed it up using his production company to create the ultimate scare experience. Originally, he wanted to use an 'actual' haunted house but gossip in the press seemed to suggest that his publicist could not locate one for this extravagant party. Apparently, many of the so-called 'haunted' places in New York were either busy, didn't want the attention or did not have sufficient plumbing (one did not have running water or bathrooms). In the end he settled for 7 East 80th Street, and instead of 'actual' ghosts he decided to create his own. The invite list included Hollywood's elite, Studio executives and members of the press. Each invitee received a blood-stained tomb-shaped invite in the post that doubled as a 'menu of horror'. The idea was to turn the lofty town house into a Halloween-themed maze where successful entrants would find a dining room in the final conclusion of the maze. Hitch placed coffin-shaped bars around the lofty townhouse so *"guests could drink up courage before the next room"*. He also placed speakers inside the walls that would emit random groans from passing ghouls throughout the building. Using the dilapidated furnishings, he trailed cobwebs throughout and added dust and footprints to old paintings, antique chandeliers and velvet drapes. He installed special effects such as professional lighting, with one room simulating thunder and lightning. Scareactors and dummies were also deployed. One trick involved placing a simulated corpse in an upstairs bed that looked as though the body had never been discovered. The event's menu read *"Morgue Mussels, Suicide Suzettes, Consommé de Cobra, Vicious-soise, Home-made fried homicide, Corpse Croquette, Gibbeted Giblets, Ghoulish Goulash and 'Fresh-cut Lady Fingers (in season)' with a Ragout of Reptile."* Dessert would be followed by coffee and a slice of a cake that was made to look like a decrepit church and graveyard. *Life Magazine* was the official photographer of the event (photos can be found online), and their photos show various A-list guests dressed in horror-inspired costumes navigating cobweb-filled halls and ghostly rooms.

While Hitch planned his Halloween parties at the Bungalow, further up the Lot Universal were planning their own. In 1972, over the weekend of October 28th and 29th a costume contest for children was held in the Studios. Marketed as 'The Little Monsters Halloween Party', the event encouraged children who had come for the backlot tour to dress as their favorite monsters to gain free admission (so as long as mom or pa was paying for full admission with an adult ticket). Each child was given a token after the tour for a free ice-cream. Every hour, a best-dressed young goblin would then be awarded a prize, the judges being Frankenstein's Monster and the Phantom of the Opera. All the hourly prize winners would receive another voucher for a free ice-cream and would be entered into a grand prize raffle. The winner of the grand prize draw would receive a private viewing in the Universal screening room of the movie of their choice, and dinner in the commissary with 50 of their friends. The vouchers would only be redeemable at Farrell's Ice-cream Parlors and were only awarded to the children under 12 who looked "the most original". All the winners would also be later invited to stand on the Universal Christmas Float in the Hollywood Santa Claus Lane Parade. The Halloween party was very successful and was repeated the following year in 1973. This time slight changes were made; instead of free ice-cream, winners would receive theater passes and the overall winner would win a combination of three prizes: a weekend vacation staying in a lodge in Yosemite National Park, a Halloween makeup makeover to make the winner 'the scariest ghoul in town' and space for them and their family on the aforementioned Christmas parade float.

Hitchcock posing at one of his many Hollywood parties

It was during this time that horror became big business. A baptism of fire from 1960's *Psycho* had led to any number of horror, chiller and thriller pictures going into production. A new wave of more graphic and gory horror was balanced out by a return of the classics, such as the Universal Monsters; the Monster Kids of this time lapped up all things horror and many of the tourist hotspots nationwide sought to profit from this interest by organizing their own unique Halloween festivals. One of the new wave of autumnal festivals began in 1973 at Knott's Farm with *Knott's Scary Farm*. As with Universal, they started off small and appeared for only a few nights. However, the success of their humble event grew and grew, to the point where commentators have said that Knott's is currently the first and longest-running Halloween event to be held at any theme park. Whether they are the largest is debatable, but they can be accredited as being the most long running, as the event has returned each year since 1973 to the present. The ongoing success of the Knott's event can be seen as a catalyst for Universal during these 'dormant' years to revive their event and show Southern California just who the king of Halloween actually is.

A couple of years later in 1975, Universal added a new attraction to the backlot tour just in time for Halloween. This new attraction, named 'Land of a Thousand Faces' (in reference to Lon Chaney's nickname of the 'man of a thousand faces), ran until 1979. It was specifically opened at this time to show that for Halloween fun and games, you "had to" go to Universal Hollywood. The new attraction was a follow up to a former successful make-up show that ran for a number of years previously. Two years before, during 'The Little Monsters Halloween Party', Universal had added makeup tutorials and a behind-the-scenes look at Lucille Ball's former dressing room. It seemed that whether it was Halloween or not, people seemed to be very interested in the art of how ordinary-looking people could be transformed by makeup and prosthetics. The new horror makeup show would seat around 1700 guests and was played around ten times a day, allowing performers to go into more detail about the makeup process. As well as describing the makeup processes of some of cinema's most iconic creations (Lon Chaney's *Phantom Of The Opera, The Incredible Hulk,* and T*he Wizard Of Oz* character The Lion, plus others on a rotation), the show would also pluck worthy volunteers from the audience to have them especially made-over live on stage. Usually this would be a couple of 'lovebirds' who would be transformed into Frankenstein's Monster and his Bride. Once complete, the finale of the show saw the couple placed on a specific prop stage where a flick of electricity and some Hollywood magic would see the couple switched out from a puff of smoke into charred human remains. Towards the end of the show's run, an actor depicting The Hulk would run on stage smashing walls and causing chaos. You can see from the ingredients of this early show how these would later transform into the Horror Makeup shows we know today. Along with the new show for Halloween, Universal offered free face painting to kids who wanted to look like their favorite Universal Monster, and a new addition to the tram tour saw guests enter into a spooky ice-glacier. Celebrity autograph sessions were offered on select days where famous actors from a variety of shows that were in production on the backlot would come up to sign whatever people wanted. You also got the chance to 'spy' on Alfred Hitchcock as he shot his 'latest blockbuster', *Family Plot,* which sadly was his last.

The Land of a Thousand Faces logo from the park map

One of the very first icons for their Halloween events, and some might say the first possible *official* icon, was 'Baby Frankenstein'. As the event was marketed directly towards children, the scary-with-a-small-'s' events were an opportunity for Universal to bring more locals, particularly families, into the studio. 'Baby Frankenstein' or 'Baby Frank' was nearly always on hand for a photo opportunity with his father, Frankenstein's Monster, though most people incorrectly called him just 'Frankenstein'. The duo would appear during the year but most particularly at the Halloween event days (none of which were offered as separate tickets) and would delight and thrill guests in equal measures. Although Frankenstein's Monster is still a mainstay of Universal, Baby Frankenstein appeared only throughout the 1970s and early 80s.

1980 rolled around and the Studio continued to offer makeup tutorials, but this time in connection with the opening of another horror-based attraction: *Castle Dracula*. The Halloween festivities took place every weekend in October and offered extra runs of this new show plus 'Monster Sweepstakes' that were run in partnership with Sprite and Coca-Cola. This was the first time that Universal had partnered with the soda company for such Halloween events, and it is a partnership that continues to this day; the latest HHNs are all sponsored currently by Coke Zero.

Castle Dracula was built on the site of *The Land of a Thousand Faces* and was a more comfortable venue, with enclosed walls and air-conditioning. The 20-minute performance cost $3 million to build at the time and ran up to twelve times daily (a few more on selected October weekends). The now-expanded 2,500-seater venue would actually soft open on Friday 13th June 1980 (yep, Friday 13th!) and instantly became very popular. The show combined practical effects, real actors and animatronics, and a beautifully bedecked entrance foyer housed various recreations of props from the classic Universal Monster movies. Although the show was a retheming of the '*Thousands*' show it still contained the same basic elements of making-up a couple from the audience and a late wall smashing scene with the Incredible Hulk.

The very first Caste Dracula logo from the park map

During the early 1980s Universal had invested in full-time attractions but hadn't really got onto the Halloween gravy-train. Just down the road at Knott's, their *Scary Farm* hard ticketed event had been running since 1973 and had literally sold out every year for nine years running. Not wanting to get too horrific too quickly, they still marketed their Halloween activities towards locals and families and by 1982 they had upped the offerings. Local newspapers and radio stations ran commercials about the re-themed 'Halloween Backlot Tour'. The rethemed tour ran throughout October and included spooky surprises. One such surprise was seeing the long-awaited first sequel to *Psycho* shot almost entirely on the backlot during this time. The Halloween festivities were also tied into another movie franchise and would mark one of the first times that Universal had tied a movie franchise to its Halloween celebrations. The movie was *Halloween III* (a Universal production) and it was released on October 22nd. Various set reconstructions were constructed, along with props from the movie. Kids were encouraged to attend the month-long Halloween party and in return were given free Halloween masks based on characters from the movie. A series of free trick or treat locations were also set up at various locations around the park (sounds like Mickey's Not So Scary!). The main events occurred at weekends in October with especially-created *Halloween III* merchandise available to buy. The events were popular for Universal, but they felt they could do more to directly compete with Knott's; this, however, didn't happen immediately. During the following two years Universal kept their Halloween events to a minimum as backlot expansion and alterations ate into their budgets. By 1985, it seemed many of their local competitors were getting into the Halloween business, and that year Universal half-heartedly sent a couple of their makeup artists to a local mall to demonstrate 'monster makeup effects' to volunteering members of the public. It was after this washout that they knew they had to get into the Halloween business in a bigger way, and they decided to make plans.

1982: "Trying out a new horror experience..."

Since October 26th, 1973, local theme park and Southern California mainstay, *Knott's Berry Farm*, had been running a small Halloween event that had been growing in popularity with local residents. The event, *Knott's Scary Farm*, appointed actor and song-parodist Weird Al Yankovic to become the event's icon in 1981 and the focus of their marketing, with 1980s glamour-puss Elvira taking on the mantle the following year. Soon the event was bursting with guests and quickly sold out.

Upstate Universal Studios' parent company head, Lew Wasserman, had noticed the fleets of guests making their way home early from the park in order to make their way to Knott's Berry. This simply would not do. As early as 1985 plans had been made to create a series of Horror Nights around the traditional Halloween holiday, to try to combat the perceived loss of trade resulting from the popular event held at Knott's Berry. The plans didn't take off in 1985 mostly due to increased studio requirements for shooting. Missing their window of 1985 did not deter the company though. The following year a bold decision was made to enable the event to take priority over any filming for the 1986 Halloween holiday season.

On October 8th 1986, the *Los Angeles Times* reported that the local studio would run 'Horror Nights' where 15,000 'frightniks' could part with $14.95 to attend a specially ticketed event to be run in the evenings after park close. The marketing for the event, which included newspaper adverts and radio commercials (Power 106 FM and others), promised guests the chance to spend an evening with Dracula, the Mummy, the Wolf Man, the Phantom of the Opera and even Norman Bates' dead mom! Over 70 costumed characters would roam the expansive backlot and the studio tram tour would run at night for the first time in Universal's history (it happened first here in 1986 and not in 2015 as some believe!).

A newspaper advert from the time for Knott's Halloween event

A Universal spokesman announced to the local media outlets that the event would run from 7pm to midnight on both October 31st and November 1st, 1986. They advised that the tickets would be sold on a first-come-first-served basis, with a limit on ticket sales of just 7,500 per day. This event would be a one-of-a-kind event utilizing Universal's impressive back catalogue of monster heritage to its full strength.

"We're getting set up to scare up the devil out of people" the spokesman for Universal said, *"so please, do not bring your children."*

The plan for the event was to utilize existing park assets such as the Bates Motel, which had recently enjoyed increased popularity with the summer release of *Psycho 3* that year. *Psycho 2* (1983), which had been released a couple of years before had, at that time, been the longest awaited sequel in film history. The newly formed *Psycho* franchise was drawing on the new wave of 'slasher' and monster movies that were becoming extremely popular. Since creating the format in 1960 with Sir Alfred Hitchcock's original masterpiece, *Psycho*, the niche genre - a combination of a thriller and horror (usually with a knife-toting psychopath in tow) - had gone from strength to strength in the 1970s and 1980s with classics such as *Friday 13th* (1980), *A Nightmare on Elm Street* (1984) and *Halloween* (1978) all proving popular with audiences.

Other popular areas included Courthouse Square, dressed to look as if a killing spree had occurred, and the Court of Miracles, made to look like a peasants' revolt. The Court of Miracles area had actually been used to shoot the original *Dracula* with Bela Lugosi, *The Wolf Man* and most famously *The Hunchback of Notre Dame* and the original *Frankenstein*. This section of the park proved popular with horror film makers as the area was compact, with many small streets representing vague areas of continental Europe. These were all put to good use when passing trams would be confronted by hordes of village folk chasing down the monster of choice for that hour.

The event was humble in its beginnings. The aim was to allow the famous studio tram tour to be run at night for the first time ever, with a new tour guide script focused on the horror and sci-fi sights of the backlot combined with costumed characters jumping out at every turn. Local posters and newspaper adverts promised that:

"They're here. Lurking in the shadows. Hiding behind corners. Stalking dark alleys. Those terrifying monsters who haunted our streets for 60 years have come back... to get you!"

While running the popular tram tour (or *Terror Tram*) and a few select attractions in the main theme park, the park also put on a concert to keep the event relevant and young for its audience. Michigan-based R&B band Ready for the World played at the event each night on stage at the park, performing such hits as *Oh Shelia* and *Love You Down* to delighted park guests. Ready for the World were signed to MCA, the parent company of Universal Studios, and were only too happy to play to local audiences.

Using an MCA-signed musical act, costumes from their own huge costume department, and actors from their own talent agency alongside park operational staff kept costs down in what would be a water test of the local economy to see if such an event would be successful. After the first night, the studio knew they had created a hit.

The event was a huge success. It sold out quickly, due in part to the advent of the ability to call the park and pay over the phone with a credit card. Universal's excellent marketing department quickly distributed posters and radio commercials informing the local communities that the event was sold out but had decided to run one extra day on Sunday November 2nd with a slightly earlier start of 6.30pm. Posters of Jack-o-Lanterns were printed showing the popular holiday icon being destroyed from above by a chainsaw, a symbol that would be used again years later. The posters advised people to book now to avoid disappointment, as otherwise it *"will haunt you forever!"*

However, despite the sell-out of tickets and orderly manner of the guests, the event was soon marred by a very unfortunate tragedy. It was reported in the *LA Times* that late in the evening of November 1st, Paul Rebalde aged 20 of Woodland Hills, who was stationed along the *Terror Tram* route in full zombie makeup, had sadly been killed. He was tasked with sitting within a parked tram along the route with scores of mannequins which all had similar makeup applied, making the guests believe they were all dummies. Rebalde's role was to jump from the parked tram to scare guests who were passing by in another tram.

Rebalde, along with other actors, was one of the theme park attendants who had been asked to work as one of the *Terror Tram's* new cast of over 70 costumed characters that lined the route of the tram. Rebalde had been described in a *LA Times* article as *"a thin, rusty-haired youth who was quick with a smile"*. They said he had worked in the theme park at several jobs.

"He was one of the sweetest kids that worked up here," one fellow employee said. *"He was the kind of guy that always walked around with a smile on his face. Everybody liked him."*

Rebalde was believed to have jumped from his stationary tram at around 8.30pm to scare one of the passing trams when he became trapped between the third and fourth sections of the moving four-part tram. He was likely crushed to death and then sadly dragged some 100 feet. He was pronounced dead by local medics at around 9pm.

An investigation was quickly set up by officers from the Los Angeles County District Attorney's Environmental Crimes and Occupational Safety Division, headed up by John F. Lynch. Joan Bullard, marketing and publicity director for Universal Studios, said *"There was no indication that the tram had a problem or anything like that. The sheriff has told us that it was an unfortunate accident."* She continued, *"The tour's safety record is exemplary and that we (Universal) have never had an incident like this in our 22-year history. We're all very sad."*

The *Terror Tram* was abandoned for the rest of the night and additional safety measures for the final extra night were put into place to protect both actors and guests. Essentially, this meant that no actors were allowed to 'jump or attack' any moving trams and that only stationary trams would be allowed for scaring purposes.

Rebalde had worked in the merchandising department for the Studios since the beginning of May 1986. His role was defined by a spokesman for the park as being "*very broad,*" but several studio workers interviewed at the time said that Rebalde's job included selling a variety of merchandise to park guests and serving as an assistant manager of a stall that sold film near the famous front gates of the park.

A combination of expenditure required for park refurbishments and backlot availability due to feature film and television requirements, plus the tragic consequences that occurred on November 1st, led to the event being discontinued for the foreseeable future. The recent addition of *King Kong* to the tram tour required further expenditure for maintenance purposes and various popular stage shows were being overhauled. The *A-Team* stunt show was swopped out for a *Miami Vice* themed show; this coincided with a huge increase in shooting space required for TV shows such as *Murder She Wrote* and *Matlock.* MCA was keen for Universal Studios to be the new home of televisual serials, particularly in the niche genre of 'afternoon murder mystery', something that could be readily and repetitively syndicated (still to this day even).

Soon on the horizon MCA had a planned expansion for more child-friendly areas of the park, including *Fievel's Playland.* Seeking to distance its image of a park that was built mostly for adults and teens, the park's image of horror was downplayed for some years in part due to the tragic events that had occurred but also in response to an ever-growing *Disneyland* which was drawing ever larger crowds. *Halloween Horror Nights* or *Horror Nights* (as it was dubbed at the time) was not expected to return; indeed, it simply did not fit with the park's revised family spirit.

Reflecting on the event, some insiders said the scheme was too costly for the little financial return it made. Others pointed to the fact that policing an event on a huge studio backlot such as this was near impossible. Whatever the true reason, in 1987 no Halloween events took place and in 1988 they were limited to just one weekend in October with various meet and greets, featuring their famous monsters. The monsters were also relegated to just handing out discount coupons at local malls to attract locals to the park over the festive period.

Frankenstein's Monster meeting a fan in 1987

By 1990 the new Florida edition of Universal Studios was about to dip its toe into the Halloween business but Universal Hollywood was still reluctant. Park redevelopment and shooting schedules ensured that very few resources could be committed to any company business that wasn't a reliable source of revenue. A complete coincidence in the horror business did happen in this low point of a year, though. Universal hosted the inaugural 'Horror Hall of Fame'; an annual Oscars-style awards show hosted by Robert Englund (aka *Freddy Krueger*) which honored the best horror films, television series, actors, producers and special-effects designers from across the industry. The event is noteworthy as it must have been witnessed by many of the folks that would later produce HHN in that it had some very similar ingredients to the event we know and love. For example, it had a foul-mouthed audience interacting section hosted by Chucky (*Child's Play*); the *Psycho* house and Bates Motel were used to introduce the awards; and it even had portions of the show where The Cryptkeeper would interrupt proceedings to give his own spin on the horror genre. All of these were elements of the Hollywood event that would show up time and again. The show would also feature many special previews including one very special section about the upcoming *Psycho IV: The Beginning.* The audience learnt how it was being exclusively and entirely shot in Universal's new production facility and theme park in Orlando, Florida, which acted as a kind of advertisement for the new fledgling park. The award show would continue for a further two years before it was cancelled.

1991 rolled around, and as anticipation continued to grow for the successful Halloween event that had been demonstrated in Florida, it felt that finally Hollywood should return to the fray and host their own event. Tentative plans were drawn up, but were put on hold for 1991. These same plans, however, were finally realized in 1992.

1992 to 1996: "Reviving the horror..."

Universal decided that 1992 would be the year to revive the Halloween industry. Spurred on by the success of the Florida version, executives used ideas and plans from the past few years to create their own version of *Halloween Horror Nights*. The announcement that Universal would go into direct competition with their neighbor, Knott's, sent shockwaves through the local tourism industry.

The *LA Times* wrote:

"Halloween has traditionally been the domain of Knott's Berry Farm, which has staged "Knott's Scary Farm" for more than a decade. But now the

Universal Studio tour is calling on its own goon squad—Frankenstein, Dracula, and the Phantom of the Opera—to muscle in on the action."

The plan was to utilize as much of the park as possible, bring in extra security to manage the event, and bring about a true party atmosphere. It would also capitalize on proceedings by selling the party as a separate hard ticketed event to make the public believe it was as exclusive as it would be outrageously scary. In Florida, as with Knott's, they built houses or (as many Hollywood HHN fans would call them) 'mazes'. Hollywood knew that mazes could be built relatively cost-effectively and they would eat up crowds, they also knew they could control the crowds better if they had special attractions such as these. The mazes would be built in the parking structures. Two mazes side-by-side were entitled *Maze of Maniacs* – *"Take a turn for the worse in this wicked, winding asylum of murders and misfits"* and *Nightmare Alley* – *"A house of horror where movie monsters and maniacs invite you in for a bite".*

The maze would be themed to an old haunted film vault where the horrific creations of cinema's past would come to life within their imprisonment and recreate some of their famous scenes. The special effect wizards working for Universal on a number of productions were drafted in to work some of the scenes in this maze.

It is also worth noting that it is commonly understood that HHN Hollywood's first maze that went into production was *Maze of Maniacs* and this is probably where the name 'maze' came from in reference to these haunted houses. Orlando has traditional preferred the term 'house' and Hollywood has used the term 'maze'.

The mazes would be an assortment of murderers and maniacs sourced mostly from cinema and television (Universal was less strict with external IPs back in those days). Scenes of torture, peril, disease and an asylum were depicted in the mazes. Props from Universal's prop warehouse (the largest in the country) were used to fill the mazes, which were built by television crews between productions over the summer months. By September 14th, Universal began to run adverts in local newspapers inviting youngsters and performers to audition for their 'Scream Academy' and earn a position as a 'scareactor' (a term borrowed from Orlando). Thousands descended onto the auditions to gain their role as the next Hellraiser or Jason Voorhees (Frankenstein's Monster, Dracula or even Baby Frankenstein were considered too tame for this horror event!), with 300 roles on offer. Along with the actors, props and sets, the mazes (as well as the *Terror Tram*) would include 4,000 gallons of fake blood, 2,000 gallons of green slime and 1,000 trained rats – Universal was not pulling any punches here!

As just mentioned, the daytime tram tour would return at night rethemed as '*The Terror Tram*'. It was the first time it has been reutilized at night following the accident in 1986. The tram would feature a number of horror surprises, all of which could be swopped out during the day so as to not affect the daytime family guests. Beetlejuice would be your guide for the evening and he would escort you through a more murderous looking Bates Motel, a mad scientist's lair, a tram car wreck and past a vampire's feeding ground. The attacks on the tram were also scaled back, with all scareactors being strictly told to keep back from a moving tram to within at least 5ft, in order to avoid a repeat of the tragic accident of 1986.

Universal wanted to be different from their competitor; they wanted to use their film making know-how to set them apart. Their expertise in horror - and a solid budget (rumored to have been $2 million) - was going to show California that Universal knew Halloween. The then Studio General Manager, Terry Winnick, explained: *"We have the use of all our motion picture techniques. All the fires, smoke and explosions and re-creations of great scenes from the movies – that kind of stuff is different from putting up cobwebs and just having monsters jumping out of the fog."* The result of this hard work and dedication would see the whole 425-acre studio being completely re-themed for the festivities. Priced slightly higher than Knott's at $27 (Knott's was $25), the event would run on October 22nd, 23rd, 24th, 29th, 30th and 31st.

Other attractions included *Chucky "In-Your-Face" Insults* which was a much pumped-up version of his segments from the Horror Hall of Fame Awards. The internationally renowned magicians (and now huge HHN lovers), Penn and Teller also performed their 45-minute show four times every night in a packed Star Trek Theatre. The show was entitled '*The Bad Boys of Magic*' and was undertaken in their unique, gross-out style of magic. It featured all sorts of mind bending tricks, with the 'needle and thread' swallowing trick, fire eating and even sawing a woman in half only for the trick 'to go wrong' and for fake blood to be splattered around the stage. Whereas Orlando used their Wild West Show to try a new show called *Bill and Ted's Excellent Halloween Adventure*, Hollywood decided to re-theme theirs to *The Wild, Wild, Wild Witch Hunt* which, like the Orlando version, used the same western sets, the same actors and just re-tweaked the story (yes, the original Bill and Ted in Orlando were stunt performers!). *The Fright Forum* and *Mutation Pit* were walk-through shows that appeared to trick guests into thinking they were about to fall into a pit of boiling oil.

The famous mentalist Glenn Falkenstein was drafted into proceedings with *The Amazing Falkenstein Show* performing four shows per night. Falkenstein was a regular at Universal as he hosted a weekly radio show from one of their backlot studios. His HHN shows would include reading people's minds to reveal "dark secrets" and predicting their futures, often with a joke that their future was grim "*as they were about to enter one of Universal's haunted mazes!*". *The Tower of Torture* was a sideshow that played continuously throughout the night. Acts included the Glass Walker – a professional strolling barefoot on a bed of nails and broken glass; the Serpent Sorceress - a fire-breathing Lady Lucifer and her two boa constrictors who "*would dance you to death in the Tango of Torture*"; and the Saber Eater – a sword swallower removing impossibly large swords from his throat. *The Zombie Spooktacular* would also take place and was another stunt show intermixed with saving the world from brain eating zombies. Think *The Walking Dead* meets a water-based stunt show.

A familiar name to many of us was the *Carnival of Carnage* show, that ran continuously through the night. The show featured an assortment of carnival-type misfits who performed a number of gross-out features through the night (nails through tongues and the like). *Ghoulia Wild's Roadside Cuisine* was a small show that ran six times per night and was basically another gross-out show that featured a mad cook providing dishes made from mostly roadkill and cockroaches. A run-over dead hitchhiker was also used to make a very special pie and the front row were guaranteed to get splattered with the contents of her larder. *The Death Globe* was presented four times per night and was billed as "*A devilish spectacle of stunts even Lucifer wouldn't try*", very much in the style of the motorbike stunt shows that use a metal globe to cycle within. *The Living Deadheads Review* was a musical trio that performed ghoulish hits from the last few decades. This show, along with *Burn and Bury Swap Meet, Country Music at the City Express,* and *The Voodoo Gurus* were deemed as the four attractions that the scaredy-cats amongst us could attend without the fear of a zombie breathing down your neck. *Burn and Bury Swap Meet* were a comedy duo, *Country Music at the City Express* was housed in the Victoria Station and played hits from the country western music scene, and *The Voodoo Gurus* were a Caribbean-style reggae band. *Club Fright* was also offered throughout the night; a happening dance party that grew more popular as the nights wore on. Likewise, *Studio Center Salsa* was performed at select hours each night, featuring an array of different Latin dancers garbed in reminiscently styled 'Day of the Dead' attire.

The *Backdraft* portion of the Tram Tour stayed open, *Beetlejuice's Graveyard Revue* performed five times nightly (when he wasn't hosting the tram tour obviously!) and for reasons unknown, the *E.T Adventure* which has opened the summer of the previous year was also open. Interestingly, Universal also promised the crowds in a publicity stunt that Guest Services would also be staffed with a number of professionally trained psychologists just in case guests were traumatized by the event.

Another event that coincided with the festivities was *Halloween Jam at Universal Studios Live,* which was presented by Woody Harrelson and Elvira on NBC at 11.30pm on October 23rd. The show toured the event and featured additional acts such as AC-DC, the Black Crowes and Ozzy Osbourne. The 90-minute show saw presenters attempt the haunted mazes, an interview with Beetlejuice and even a special performance by Penn and Teller.

The demand for tickets to the newly -devised *Halloween Horror Nights* was huge! Other than the first night, the event quickly sold out with security teams having to turn crowds away most nights. Some 16,000 guests came to the event during its run. Trespassing was alleged to have occurred and the event's management were accused of being 'overwhelmed' by the size of the event by many local commentators. Universal wanted to test the water and get in on the Halloween industry action but instead the event in 1992 became hard to manage and guests complained that they literally couldn't see everything they wanted (it's often you heard that sort of complaint!). Universal needed to learn lessons before they offered the event again, but in the meantime at least they praised the hard work that was done.

"It was extremely successful for us," Joan Bullard of Universal said of the venture to the *LA Times. "The entertainment was well received. We found that guests actually wanted more mazes. Next year we will have more entertainment."*

There definitely wouldn't be more entertainment in the following year, though, as while Universal worked out how to better manage the event they shelved it. From 1993 to 1995, Halloween was 'dead' at Universal, whilst in Orlando the event began to flourish. Orlando's better laid out and more secure theme park meant that they could control the crowds better. Hollywood would put on the *Halloween Jam II* in 1993 (which also went live to Orlando during the broadcast) and in 1995 they had a monster makeup contest and trick or treating in their fairly new City Walk area. As the Studios transformed from a studio that had a few rides to a studio with a resort destination attached to it, they took the time to plan their next Halloween venture with greater consideration.

Many people overlook this, but *Halloween Horror Nights* unofficially came back to Hollywood in 1996 (countless other websites will tell you it was 1997 but they are wrong – kind of). Not wanting to repeat the sprawling and uncontrolled event of 1992, they settled on a low-key event on selected nights and concentrated mostly on the City Walk area. They still demanded separate tickets, though! This time a haunted house would be built in the parking garages (like they did in 1992) but instead of two it was just one, bigger version. The change in tack here was to attract the people who came to the previous year's festivities on City Walk (which were mostly families) but also to cater to the teenagers and young adults that rammed the Studios in 1992.

The solution? Well it was a unique one that hasn't been tried since. An article appeared in the *Santa Cruz Sentinel*.

"Universal Studios Hollywood is operating the Chamber of Chills on Universal Citywalk nightly through Halloween. The attraction, a Hollywood version of a haunted house features Universal monster characters as well as newer, more icky creepers like chainsaw-wielding maniacs. Parents take note: a gentler version of the experience, the Children's Chamber of Chills, with clowns and non-horrific effects, is open on Friday, Saturday and Sunday afternoons."

To cater to both camps, they ran a gentle version during the day with the classic Universal Monsters and a more horrific adult version in the evenings. The adult version was actually billed as "*The Scariest Haunted House in North America.*" The other unique concept for the maze that was reportedly signed off by Ron Howard himself was to step away from the 'conga-lines' of the past and take guests on a guided tour with 'ghost-hosts'.

Kristen Kress was an actress drafted in by Universal to portray Linda Blair's character from *The Exorcist*. She recalls a milder tack was taken during the day and then at night things got a whole lot grosser, *"I was so young, I barely remember! I had a levitating body, and had to throw up regularly on a Priest every single night!"*

One of the main problems of the 1992 event (security aside) was that the event was too expensive to run. Universal knew that if they wanted to put on a decent event in 1996 they needed to reach out to industry partners and get other stakeholders involved in the production. Many companies were initially interested but eventually Universal signed a contract with merchandise producer Spencer Gifts and Ron Howard's production company Imagine Entertainment.

Between the three of them they wanted to create a smaller scale event for the day time and then morph it into a "scarier than hell" event in the evenings.

The park would not be open in the evenings and a ticket to the haunted house also admitted guests to the festivities and games planned in City Walk. The maze was constructed on the first floor of the main parking structure nearest to City Walk, so it was only a short trip away. Whereas Knott's was becoming bigger and grander at each event, with tickets now as high as $29.95 per person, Universal was becoming more modest and scaling back to just $8. Dick Costello was head of MCA's marketing at the time and said the change in strategy wasn't just about control but it was also Universal's wish that the maze would be so good that you'd want to come to see it again and again. He argued to the press that although Knott's offerings were very good, could their style and cost be 'one and done'? Universal also launched the maze ready for opening on September 13th (yes that was a Friday too!) which enabled people to see it first hand on opening and then come back again during the more traditional Halloween period. They also had a 'Spooky Sunday' add-on event that was just for children to trick or treat, with a treasure hunt-styled map route around City Walk.

The logo for the new maze (later reused in Orlando for their HHN)

While Imagine Entertainment designed and built the maze, Spencer designed the gift shop and sited it right next to the exit of the maze, filling it to the brim with all kinds of horror-related merchandise. From noon to 5 pm, Fridays through Sundays, the maze featured clowns, fairies and "gentle spirits" who reflected the lighter side of the fright season. But from 6pm onwards, Universal strictly recommended that the maze was so terrifying that nobody under the age of 12 should enter. From until 2am Mondays through Sundays to October 31st, the maze turned sinister, with live monsters including Frankenstein, Dracula, the Wolfman and a legion of undead ghouls. Universal were attempting to create 'the world's most frightening live-action haunted house ever.' And from the reports we've seen, they succeeded!

The maze had 9 corridors, 11 main rooms, was 6480 square-foot in size and was staffed with over 130 scareactors. The centerpiece was the elevating bed complete with sick sequence from *The Exorcist.* Crowds were appalled and terrified by the scene. Other rooms included:

- 'The Trophy Room' which was a homage to the *Texas Chain Saw* movies
- 'Pumpkin Patch' where cute jack-o-lanterns were lit up, while a repetitive Halloween jingle was played before a tall scarecrow burst out of a shed with a running chainsaw
- 'Reflection Room' where mirrors were used to reflect a waiting wolfman scareactor, before the lights went out and the actor was standing in front of the guests
- 'Pitch-black Room' where the walls were sticky and SIF (stuff in face) were hanging everywhere
- 'Jail Room' where a Michael Myers lookalike would jump out at guests *and*
- the 'Execution Room' where a lifelike dummy would simulate being electrocuted.

The classic monsters drew guests into the maze and then the more modern horrors sent them screaming from it. The finale of the maze was an ordinary-looking living room that, to unsuspecting guests, quickly turned into a nightmare with Freddy Kruger jumping out from behind a false wall.

Leonard Pickel was drafted in by Ron Howard to work as a consultant for the design process of the Chamber. He later recounted to *Colorado Springs Independent* that on completion the maze was scary but that he felt that the merchandise tie-ins lessened the impact of the scares he wanted to achieve. Because of this, the project was, in his mind, 'a fail'. He said, *"[People say] 'It's just a haunted house? How hard can it be?' Howard expected patrons to readily context-shift between mall shopping and a 'date night' attraction in order to draw an audience. Pairing patrons with a guide slowed groups down, increasing wait times and, by introducing a friendly presence, making the attraction less scary."*

The combination of reportedly overly merchandising the event and having this system of guided tours rather than a continuous line meant that the maze backed up at the exit and huge queues of people built up. Guests were intermittently taken into the maze every ten minutes or so with tour guides. This meant that the line for the maze would consistently be over a three hour wait after 9pm. This, combined with the store at the end of the maze, meant that at times, guests were held up in T*he Exorcist* and *Freddy* rooms while people worked through the store buying up horror merch. Pickel recounted that the ideas were right, but that they were just not executed in quite the right way.

The other issue might have been that the haunted house was replicated too fast and was built as one of many across the US. Twelve of these *Chamber of Chills* were built at the same time across various cities in the US, all opening for Halloween 1996, with some staying opening until January 1997. Outside of Hollywood, they were known officially as *Universal Studios' Chamber of Chills* and were located in 12 different sites across the US, including: Kentucky, Indiana, Minnesota, Pennsylvania (Pittsburgh and Philadelphia) and Massachusetts. All were identical, and all had the same 11 rooms and 130 scareactors with the finale gift shop. On average, it would take each party of 8 guests around 15 to 20 minutes to go through each 6,480 square-foot maze. Each location, including the Hollywood version was built and run by outside contractors.

The lessoned learned from the previous decade showed Universal that they could pull off some great Halloween experiences. They were starting to work out exactly what did and didn't work; though more could always be learnt. The one shining reality within the confusion of both events of 1992 and 1996 was that there was a huge demand for Halloween events! And because of this Universal were about to dive straight back into the market...

1997: "The Cryptkeeper cometh"

Universal planned two events for 1997: *Halloween Horror Nights* and *The Halloween Festival for Kids*. The mazes would be moved into the park on a separate hard ticket and would be for teenagers and older, while the children's activities would be restricted to City Walk. The latter event came from the 'Spooky Sundays' that were held in 1996 which were almost as popular as the maze of that year. Lauren Schwartz, Universal's then event manager, told the *LA Times* *"It was very successful, and that told us there's a huge need for children's Halloween activities. One of the more attractive features is that the festival is free. And it has transformed a sandy area across from the Hard Rock Cafe on City Walk into a festive Halloween headquarters decorated with orange and black balloons. The approximately 2,500-square-foot patch is called Light House Beach, and every Saturday and Sunday this month there will be live entertainment, cookie decorating, arts and crafts, and face painting. The opening act Saturday and Sunday consists of three performers called the Scared Silly Singers. On October 18th it will be singer Lori Richards; October 19th, singer Bob Harrison. Twinkles the Friendly Witch will close the festival with performances October 25th and 26th. All of the acts will include interaction with the young audience. They're very fun to watch, even for adults!"*

While the kids were taken care of, the teens and everyone else were in for an impressive mix of horror and party. The sprawling heap of sideshow after sideshow of 1992 was replaced with 4 mazes and 6 shows. Everything would be planned by a small team of just six Universal employees led by longtime Universal employee Cory Asrilant. He said at the time, *"They brought me in in December. For the first three months we built a creative team of designers, effects people, lighting guys, makeup artists, other kinds of specialists, to come up with the scariest most-intense experience available. We sat down and drew pictures, drafted ideas and concepts, wrote some creative treatments, then proposed it to the company. Basically, we had lots of meetings and received evaluations from different company executives and we convinced to need to do this."* It's hard to believe but if it wasn't for Asrilant and a bunch of other dedicated horror genre fans the whole event at Hollywood might never have come back.

The ticket numbers were restricted and pre-sold, extra security was brought in and all alcohol sales were strictly controlled to wristbands only (much to the annoyance of anyone who looked more than 30 years old). Running from the beginning of October on 12 selected nights (mostly weekends), the event's planning process started as early as January. More managers were brought in, with an impressive team of 350 scareactors, 700 members of operations and technicians, 40 stunt performers and a whole hoard of security personnel. Ticket sales and auditions would both begin in August of that year. Universal knew what had gone wrong before and this time they were going to ensure the event was a huge success. By bringing more staff in from their own production houses, they knew more 'movie magic' could be deployed to give them the edge over their haunt competitors.

"We're doing mazes that bring the magic of the movies to life around you," said Norm Kahn, then vice president of Universal Studios Hollywood. *"You'll walk into a room and we will re-create a scene from a movie with the main character. Rather than watching or explaining a character, we are taking the mazes to the next level and putting you in the movie."*

If Universal Orlando at the time was the place where you could 'ride the movies', Universal Hollywood's Halloween Horror Nights were going to be the place where you 'got scared from the movies'. The first maze to be constructed was *The Cryptkeeper's Film Vault* and it certainly produced the longest lines of all the mazes of that year. It was a combination of great scare scenes from an assortment of recent horror movies. One scareactor told us, *"It was one the best they ever made and so cool! I was a swing actor for the cast so I got to fill in the empty positions for the night (if someone got sick or were absent). Back then the maze walls were standard black painted plywood without much set decoration, nothing like it is now. My favorite scenes that I worked were 'The thing' (breaking out of the ice), 'I Know What You Did Last Summer (or some killer on a bridge with fog and a hook), an 'Evil Dead' scene where a Deadite creature runs out from a spraying fridge, Freddy's basement and furnace scene (I played a victim most nights), and 'Psycho' (Norman Bates as Mother with a knife).*

Operationally the maze, as with many of the others, was well organized with various crews there throughout the night. It was also the first time the technique of having 'fake victims' was used. She continued, *"If I wasn't filling in for a missing person, the lead had me dress as a victim and jump in line with the guests and the cast could pull me out of the line and interact with me. Freddy would always pull me out, every single time. There was a weird plexi-glass room with bad house music, fog, and club lights that the victims would congregate inside and slam against the glass when guests would walk by, never got that scene but it was so cleverly done. There was no makeup team back then, each cast member would get a makeup box with your name on it and we would do our own makeup, which was pretty much black eyes. I would make an edible blood concoction out of peanut butter and give it to the other victims, everything smelled like peanut butter by the end of the night, especially the plexi-glass room. Our green room/break area was the back part of the men's locker room when it used to be a separate room, (across from the employee cafeteria) you can still see the sidewalk going up to the side door of the locker room, which used to be front glass doors. There weren't many rules back then, a lot more gung-ho where scaring the guests witless was always the prime objective!"*

Freddy, Jason and Myers were all in there doing their unmistakable horror best to scare the hell out of guests. One of the more memorable scenes was the bathroom scene from *Scream* where guests had to squeeze down a corridor filled with toilet cubicle doors but not knowing which door had Ghostface hidden within. One guest at the time said of the scene *"I think I need to use the restroom after being in that restroom scene!"* The maze was also 'bookended' at the start and finish with puppets from the old Cryptkeeper himself. Worked off-stage by four hidden technicians, the puppets would speak a recorded dialogue by the original actor to play the character. They would introduce the scares and at the end provide typical snarky comments before giving that unmistakable howling laugh as guests ran out the door being chased by Ghostface. We can appreciate why this perhaps had the longest lines!

A popular scene from the previous year's *Chamber of Chills* was a 'live execution' scene where a mannequin dummy with some moving parts appears to give the illusion of a man dying by being hit with thousands of volts of electricity. The scene was so popular that they reworked it and placed it within the Cryptkeeper's maze. The attention to detail was astounding and started a new *Halloween Horror Nights* tradition.

"With the lighting, the sounds and the smells, we really wanted to touch all the senses," said Cory Asrilant, *Halloween Horror Nights* production manager to the *LA Times.*

The scene was inspired by Wes Craven's *Shocker* which was a Universal picture and enabled them to draft in some of the original production crew to create this live, special effect. The effect was so successful that some guests were known to vomit. The use of mechanically pumped-in smell technology contributed to the effect on guests. *"I don't know where they found the chemical, but there is some chemical out there that smells like burning flesh and we used it to the max."* Asrilant said.

The same Cryptkeeper scareactor from earlier told us about how scary the maze would be, with literally every room giving nearly every guest a big scare, *"'The Thing' gave some of the biggest scares, the costume was pretty gross and I sweated through the entire thing. Whenever I would break through the ice the sweat in the mask and arms would pool in the bottom of the mask until I would turn my head or arms, and it would just come dripping out, people say that and their eyes would just get huge, I would get pretty close to the guests and they would freak out and back up into the set behind, people would just scream 'nah nah nah' or 'that's messed up'. I'm sure I stunk pretty bad too. People just thought I would be staying behind the ice and when I would come around, stretched face with tentacle hands, sweat pouring out they would just run away. I loved that room and I loved that maze."* And love it the people did, with it always having the longest lines of any maze that year.

Next up was the *Classic Monster Maze* which was located right next to *The Back to the Future* ride, which had only just opened that previous summer (it was also open for this HHN too). Guests started off in an old, decrepit theater which was showing reels of old black and white monster movies. As guests walk down the aisle they enter the screen and literally into some of the most famous scenes from horror history. The whole maze was presented in a novel manner in that every room from the cinema screen was in full black and white. It was a technique that required a great deal of planning and was not as easy to achieve as you might think.

"When you're not used to being in a black-and-white world, the lighting can really play tricks with your mind," Asrilant said.

All the classic monsters were represented. One of the memorable for guests was a 6ft 5ins tall Frankenstein's Monster who would hold up the lines of people inside the house by blocking their path and growling at unsuspecting guests. The maze was squeezed into this space and was not overly long. Once most guests had been through the maze they joined *The Back to the Future* ride queue which was near the exit.

Area 51 was the next maze in the lineup this year and would take guests away from classic horrors and smack them down into the sub-genre world of science-fiction horror. The maze is designed as a secret military site in the Nevada desert. The maze starts gently with the concept that the US government has finally decided to reveal a peaceable alien spaceship to the public. What could go wrong? As you might suspect, things go awry, leading to a medical containment holding room, an alien autopsy and an alien morgue complete with real refrigeration. Nods to popular science-fiction TV shows were seen throughout, with a heavy nod towards *The X-Files* and other 'found footage' shows thought to show extraterrestrial encounters.

The final maze was *Creature from the Black Lagoon's Monsterquarium* which was presented in the *WaterWorld* theater. The premise was that you were taken into a haunted aquarium where some of the world's most diabolical creatures have been collected for your viewing pleasure. The only problem is that they have broken free and are running amok within the facility. Some actual real tanks of water were used and others just fabricated the look of underwater scenes.

Production designers who had worked on older movies were drafted in to create some of the scares, including a moving giant squid and various flying devil fishes. Inside the tanks, haunting mermaids swam and sang various melodies which used actual scareactors. Meanwhile the host of the maze, the Creature, swam inside the main tank and would splash unsuspecting guests – many people exited this maze sopping wet!

Lisa M DeHaven who worked as an assistant to the makeup designer recalled, *"When you walked inside, you knew you were in for a treat as guests were greeted by your master of ceremonies – this strange looking creature who sort of does this nightclub standup routine for you as you're waiting in line. The floor was all wet and jet would periodically spray guests. You enter into the area where all this seaweed looking SIF is hanging down from the walls and you have to find your way out of it to get to the main viewing area, of course there's the Creature' lurking in there too! The Creature would grab at you if you're not paying attention! As it was built in the 'Waterworld' venue so all of the strange sea monsters were around inside the water area, on the edge, in different cages or in display areas. It was brilliant to see as I have no idea how they built these wonderful props. I got to go through this maze tons and tons of times because I was in charge of a lot of the masks for that maze. It never got old and it was as scary from day one as it was at the end of the run!"*

A fine roster of shows was presented that year. *The Circus of Horrors* was a freak-show where instead of using scareactors, Universal actually recruited professional freaks to perform. Various acts included a guy who could stick pins through his cheek, a man who could lay on a whole bed of balloon-popping nails while a member of his team walks across his torso, and a woman who could eat whole lightbulbs. Universal felt that drafting in professionals to gross out the crowds would really 'freak' them out.

"This is real stuff and it's really gruesome. Some of them I couldn't even watch," Asrilant said. *"And I had to audition all of them!"*

Another show that shocked audiences for entirely different reasons was *Chucky's Insult Emporium* which had been resurrected from 1992. The unmistakable foul-mouthed doll was again brought back to goad and provoke audiences for another year. Three smaller sideshows were also offered. These included: *Boogie Knights, March of the Zombies* and the *Creepy Animal Show. T*he latter was a jazzed-up horror version of the daytime show, along with *Beetlejuice's Rockin' Graveyard Revue* which was played out during HHN from the daytime too. The final show that just happened to be borrowed from Universal Orlando was *Bill and Ted's Halloween Adventure.* The show in Orlando was wildly popular and was onto its sixth edition when Hollywood began putting it into their HHN. The show's script was unique to Hollywood and not copied. It centered around the premise of trying to 'save TV' from the evil 'Cyberspace Witch'. As with the east coast version, lots of popular culture and political satire were intertwined with the bodacious duo trying to save the world. This was all topped off with a number of dance routines and some exceptionally great pyrotechnic effects.

Rides that were open this year were the *Jurassic Park The Ride, E.T Adventure, Back to The Future: The Ride* and *T-2 3-D: Battle Across Time.*

As with previous years there were a few areas that needed to change. One of the biggest reasons that the Cryptkeeper's maze was so popular was that the other three mazes were considerably shorter (though it did have the best scares!). In an effort to reduce line lengths, Universal employed a new idea of mirroring the mazes so that two lines of people could walk through identical pairs of rooms with the same actors in each. Unfortunately, due to lack of space the idea backfired as the mazes were just too short. The Cryptkeeper, whose maze didn't have this design, proved to be the most popular, with people preferring to wait longer for a longer maze. The idea would never be employed again.

1998: Halloween Horror Nights II - Primal Scream

In 1998 the event followed the fairly successful pattern of its previous year. Many of the houses were slightly re-themed and relaid, the duo experience lines were scrapped, and instead additional rooms were added where possible. The sci-fi maze was renamed *Alien Assault* (the tongue-in-cheek tagline read *"You'll be abducted by the extraterrestrials and travel deep inside a spaceship to experience inhuman terror that would make Mulder and Scully weep!"*), the classic monsters came back with *Classic Creatures Features* and the good old Cryptkeeper returned with *The Crypt Keeper's Screaming Room*. The Creature's weird and watery maze was scrapped due to the length of time it took to strike (close out) every night in order to allow the *WaterWorld* Show to run each day. Wanting to keep the number of mazes the same as 1997, they decided to change the location to enable a larger maze to be built. Reaching out to the horror industry they entrusted *Candyman* and *Hellraiser* creator Clive Barker to come up with a suitably demented addition to the event. That maze was *Clive Barker's FREAKZ Maze*.

Whereas with *Chamber of Chills* in 1996 they enlisted Ron Howard who then brought in a team of people to design the maze, Barker wanted to design every last detail himself. Taking over an entire soundstage, Barker scripted, storyboarded, sound tested, designed the makeup, costume designed and even helped score the music for the maze. He created a character by the name of General Santiago who would guide the guests through the 12-roomed maze. Inside, an assortment of 35 professional freaks and special effects were designed to scare and assault the senses of the visiting public. Doubled headed freaks, a woman giving birth to a live alien and one even pretending to eat a living chicken were hidden with the maze's layout. Santiago would be revealed at the villain of the piece, with hero Tamara turning out to be the person trying to escape this hellish nightmare brought to life.

The maze was designed to be a 'living movie' and Barker was the master of ceremonies directing every scare to get every last scream out of every guest. In a press release at the time Baker said, *"Audiences have become accustomed to experiencing images of extreme intensity and violence, so we've had to go in a more dramatic and unique direction to create this environment at Universal Studios. I intend to take away the audience's sense of control, take away their zone of comfort. In 'Freakz', every corner is loaded with something that will make their adrenaline rush, make their palms sweat, truly put them in a state of fear. My work in [theatre] has left me with an appreciation of things that can be done in a 'live' medium that simply cannot be done in movies. In 'Freakz', there will be the dread of physical contact, the chance that this thing is going to touch you. There will be the sense that these creatures will be coming at you from all angles. Although the audience will have the choice of where to look, they won't be able to simply avert their eyes from the screen as they do in the movies. An important element of their safety net will be removed. It promises to be a far more physical experience than the cinema affords."*

Norm Kahn, then Universal vice president of entertainment said, *"About 15 minutes into the meeting with Clive I knew we had the right person, he understands how to build horror and tension. Freakz is an assortment of horrific oddities that Clive has gathered from around the world."*

The shows seemed to follow the format of the mazes, with some being rethemed and others being brand new. *The Ultimate Tribute to KISS* by cover band Black Diamond (who apparently are still touring) was one of the new shows. They pushed out all the greatest hits from KISS and it was rumored that KISS front man Gene Simmons was actually in the crowd on some nights. Simmons is apparently a huge *Halloween Horror Nights* fan. Another new show was *SlaughterWorld* which used the now empty *WaterWorld* stage to host a show that was similar in quality to the daytime show but with a more death-defying edge. Returning too was the *Carnival of Carnage*, albeit with a name change. It was still a similar show with professional freak doing their usual thing of sword swallowing and glass eating, and human pincushions putting their battered bodies through acts of brutality for your viewing pleasure.

Chucky returned with *Chucky's Wedding Chapel*, where he and his blushing bride Tiffany got hitched five times every night. People were even plucked out the crowd to help with the ceremonies and were embarrassed into acting like jackasses for the gathered crowds. Universal also undertook a lot of cross marketing for this show to tie in with the recently-released *Bride of Chucky* that hit cinemas during the event's run. Bill & Ted's *Excellent Halloween Adventure II* returned with a new script that saw the duo pack in the laughs and the dance numbers in equal measures. The main gag of the show seemed to be lauding the movie *Titanic* which had hit theaters in the previous year but was still breaking box-office records. Finally, a small sideshow entitled *Small Soldiers – Behind the Scenes Experience* was offered both during the event and during the day. Universal described the experience thus: *"The Experience is inspired by the DreamWorks Pictures-Universal Pictures co-production of Small Soldiers - hitting screens nationwide on July 10. Many elements of the new film - which will blend live action with state-of-the-art computer animation - will be included in this exclusive, hands-on experience of high-tech movie magic, which features a video narration by the film's star, Phil Hartman and "live" appearances by the film's colorful characters."* Along with the following rides being in operation: *Back to the Future: The Ride, E.T. Adventure* and *Jurassic Park The Ride.*

Another tradition that started this year was the horror industry's *Eyegore Awards* where honorees are awarded little goblin-like statues (akin to the *Oscars*) for their work in the horror genre. Winners in this inaugural year were Janet Leigh, Jennifer Tilly and Clive Barker. As with this year and the many times it has returned, it has been held to also publicize *Horror Nights* and give it a peppering of Hollywood glamour that other haunts around the country could not compete with.

The event ran on October 16th, 17th, 23rd, 24th, 29th, 30th and 31st from 7pm to 1am. Universal believed that crowds totaled just over 100,000 for this short run. In order to retain the daytime park guests, which had vastly grown in numbers during this time, they introduced *Stay and Scream* tickets for the very first time. This allowed day guests to add to their ticket at a reduced cost to keep them in the park on the event nights. Interestingly, this year also utilized more soundstages to house the various haunts than any year before or since. Universal had a huge Halloween hit on their hands!

1999: "Five times the horror!"

The year 1999 rolled around and whilst everyone else was preparing for their millennium celebrations and avoiding the 'dreaded' millennium bug, Universal was quietly planning their Halloween event. Plans had been realized much earlier than before, with the scope and popularity of the event continuing to grow. The success of working with recognized experts in the horror genre in the previous year was set to continue, and by August the news via the *LA Times* was leaked as to who one of these experts were. *"Rob Zombie is being given free rein to fashion a fright-night extravaganza in a sound stage, which will open Oct. 15 and run the three following weekends, culminating, of course, on Oct. 31..."*

Following in Barker's footsteps, Zombie wanted to take the haunted house and move it to next fright-filled level. The maze would officially be entitled *The Thrilling Chilling World of Rob Zombie* where people will *"Tunnel deep inside the most depraved realm of all -- Rob Zombie's brain -- where the living dead reign supreme!"*

Zombie, playing an exaggerated version of his horror personality, would welcome guests into a fun-filled, murky world full of demonic possession and brimful with the deadliest of sins. Zombie would deploy bungee jumpers to jump down at guests (something that hadn't been seen before at the Hollywood event), complete with demons poking body bags that were suspended from the ceilings in a nightclub setting with a go-go bar. Even some murderous robot servants were thrown into the mix. The house was confusing and horror filled, but in a mix that terrified guests as they didn't quite know what would come at them next.

Zombie approached the design of the maze as he would if he was designing one of his many music concerts. At the time he was known mostly for his music and had just moved his *Zombie A Go-Go* label to the studio. He had worked with Universal in the previous year where he produced soundtracks from three of Universal's classic Frankenstein films. Universal asked Zombie to take the lead on one of the mazes for 1999 after they saw how much passion he had for the genre, and it would become a role that Zombie would truly relish.

The iconography and design would need to be tailored to Zombie's own interests, fears and insecurities. Zombie took the role of maze designer very seriously and spent months pouring over every last inch of the design.

"I wanted it to be like a trip through the album. It won't be like rock music pumping through because that's not scary at all." he said.

In fact, it would be a mashup of sheer terror where rock music was the servant to the scares within. The façade was a giant 30ft replica of Zombie's face where guests entered in via his mouth (well, you are literally entering his head!). The route took you via a darkened tunnel that was the slimy throat of our maze's host. The walls dripped with a green ooze and then led through to the guts of the maze. Memories of past horrors were brought to life and even a 'hellbilly deluxe' portion of maze would terrify guests. Other rooms included a 'superbeast' room where the membrane-dripping intestinal Man Monster dwells. Past this, a room dedicated to female zombies was found and then a true meta room was found where the artist could be seen struggling to make a monster.

"It's not supposed to be for young kids," Zombie warned at the time. *"It's not meant to be silly; it's pretty bloody."*

To compete with Zombie, Clive Barker also returned for another year of 'Hell on Earth' and that was exactly his theme for this year. *Clive Barker's Hell* debuted on the upper lot where guests would, *"Dare to enter the putrid put of infernal damnation from the Wizard of Wickedness."* *Hell* would prove to be the most popular maze of 1999, and queues would regularly extend to three hours in duration. One attendee of that maze told me, *"Hell was being whipped up in the local media, rumors on how warped the maze from the previous year was definitely propelling more guests to attend in the following year."*

Barker told the *LA Weekly*, *"In England, we don't have a lot of this. When Universal asked me if I'd be interested in doing one, I said, 'Sure, I'll give it a crack.' I saw it as a four-minute piece of theater that loops. David and I went through it and talked to the actors, and gave them their motivations. So I took it very seriously. You know, the Halloween maze is a very American form. To me, they're like sculptures in a way. In fact, the people I know who are most interested in them are visual artists and writers. We go around in gangs every year seeing as many as we can, and we study them. When I started doing mine, people would say, 'Why are you doing that?' They thought it was silly. But there are a lot of things you can do with them. To me, they're like what you thought horror movies would be like before you saw a horror movie. You know, 'They're coming after you - they're coming after you, and you won't be able to stop them.' Their interactivity is interesting, too, and their density."*

The maze would develop from Barker's previous attempts, with him using what worked and honing what didn't. Universal were acutely aware of waiting times and the need to send a consistent line of people through the maze so as to not back it up too much or to keep the crowds waiting too long. Although this was the primary design consideration that Universal passed to Barker it would actually work differently in practice. Barker found that scenes that really 'got under people's skin' or turned their stomachs would propel guests faster through the house. But when larger set pieces were involved or curious scenes were deployed this would slow the movement of the maze down; one such scene featured S&M and it very much slowed down the 'conga-line' effect, with everyone gasping and saying, "what did I just see?"

Barker re-used the 'tour guide' pulsing technique for the maze which had been seen in his previous attempt *FREAKZ* and at the *Chamber of Chills* before that. Various characters that were reminiscent of Barker's *Hellraiser* movies were present in the maze to direct the action. Sound and strobe lighting had been used to confuse guests within the mashup Satan's palace portion of the maze. A number of puppets were also devised to act as Satan's minions jumping through boo-holes located in the walls of various tight passageways. No one was safe in this maze! A press release issued at the time said, *"Clive Barker, best-selling horror author and creator of the "Hellraiser" and "Candyman" films, spawns his twisted terror upon an unsuspecting crowd. He douses guests in the heat of Hades, engulfing them in the fiery flames of ... his HELL!"*

Another filmmaker working on the lot was also drafted into design duties. Stephen Sommers, who had directed the Universal smash-hit *The Mummy,* was asked to bring his vision of the movie to the Halloween event. Sommers had been in the middle of pre-production for its sequel when Universal floated the idea of him pausing that to make this maze. It would incorporate many of the main set pieces from the original movie and would also utilize a number of props and costumes left over from the actual production. The maze was designed to be claustrophobic in places and with larger, grander scenes in others. For example, in one corridor, sounds of scratching scarab beetles gave the impression that a wall was fit to burst with the critters, and dimming lights and projections with SIF were deployed to make all guests believe they were being covered with flesh eating bugs.

One former guest told me, *"It made my flesh crawl and it gave me nightmares in that darn maze!".* The nightmares of crawling beetles aside, guests would literally come face-to-face with members of Imhotep's undead army. *"I was mostly interested in things that make people jump,"* said Sommers. *"I like to add texture, like the crunching [which simulates bugs underfoot], the walls of slime, anything that will make people scream. If we can get people laughing and screaming, that will be great."*

One of the most popular scenes in the maze was the 'mummification room' where guests saw horrific displays of people being mummified alive. Tongues were being unwillingly pulled from people's mouths, red-hot pokers were being pushed into noses and others were being seen locked away in air-tight sarcophagi. Water sprays to simulate pouring acid, a blood-filled fountain and an assortment of mummies would propel frightened guests into the final room, where the high altar was relocated with Imhotep seeking to bring his love back to life. As guests stared at the impressive set piece, other bandage-clad mummy soldiers would jump out at guests to ensure they made the exit in good time.

A rare cast photo from 1999

Creature Features would appear this year, where guests were asked to, *"Step through the movie screen to rub elbows and other body parts with classic*

Universal Monsters like Frankenstein, Dracula, and Wolfman." This was largely a repeat of the previous mazes that featured the classic Universal Monsters. Whereas Orlando has hardly ever repeated houses, it is fairly common within the wider industry that some houses/mazes get tweaked and repeated, particularly as it saves budget and makes sense if they are popular.

A new maze for the lineup this year was *Cleaver's Meat Locker* where "*Bloodthirsty butchers hack their way through various cuts of meat, including human flesh!*" It was located right next to the exit for Barker's maze on the Upper Lot which meant it was able to feed off the popularity of Barker's. *Cleaver's* was a relatively short maze, which was not unlike the later versions of this maze that would re-appear in Orlando years later. The premise was that a modern-day butler had become demented and started to use humans, rather than animals, as his prey for his warped meat factory. One of the most longstanding memories of this maze for many of the guests was the use of smells. Somehow, somewhere, a company had to produce for Universal Hollywood a 'human flesh burning' scent – gross!

As with the Universal Monsters maze returning (with two Alfred Hitchcock rooms added), a number of shows returned for 1999. These included: *Chucky's Insult Emporium* (Petrifying put-downs to offend everyone!), *Animal House of Horrors* (Wild, man-eating beasts unleashed to run amok!), *Bill & Ted's Excellent Halloween Adventure III* (The boys are back trashing media celebs in a most excellent, all new adventure) and the *Carnival of Carnage* where you could "*Freak out at the sight of this gory collection of sword swallowers, glass eaters, and human pincushions torturing themselves into a tizzy!*". All of which, excluding the Bill and Ted Show, were more or less repetitions from the previous year. *Chucky's* Show had become less about Tiffany and more about goading the guests, whereas the Bill and Ted Show was on the same wavelength but was taking aim at the celebrity culture of the time.

The event this year had upped the scares and focused on a target audience of late-teenagers to young adults. A conscious decision was made to reflect this targeted action by upping the adult content of the shows and ensuring the mazes this year were incredibly scary. Various signs were deployed to reflect this change, with one at the park gates reading: "*Visitors Victims Beware! Take heed all ye who enter here: The masters of horror have devised the most atrociously terrifying night of your life. Welcome to Universal's Halloween Horror Nights III. Venture into a sinister and evil vortex of hideous beats. Freaks and creatures that stalk your every step! Malicious mazes of maximum monstrosities! Thrill and chill rides that'll have you screaming for mercy! Wicked bands and horrifying shows to rock and shock you to your senses! After this night of mayhem, you'll be lucky to rest... in pieces. Sweet nightmares!*"

So while *Woody Woodpecker* would host *City Walk's* 6th annual Halloween event for kids entitled '*The Wacky Halloween Fest*', things were getting decidedly more grown-up in the main park. Another more adult-like choice made this year was the introduction of yearly cocktails. They were: *The Rob Zombie, Mummy's Curse, Pirate's Revenge* and *The Werewolf's Bark*. The rides were scaled back and the event closed at 1am most nights. Universal had taken aim at the slightly more mature market and, for now, it appeared to be working.

2000: HHN IV – Unlocking the Gates of Doom!

The world partied hard in 1999 when the millennium occurred. And although there was talk of the computer systems of the world failing or the world as we know it coming to an end, it didn't happen. People generally celebrated with gusto to welcome the new millennium and by September 2000 everyone had just about recovered and looked to Universal for their next major party. And they were in luck, as Universal had been planning the 2000 event since the 1999 one ended. It was promising to be Hollywood's biggest and 'baddest' year yet. Little did they know the event would literally fall into both categories. The action started on Friday October 13th and continued for seven further nights on October 14th, 20th, 21st, 27th, 28th, 29th and 31st (all 7pm to 1am). Tickets were $39 and were purchased through Ticketmaster, at Universal Studios Hollywood front gates or at Spencer Gifts. 'Stay & Scream' tickets were reintroduced for just $20 with a full day ticket. And Celebrity Pass holders (the annual pass holder ticket name at the time) could have bought an HHN ticket for just $19 for themselves and $25 for their guests.

By this time, Cory Asrilant had been promoted to 'Creative Director of Halloween' which essentially meant that he was now in charge of the event's creative direction. Asrilant was working around the clock when he was interviewed by the *LA Times* in September, telling them that he was putting in over 100 hours a week on occasions, and had even slept on his office floor as he finished so late into the early hours of the morning. "*It's one month out of the year where I get no sleep and I have no personal life*," he told the paper. Asrilant prepped the local media outlets that once again it would be the scariest yet, the largest yet and that it was definitely not for children. He even remarked that for this year, "nothing was off the table" in terms of scares, and that he and the creative team did not reject any ideas on how to terrify everyone who came through the park's gates.

"We sit in a room with a big board in front of us and we literally list every different way we can scare people. We look at all the different properties we'd

like to work with, such as Rob Zombie, 'Buffy the Vampire Slayer', and the World Wrestling Federation. Then we try to figure out ways we can incorporate those into haunted attractions. We develop them room-by-room, idea-by-idea. Then we go to character development and specific scares, the animated elements," said Asrilant at the time. By June all these ideas had morphed into full designs that were being built across the Park and backlot. And as October rolled around, guests would take their first steps into the horrific worlds that he and his team had created.

The first of five mazes that enthralled guests was *Buffy & Angel: Hellmouth Haunt* which threw guests right into the middle of an episode of the wildly (at the time) popular horror/fantasy show. Using almost carbon-copies of the original sets, including Buffy's dorm, Sunnydale, a ruinous high school, a park, and a subway, guests would come face to face with a variety of Buffy's fearsome foes and see her do battle. Eventually, the maze would merge into the popular spin-off show *Angel* and guests would see some of the familiar faces from his popular program. Asrilant said at the time, "*We came up with the idea because of the popularity of the Buffy and Angel shows, so we went to Joss Whedon and pitched him the idea. He fell in love with it. We got two minutes into the meeting and he was loving every second of it. Then it suddenly became his idea! We let him roll with it, and he was saying, 'How about this? Let's do that.' We came up with the original concept and he developed it.*"

Special effects and live stunts were added into the scare mix to produce this rather unique experience. It was unique in this combination of action and horror (much like the show) but it was also unique due to the fact that before and since, no live action *Buffy* mazes have ever been produced. A Universal press release at the time said, "*Combining narrative story elements with visceral "scares," the attraction will mark the first time that current television programs are adapted as a Halloween attraction.*"

Whedon was protective of his show and wanted to ensure the best maze possible was built. As Asrilant told the *LA Times* at the time, "*[Guests] will walk through Buffy's dorm room and you see an image lying on the bed with blond hair. So you're walking by it not quite knowing what to expect but, of course, it pops up and it's not Buffy, it's some evil creature with blond hair. Characters jump out at you from air vents, and floor hatches, they even come down at you on bungy cords. One thing that Joss stressed to us is, being that his shows are on national television, he can't take it as far as he would like in terms of scare factor, so this is his opportunity to really scare the crap out of people. So this takes it a step further than the regular show in terms of scare; there's no romantic storyline in our maze, it's purely in your face scare, scare, scare! We don't recommend this event for under the age of 12. There are no restrictions, we allow anybody in, but to tell you the truth we do gear towards 12 to 24 year olds. So we don't hold back on the scares, we want this to be as scary and as ferocious as possible. So if* you do bring your three or four year old, we have many emergency exits for you to escape from if necessary..."

Lisa M DeHaven was a makeup designer this year for the event and she adored this maze. She said, *"I loved the Buffy/Angel maze. That was my favorite. It looked a lot like Sunnydale from the show. They had the park, the school. And I remember they had at least a few actors that were the spitting image of Angel and Spike! It really was like you were walking through Sunnydale and encountering all your favorite characters and few unsavory vampires too! Again, Michael [Burnett] and his team did a great job with the prosthetic pieces...there were a LOT of them in this maze. At one point you'd be walking thru the maze and all of sudden this school yard fence would separate you from your group so you'd be walking and all of sudden you're look at your friends on the other side of the fence! And you just know the vamps are out there waiting for you! It was a great maze."*

Not only were the makeup applications completed using a more Hollywood/film style application, where prosthetics are applied direct to the actors' faces/bodies (with no masks), but this was combined with film-like sets that looked as if they were right out of the show and made the maze so special.

A number of mazes ready for use at HHN 2000

DeHaven continued, *"The one scene that sticks out in my mind was when you enter into the park area and everyone gets separated by the fence. So you end up getting split up and "alone" in the dark park...kind of like vampire bait! The park even had this sense that it was huge and you were stuck in a small corner of it. The one main thing that always impressed me about all of the HHNs in Hollywood was the attention to detail in all of their sets. I know that coming from a theatrical background myself, that was something that always impressed me so much. They just made the experience so real. And being a huge Buffy/Angel fan myself I can tell you, I was very impressed."*

The maze featured all of the most enduring characters and villains from the show's run. The Judge, the Gentleman (who Orlando fans will know better as the *Body Collectors*), the portal and even a horde of werewolves doing battle with a group of vampires. A very good Buffy look-alike actress would fend off the hordes of monsters with her trusty crossbow. The battle sequences really required guests to take additional trips through the maze to appreciate every nuance of the design. On opening night if you had survived the demons, vampires and werewolves, guests were in a for a great surprise as Joss Whedon, Alyson Hannigan and Amber Benson (all from the show) performed an impromptu meet and greet for fans, signing their park maps signed and posing for photographs. *Buffy* creator Whedon had worked closely with the park to ensure the maze used all the original *Buffy* ingredients in an authentic way but to give fans something entirely new to experience.

"Our primary interest was that it doesn't suck," said George Snyder, then director of development for the shows to the *Daily News LA*. "*What we didn't want is something cheap and generic*", which had supposedly been Wheldon's main concern. Snyder continued, "*I have to say I've been over recently to see it in its final stages, and it's impressive. They've spent a lot of money on it. It's intriguing and true to the show. They came and toured our sets, worked with our set designers, worked with our makeup and special-effects artists, stunt coordinators. It captures the mood for the show."*

By this year the scale and scope of employees working on the event was huge, said Asrilant as he described the process behind this one maze to an online magazine, *"We start designing it in January, and we actually start construction in June. We have a construction crew of about 40 people, we have a make-up crew of 30 people, an effects crew of 10 people, not to mention hundreds of actors."*

Another creator who was always keen to keep a sharp eye on the fright details was Clive Barker, who returned to the event for his third and final time with *Harvest*. The inspiration for the maze came from a nightmare that Barker had which had been so detailed and horrifying that as soon as he awoke he wrote down what he could remember and faxed it to Universal with the header 'a great idea for a maze'. Universal positively replied and Barker added more notes and sketches. By January, a full creative meeting had been held and every room and idea was 'fleshed' out.

Barker spoke about his work with Universal at the time to an International Toy and Memorabilia Festival, "*Every year for Universal I do a Halloween maze. Our brief from Universal, which is a very big family-oriented organization, is come*

Halloween Barker should do his worst. Last year we had 68% of the people going through the park one night went to my maze. All of them went through, and then 68% went. It was a disgust-fest, and extreme. My point is that there is a part of the human heart that wants 'Romeo and Juliet', and there is another part of that heart that wants 'Macbeth', or 'Titus'." He continued, "When people come out of the Clive Barker Halloween Maze they've had blood, screaming, madness and monsters. They've survived. There is a sense of, 'I came out the other end of this and I survived'. I would sit at the end of my maze, with this big 'shit-eating-grin' on my face, and these giggling people come out having just had that popcorn moment. We take a sound stage every year, and all you can hear are screams coming out of this place. It's like a slaughterhouse. These folks come out the other end with these grins. There is something cathartic, something incredibly healthy, but it's not for 6-year-olds. It's for us."

The maze logo from the event map

The maze was themed to a decrepit mausoleum with a large aperture in the wall that transferred guests from the real world into another plane of existence. The effect of transitioning was fairly unique; they utilized a vertigo tunnel (a spinning tunnel) which guests walk along the traditional ramp inside. However, the difference here was that the tunnel was lined with earth and burlap and technicians above were periodically pouring sand into the tunnel which, as it turned, would fog up and incredibly disorientate guests. Inside, guests found a dilapidated crypt that led to a mysterious graveyard where an assortment of various monsters, including the Vipex (a character that Barker worked on for a movie that was never released) were harvesting souls from the recently deceased.

Past this, guests saw a larger Vipex depositing eggs (much akin to the *Aliens* movie) in a special egg chamber where eggs were literally bursting open and spraying their goo (actually just water) over the conga-line of guests. The maze then followed the hideous waking creatures as they entered from their chamber into the real world via sewers and service tunnels where city workers on a construction site were being attacked. The Queen of these monsters then returns for one final attack before the reanimated corpses of the construction workers - now under the control of the Vipex - also swing at guests. As with Barker's first two mazes, this maze was incredibly popular, with tremendous lines on every night of the event.

Also returning to the event was Rob Zombie with a maze that has possibly become one of the most notorious from these early years of the event. That maze was *Rob Zombie's The House of 1000 Corpses*. The maze was extreme. Zombie warned Universal that in the first few years that he was just learning his craft but by this maze he wanted to 'open the horror taps' and really go for it. Blood and gore abounded and the public lapped it up. HHN Makeup artist Lisa M DeHaven recalled, *"That was a maze I didn't go in very much, honestly (and I can handle a LOT of scares) it was just so gory!"* Despite this, the gore didn't deter guests; they lapped it up with one insider remarking to this author that the maze almost had a cult-like status at the event that year.

Universal executives greenlit the film production based solely on how popular the HHN maze was which made the maze the first maze/house to ever inspire an actual movie. The sets, the characters and the props were all created for HHN but were then used in the production of this movie. *Captain Spaulding*, the *Firefly family*, the *Murder Ride* and *The Museum of Monsters & Madmen* were all created especially for the maze. The movie gestated for three years on the Universal Studio backlot. Universal executives interfered with the production, worried that the movie would get an explicit rating for the violence and graphic scenes. The then Universal Pictures Chairman Stacey Snider told the *LA Times*, *"We have the utmost respect for Rob, who made a really intense and compelling movie, but it turned out far more intense than we could have possibly imagined. When I looked at the cumulative effect of the entire film, it was clear that the best version of the movie would end up getting an NC-17 rating, and we felt that would make the marketing and distribution of the movie impossible for us."*

It seemed that at the time that Zombie was not entirely surprised by the studio's sudden case of cold feet. He said, *"I have to admit that it would've been great if they'd released the film, but it felt weird from the get-go. Here we were, making this crazy [expletive] horror film, with this big corporate entity behind us. If you look at the history of horror films, the really scary ones, like 'Texas Chainsaw Massacre,' were made by little independent companies, not big corporations. It was obvious that Stacey was disturbed by the movie, which I took as a compliment. It was like, great, she's really freaked out by it. It must be a really*

58

scary movie. To me, what was most important was that the audience dug it. My feeling is that horror movies are like heavy-metal music. If you show it to the wrong person, they're going to be disgusted by it. Horror movies are supposed to be dark and disturbing. What offends some people is exactly what makes it cool to other people. So for me to cut out all the violence would be like saying, 'Hey, we made a porno movie, but we're taking out all the sex scenes.' I mean, why do you think people are going to see it?"

Still, Snider wasn't alone in her reaction. Terry Curtin, Universal's head of publicity, also agreed that the movie had gone too far and told the *LA Times*, "I'm not sure where the line is, but it was clear from watching the film that it had crossed it. It's probably the first time in my career that I felt I'd have trouble working on a movie. What made it even more bizarre was that it didn't seem to offend the audience a bit, which disturbed me even more." At the time Congress had been actively considering violence in movies and the effects it had on wider society. Not just this movie but scores of others were all called into question as to their 'appropriate' levels of depictions of violence, sex or drug use. Snyder continued at the time, "[sic] The conceit of Rob's movie, which has no recognizable stars, is that it's not a fantasy. It could be real and that's what makes it more upsetting. But with Rob's movie, I was concerned that there was just an uber-celebration of depravity." And although the movie was submitted for rating by Universal it would later be pulled and placed on hold, causing further delay.

These delays would eventually see the finished film move from Universal to MGM and then to Lionsgate – nobody in Tinsel Town was quite sure whether the movie should see the light of day. Zombie finally relented, trimmed the movie up and it was released to a solid R-rating. Within days Lionsgate had a horror hit on their hands. Interestingly, when Universal decided they would not distribute the movie, the maze had a last-minute name change to *Rob Zombie's American Nightmare*.

A new outside member to the horror team-up this year was *WWE*'s (as the organization was known then) The Undertaker who had his own maze in a lower lot soundstage with *No Mercy*. As with the *Buffy* maze, it did feature an impressive façade of a steam-punked type machine. The premise was that you were entering the machine that is The Undertaker and would see his life before you. The maze was fully narrated throughout, which gave an interesting dynamic to the artform. Through the façade, a funeral home was the first stop where guests would witness the creation of the demonic wrestler surrounded by rotting corpses. After this, a boiler scene with nods to Freddy showing where his 'parents' apparently died scared guests into the wrestling area, where other large wrestlers were waiting to seal your doom. Various fights are witnessed with actors portraying the behemoth man-monster, before leaving via the exit where a Kane lookalike is impaled on a sign advertising The Undertaker. The message to all visitors was clearly that the best wrestler was indeed The Undertaker.

The Classic Universal Monsters returned with *Theatre of Blood*, though this time they weren't on their own and some more modern horrors were presented in the museum-type maze. One of the memorable set-pieces within the maze required 3D glasses and was a reproduction of the classic Hitchcock shower scene from *Psycho* where instead of Janet Leigh, the mother was in fact after the guests. Strangely, Universal insisted that guests brought their own glasses to the event and did not, as with modern times, hand out for free the temporary cardboard glasses. For many guests the maze was just a collection of carnival-styled scenes (mirrored corridors to get lost in, and various sideshows) that, if you didn't happen to own some 3D glasses, appeared to fall a little short of the mark.

One of the Undertaker's scareactors posing with a fan

Hollywood, unlike Orlando, had never had a proper scarezone before, but that was all about to change with *Nightmare Creatures II*. This was not only the first scarezone at the Hollywood event but it was also the first time that Universal had used a computer game-themed property at the event on either coast. It was presented in the Upper Lot and Universal invited visitors to, "*Help destroy the evil Adam Crowley and his hideous board of lab experiment creatures as they prepare to take over the world... beginning with you!*" It wasn't large and it was tucked away at the bottom of the then Moulin Rouge area. The developers of this Playstation game had approached Zombie who had worked on the game's score. Universal came to an arrangement with the game's designers as they wanted to create a living commercial for the game as it had just been released prior to the event's opening.

Six different shows were presented in 2000. *Bill and Ted's Halloween Adventure* saw the bodacious duo back with another show lampooning the celebrity and political culture of the time. Chucky returned for yet another spin at *Chucky's Insult Emporium* and likewise so did the various creepy animals of *Animal House of Horrors*. A *Dance Party* headed by a DJ spun tracks all night long until park close in the Upper Lot by the entrance. The professional freaks returned with their *Carnival of Carnage* performing shows seven times per night and featuring the usual cacophony of weirdos and stunt wonders. The high-budget freak show featured medieval torture, sword swallowing, fire eaters and human pincushions. The unique talent of George the Giant stole the show, where he would hammer a nail into his nose and then proceeded to eat live cockroaches, worms, and maggots. In a similar vein, *Z.com present's Bobbing for Maggots* was as disgusting as it sounds. Guests were invited to undertake wickedly awful tasks to win small prizes. It must have been interesting to see how far people would go just to win an E.T. plush! But that wasn't the only disgusting feature of this adult-centric event; event cocktails got a disgusting upgrade where some of the versions available included 'blitzed bugs': yes real 'bug juice'. Delicious.

Another smaller event that occurred was the celebration of Hitchcock's *Psycho* on the backlot to mark its fortieth anniversary. The film's star, Janet Leigh, returned to the backlot to see the now infamous 'Room 1' of the Bates Motel. AMC had run a scream contest which had been won by Sue Pelinski, a Park Ridge, IL local. She was given the honor of recreating said scream in a replica of the famous bathroom built inside the Motel. Leigh who had been a regular on the backlot for a number of years and who had visited the sets of *Psycho II* and *Psycho III*, was delighted to be back and remarked to the gathered press that this movie is the reason why for the rest of her life she only ever took baths!

2001 – 2005: "The dark years..."

From the following year right up until 2006, there were no Halloween events at Universal whatsoever. Instead, the park drew on new and current attractions, (some of which were 'jazzed-up' a little over the period) but definitely no hard-ticketed events were seen. Nobody is quite sure of why the event did not return during these years. For many insiders it was a combination of reasons that affected their decision to not have the horror event. We all sadly remember 9/11 in 2001 but many forget the negative impact that had on vacation destinations during that year and the following years. Likewise, many point to how the park is laid out, with its separate upper and lower lots which many seem to think caused operational and crowd control issues. The business during these years was focused far more on filmmaking, with this taking precedent over any other operations the theme park was asked to undertake. Obviously, alcohol may have paid a part in the decision, because whereas alcohol was later banned at the event, it wasn't banned during these early days. One insider who wanted to remain off the record also pointed to budget. Supposedly, little was undertaken in-house using the Studio's own staff by 1999. Outside contractors were brought in to undertake a lot of the design work and it is entirely possible that budgets may have got out of control with Universal seeing their bottom line being pushed and pushed. Whatever the true reason, the park would only undertake much smaller projects for the time being.

In May of 2001 they came close to bringing the event back. They held a star-studded opening of their new in-park attraction *The Mummy Returns: Chamber of Doom*. It was essentially a walk-through attraction using sets and props used to make the sequel to the original Brendan Fraser hit, *The Mummy Returns*. Taking what they knew from their work in the haunt industry in previous years and by toning it down ever so slightly, they built a walk-through that was part-museum and part-haunted house. 190 props had been repurposed in scores of the original sets which had been moved from their soundstage straight to the Upper Lot.

Stephen Sommers, who we know had worked on a maze for the Halloween event in the past, was asked to consult on the new attraction. By May it was completed and he was cutting the 'bandage' (not ribbon) at the opening ceremony. Referring to how they toned it down he said at the time, "*I went through it, I brought my nephews through it. They were terrified, they thought it was a blast.*" Walking inside the Ancient Egyptian-type entrance, guests would see a small museum filled with mostly weapons and costumes from the movie.

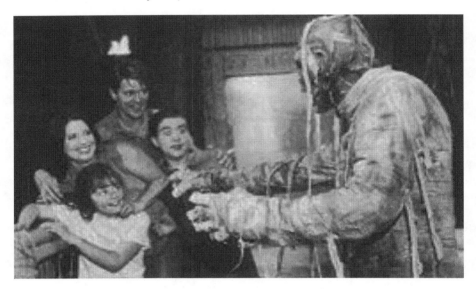

A mummified scareactor lunges at guests from within the attraction

Past the museum, the attraction turned into a haunted house where scareactors were employed as mummies to jump out from behind sarcophagi and from within boo-holes. This highly themed and dimly lit portion of the attraction was very popular. It included the spinning tunnel left over from HHN, the classic 'which-scareactor-is-real-and-which-is-a-statue' corridor and the reliable 'scare-them-out-the-door' trick but this time guests were scared down a novelty slide. An interesting feature at the beginning of the maze was a section where guests could control scares from within the maze (similar to the red buttons in Orlando). Three buttons controlled two different water sprays and there was a prop pop-up mummy scare. The attraction proved popular with kids, who welcomed the not-so-scary style of the walk-through. Building on the success of the new attraction enabled Universal to market it as something 'new to do during the fright season'.

Likewise, later in 2004, they would also open *Van Helsing: Fortress Dracula Walk-through* which would be very similar in style and would actively be marketed as something guests could try 'this Halloween'.

Other than these two attractions opening during this time, there were no Halloween events at either the park or City Walk until 2006. And although the park's night time entertainment lay dormant, somewhere in a quiet corner of the vast backlot a small team was quietly preparing for something big.

2006: The Director's Cut

The event would finally return to Hollywood in 2006, but this time it would usher in new experiences and a total step-change to how the event had been presented in the past. Lessons had been learnt, what worked would return and what didn't would stay in the past. One of the most significant alterations to the event and the one change that has perhaps altered and defined the event more than any other was the appointment of John Murdy as the overall creative lead. Murdy, who was no stranger to the park, had worked for Universal for a number of years and had been involved in attraction and show development on both coasts. His long list of outstanding works for the company and his passion for all things horror ensured he would be the perfect fit to head up the return of our beloved Halloween festival.

Murdy had been visiting the Studio since he was 5 years old. Whenever his parents asked him where he wanted to travel to or spend his birthday, he would always ask them for a trip to Universal. Growing up in the 1970s when interest in the classic Universal Monsters was revived and the horror genre really came into its own, he was one of a number of 'Monster Kids' who lapped up everything horror and Halloween related. He would graduate from High School and go onto College, all while combining trips to his favorite place in Southern California.

He told StudioTour.com, "*So flash forward to 1989, I had just graduated from college with a degree in Theatre and was looking for a job with flexible hours (because I was working as an actor at that time). A friend of mine had just started working at USH as a tour guide and convinced me to come to an audition. I got hired shortly after that so that was my first professional foray into Universal.*" Getting paid to share his passion for Universal on a daily basis must have been like a dream come true for the young Murdy.

Through the '90s he would move role from writer to show director and eventually in the early '00s he was promoted to 'Creative Director of Entertainment Production' for Universal Creative. The attraction that made his name within the company and which is also an attraction that still to this day pulls in the crowds on both coasts is *Revenge of the Mummy*. Opening on both coasts in 2004, Murdy worked on this attraction as his department's offices were moved from Hollywood to Orlando. Commuting regularly between the two finally pushed him to move back to Hollywood, where he would eventually take up the lead for the return of Horror Nights. While in Orlando, he would see how the event was organized, how concepts became a reality and how the event would be managed to ensure everyone had fun. Seeing the event come together in 2004 and 2005 gave him ideas for how Hollywood's event would be different.

At the time, the Studio heads in Hollywood had mixed feelings about its return. Some welcomed the idea, whereas others were not keen on the revelry and shenanigans of the past. He recounted years later, "*It was in 2004 that I got called to revitalize Halloween Horror Nights. People said it wouldn't work, that it would never happen, and that's when I decided I was going to do it. I love a challenge. My vision was to create attractions that incorporated horror movies that everyone knew and loved. It's been a huge success and now I work on Horror Nights all year round.*" Murdy hit the ground running on his return to Hollywood. Heading up his team of busy professionals, he would oversee the successful creation and management of over 70 projects in 2005. He showed that he not only had the management knowhow but he also now had a successful track record too, and soon no executives were in doubt that our favorite Halloween event could be successfully reprised.

Throughout 2005 Murdy and his team would work on the return of HHN at Hollywood. Taking what he learnt from how the event was managed in Orlando, he considered the wider haunt market and saw a gap in the market. He told themeparkinsider.com at the time, "*I kinda looked around the haunt industry in America and the one thing I really didn't see anyone doing or attempting to do was to create what I called branded horror, which was to actually go out and license horror movies and to bring those to life as living horror movies, with a movie-quality attention to detail. We didn't that exactly in 2006 [when Universal Studios Hollywood revived the event] -- it was kind of a baby-step year, just to get back in the business.*" It became apparent to him that no one nationally was focusing on the horror movie genre when it came to Halloween styled events. Universal had for years marketed their parks as places where you could 'ride the movies', but Murdy's idea was to be 'scared through the movies' instead. The idea was pitched to the executives and it was decided that the licensing of outside properties was a great idea but the event had to first recover its local fan base and get to grips with how a Halloween event could be held within the sprawling park. Collectively it was decided that if the event was a success then

IPs (Intellectual Properties) would be brought in the following year. Essentially, 2006 would be about logistics and 'learning the ropes' before anything grander was to be presented. This tentative approach was the right one for the time as the event had been on hiatus twice before and the passion of the team was such that they had to get it right for the future of the event.

It was early August 2006 when the first news of the horrors that awaited fans was drip-fed to the eager press, "*Universal Studios Hollywood re-invents the theme park Halloween experience with 'Halloween Horror Nights' returning Universal Backlot to its horror roots for seven nights of terror beginning Friday the 13th of October.*"

The press release detailed how the event was returning for "more nightmares" and how it had been "reinvented" for today's horror-loving audiences. One of these reinventions and one of the most highly contested new attractions was the updated *Terror Tram*, which for the first time ever would allow guests to get off the tram and explore the backlot for themselves. When the idea was originally pitched it was met with some resistance from the production teams working in this area. Universal's backlot has been one of the largest and busiest production facilities in the world and one of the main criticisms from the past was around trespassers venturing into areas that were restricted. The idea of allowing guests to wander free on the largest backlot in Hollywood was a tough pill to swallow. Of course, wandering free is exactly what they would not be allowed to do. Once the trams stopped guests would be herded off into specially-created pathways that would be lined with security guards to give the utmost assurances to nearby productions. The creative team strongly believed that this was a natural evolution for the headline attraction. Since the tragic accident of 1986, it was understood that scareactors actively approaching the trams was completely prohibited, which reduced the scares. Getting the guests to disembark into the scareactors' realm would not only heighten the scares on a face-to-face basis but also, allowing them to get there via the trams ensured that all the popular portions of the tour (*Kong, Earthquake, Jaws* etc.) could also be utilized.

The press release read, "*For the first time in the studio's 93-year history, guests will be able to disembark from studio trams and walk among the historic sets of the Universal backlot, birthplace of the horror genre. The backlot experience—incorporating such Hollywood landmarks as Psycho House and the War of the Worlds disaster scene—will play a central role in 'The Director's' Universal Studios Hollywood's 'Halloween Horror Nights' production, a scenario that calls for guests to be transported into eerie, darkened sets while subjected to disorienting and unnerving interactive experiences.*"

The Terror Tram was said to be terrifying, with guests building up a nervous anticipation as video screens around the queue told the backstory of the demented auteur: "*In 2006, Universal Pictures announced the signing of Pavel*

Prancvsky. To helm a new horror movie for the studio that invented the genre. Pavel had already made a name for himself in his native country Slovakia with his controversial film 'The Widow's Eye'. Despite rumors of Pavel's unethical filming techniques, production began on June 6th 2006. A publicity film crew was dispatched to capture the moment. All three members of the crew disappeared immediately after this interview. A week later, the first daily began coming in from the set of Pavel's production. The Studio was horrified at what they saw. The production was shut down, the footage locked down in the vault, and Pavel's contract with Universal was terminated. But security was unable to locate the director, he was thought to have returned to his native Slovakia until employees started reporting a strange looking man apparently living on the Universal backlot. Soon the internet was flooded with sightings of the mysterious director. A few weeks later, this tape arrived at Universal Pictures addressed to the head of production: <Pavel's voice>' It is a shame you did not share my vision, but I cannot let you kill my masterpiece. It must continue, and it will! I don't need your money, your crew or your actors. All I am interested in is reality. <people stuck on the backlot tram are shown> These people are that reality, they shall help me complete my masterpiece, they leave their dull little lives and come here to touch Hollywood and now Hollywood shall touch them!"

To give the backstory an added element of realism in some kind of meta ahead of its time moment there was a defined marketing strategy. Universal took a leaf from other horror franchises which had capitalized on using viral internet marketing to advertise the horrors of the event as "real" (similar to how *The Blair Witch Project* and others were marketed). Their gimmick as the video narration above suggested, was to deploy an actor dressed and made up as The Director to loiter around the backlot for the weeks leading up to the event, in the hope that people would report him via social media. The move received mixed responses but it showed how this event was definitely taking the event in a new direction.

There is some argument amongst the most hardcore of HHN fans in that some believe The Director in Hollywood is not the same as the Orlando one. The character debuted in Orlando in 2003 where he was purposely designed by their team to be one of their new rota of horror icons to compete with Jack the others. The reasoning behind the confusion over whether he is the same icon or not stems from some confusion over his name. Paolo Ravinski (his original name for 2003, before 2006 changed it to Paulo – which it has remained ever since in Orlando), Pavel Pranevsky (as seen this year in Hollywood), and Billy Skorrski (for Singapore's first event). The simple answer is that nobody really knows. What we do know is that the same actor, Gianni Garofalo, portrayed the icon in both the Orlando and Hollywood versions. Garofalo, who is a native Californian, told the ScareZone.com podcast that he believed the character to be the same for both coasts and that the name was merely mixed up by the respective marketing departments.

Other than the regular tram portions, the walking portion of *The Terror Tram* was spread over five distinct areas. Whoville was made-over as a nightmarish clown emporium where clowns of all varieties were ready to jump-out or mingle with unsuspecting guests. Wrapping around from there to Norman Bates' domain saw guests placed right into the middle of a remake of the 1960 classic. A number of scareactors dressed as 'mother' were positioned at portions around the motel and main house, while the scene was completed by the appearance of various victims scattered about. Meanwhile, the original movie played out from a TV located in the motel's office and Norman began posing for photos on his front porch (as he usually does to this day). Passing this section a 'crashed' tram was broken and smoking away as a horrific butler was offering up carved-up 'guests' who weren't as lucky as other guests. Another showpiece saw a victim being tortured and filmed as guests walked-by. The torturer was a pig mask-wearing scareactor who grunted at guests as they stared in horror. The recently retained *War of the Worlds* set was refitted as a zombie apocalypse where rotting corpses would lunge at guests before chasing them right into the path of a waiting chainsaw drill team. The final act of this horrifying picture saw The Director killing a 'guest' via pushing him or her into a wood-chipper. The machine made an intense noise as the actor screamed in pain. The effect was combined with a howling laugh from The Director, as a water effect sprayed guests to simulate the splatter of blood.

The Terror Tram was by far the main attraction of the event and in keeping with the muted reintroduction of the event, it would have only two mazes, both of which were technically reproductions of mazes from the past. The first maze, located on the Upper Lot, was *Asylum* and was Hollywood's version of the popular Orlando house franchise *Psychoscareapy*. The maze utilized many of the set pieces and props from Orlando's 2003 version. Incidentally, they also had a sequel to this 2003 house with *Psychoscareapy: Maximum Madness* during their event in 2006. As guests entered the twisted world of these inmates they were immediately confronted by the formidable façade of Shadybrook Asylum that had been shipped over from Orlando. Various dayrooms would be presented showing other inmates as well as the staff of the facility being tortured and harangued in the most awful ways. The lack of mazes at the event enabled Universal to fill them with actors who preyed on the guests each night.

Jumpsuit-wearing maniacs would be seen either killing or being killed in a variety of guises, including being hung and electrified. One of the most iconic and contentious scenes ever portrayed in a haunted house was also recreated: the toilet scene. The notorious scene, which has gone down in haunt history as being one of the most gut retching scenes to ever be produced, was built towards the end of the maze. It was complete with faux fecal matter smeared on the walls spelling out various phrases. The one on the mirror read 'poo boy', and whilst the visual senses were impaired, the smell senses were also in for an onslaught (though one insider told me that he believed the smells were toned down for the Hollywood version of the maze). The mixture of scares and gross out scenes that were all reproductions from the east coast ensured a popular house had travelled well and was quickly becoming the go-to maze for the event. In at least, it reported the larger wait times of the two mazes that were presented.

Next up was an old faithful maze that wouldn't have been *Horror Nights* without it. *Universal's House of Horrors* was presented in the *Van Helsing: Fortress Dracula* walkthrough attraction. The maze was so popular with guests that it would remain after the event and be redressed into a daytime attraction. Although the maze was not as scary as the one described above, it was very authentic. It used great purpose-built sets and utilized some great special effects that had been devised for when it was *Van Helsing*. Scenes included: *The Mummy, The Wolfman, Norman Bates* from *Psycho, Frankenstein, Nosferatu*, and more recent horrors.

Unlike previous years, and knowing how wildly popular they were in Orlando, Hollywood would create a number of scarezones that were dotted around the park and themed to each new picture that The Director was working on. Plague-infected victims would beg guests for their lives while medieval doctors stood idly by in *The Black Death*. In the New York backstreets another zombie apocalypse was reported, with a version of *Dawn of the Dead*. *"Ghost town where skeletal inhabitants of the town's most notorious still roam the smoldering streets"* ran the story, as a town full of decrepit cowboys did battle in *Deadwood*. In the London streets, visitors found *Old London,* where various fog machines were set up to mask the murders of Jack the Ripper and Mr. Hyde. Finally, Studio Centre was redressed to house some of the most iconic madmen of celluloid, where Dracula and Frankenstein's monster would rub shoulders with event guests.

A number of daytime and returning shows were presented for this year. *Slaughter World* was a re-presented version of the daytime showing of *Water World*. A handful of extra gags were intertwined into the action, though the night time show was effectively the same as the regular show (much the same as the very early *Bill and Ted* shows at Orlando). The professional freaks were also back with their *Carnival of Carnage* presented in the old *Flintstones* area. The familiar sword swallowing and human pincushions were all back for their respective torturous acts. *Chucky's Insult Emporium* made a popular return in much the same way as it had in the past. Another popular edition was the revised version of the daytime show, *Fear Factor Live: Dead Celebrity Edition* where various celebrity impersonators were put to the test with nasty and yet hilarious tasks set for them. Various lookalikes including Britney, Jacko, Stern and Saddam were asked to undertake weird and wonderful tasks; a mixture of what we know from Bill and Ted at their crudest but with a number of gross-out challenges. A new show that Universal was keen to publicize was *The Mutaytor* located outside the old *Back to the Future* Plaza. The press releases read, "...*multiple performances by trance music/performance artists The Mutaytor, a multi-media ensemble that was formed at the legendary Burning Man Festival by members of Oingo Boingo, Supertramp and other musical and theatrical groups. The Mutaytor's blend of pyrotechnics, stunt performance, tribal dancers and pounding percussion--a riotously surreal techno-retro-funk-audience—will add a spine-tingling and alarming element to the overall Halloween experience."*

The five shows per night combined a great deal of theatrics with the dance-like music that filled the area. And finally, although not a show, one of the most requested and totally unintentional attractions was brought back; that attraction was *Jurassic Park in the Dark*. Much like the *Jaws* version in Orlando (*the Shark in the Dark*) the regular attraction was just run at night and added a whole new level of terror since it was being run under the cover of darkness. Guests had said how great the attraction was at night so Universal actually advertised the ride experience as 'returning' in the event guide maps.

One addition to the event that did not return (and still hasn't to this day) was the sale of alcohol. One of the key components on its return was to control the crowds better by aiming to reduce the bad behavior of some guests by limiting their chances of buying alcohol and by actively employing more security staff. The combination seemed to have worked as the level of drunken or bad guest behavior was reported as being very low to non-existent. Ensuring that everybody had a good time without a reliance on booze ensured better guest and employee satisfaction levels. These were all combining factors that ensured the event was great success for Universal.

2007: Horror Comes Home!

By most accounts 2006 was a great success for the company. *Horror Nights* had successfully returned to both coasts. Orlando by this time had become a well-oiled-machine and would already be in the throes of planning their next event way before the current one had ended; this however was not the case in Hollywood. The smaller 'baby-stepped' year at Hollywood ended and the creatives, cast and crew waited with bated breath to hear whether the event would return. Within days of the wrap party, news came down from the executives that they were very pleased and that production should begin right away for the next year's version of the event. Murdy hit the ground running. He had already pitched some ideas and knew exactly where he wanted to take the event. Prohibited from going to big too quickly last year, he finally wanted to set *Horror Nights* apart from all the other country haunt attractions by at last seeing his dream of creating a Halloween event where guests could be thrown straight into the action of their favorite horror movies. And although this had in a way been done before, this would be more faithful to the original movies, be more life-like, have more story and ultimately make the guests feel as though they had teleported right into the nightmares of the silver screen.

Murdy recounted his mission statement to themeparkinsider.com, *"I kinda looked around the haunt industry in America and the one thing I really didn't see anyone doing or attempting to do was to create what I called branded horror, which was to actually go out and license horror movies and to bring those to life as living horror movies, with a movie-quality attention to detail. We didn't do that exactly in 2006 [when Universal Studios Hollywood revived the event] -- it was kind of a baby-step year, just to get back in the business. In 2007, that was the first time we did that, with New Line Cinema doing Freddy, Jason and Leatherface. That really proved to be the difference in putting Halloween Horror Nights on the map."*

The idea of pitching to New Line Cinema to use, as the press called them, their "Big 3" would be an interesting concept. The idea was given the green-light and the pitches occurred. The business terms of the deal have never been made public but speculation has been that in order to make the deal for Universal viable, they had to maximize their use and exposure of the Big 3 to draw the crowds to the event. Their idea was to build on the previous years of collaboration between both Orlando and Hollywood by getting both coasts to share the IP. In the past, Orlando had sent props and set pieces to Hollywood (as with 2006) and they had shared creative personnel, websites and many of the best ideas but they had never shared an IP in the same year. Luckily for Universal, they were about to work with an IP holder that wanted as much brand exposure as possible and would work with Universal in a partnership capacity in order to bring their concepts to reality.

New Line Cinema, founded in 1967 by Robert Shaye, is an independent film studio owned by Warner Bros which had started out distributing art-house and educational films to colleges and schools across the country. It later went on to undertake less distribution and therefore concentrate on more of its own productions. The studio focused on lesser-known talent and allowing them to experiment and flourish, to mixed success. This business plan remained much the same through the 1970s and 80s where one movie even went on to receive a coveted Academy Award. It wasn't until 1976 that the company began making full-length, major motion pictures. Their first was a movie called *Stunts*. The action thriller did mildly well and allowed the company to invest in three further motion pictures all based around the horror and sci-fi genres, which all failed to perform to company expectations. It wasn't until 1984's release of *A Nightmare on Elm Street* and its subsequent sequels had achieved so much success it would confer the title of *The House that Freddy Built*, thus establishing NLC as a big horror player in the market. This continued into the 1980s when the third film in the Freddy franchise managed to make back nearly ten times the budget for the studio. It was also around the late 1980s, hot on the success of this movie in 1987, that the company had acquired the right to use the characters from the *Texas Chainsaw Massacre* films. Leatherface was later joined by Jason and co. when the company acquired the rights to the popular *Friday 13th* franchise in about 1989. The company went on to continue the same lucrative mix of reasonable budget sizes to these cult franchises, releasing them to good box-office returns for many years.

Long before New Line had acquired the rights to use Jason, they had tried to get a 'Freddy vs. Jason' movie off the ground. Many fans, particularly those who regularly attended the various horror and fantasy related conventions wrote to the respective owners of the icons to register their approval for such a move. In fact, due to various owners of Jason and varying degrees of success for subsequent sequels, it would take 15 years of 'development hell' before the project could be realized. New Line buying the Jason franchise was the true catalyst to the whole project. During these 15 years it would see $6 million spent on eighteen unused scripts and over a dozen writers all working on it. But the toils of the past productions were not in vain as the movie was finally finished in 2003 with the movie going on to make $114 million at the box-office. Also during this time, the Texas franchise was fully rebooted by New Line in 2006, also making solid box-office returns. The three characters were exceedingly 'hot' during this period and had made a real comeback from their earlier successes of the 1980s to draw in popular audiences around the world by 2007.

New Line, a progressive forwarding-thinking company was also looking to expand the popular characters' appeal to not just movies but also to other media. At the time, licensing agreements for toys, comics and video games were all considered, and some were put into production. It wasn't until late 2006 that the company officially licensed the use of the icons to Universal Studios for use in Halloween Horror Nights.

The official announcement came on June 27th, 2007 that the three icons of horror would be officially joining events on both coasts, with the event taking place in Orlando for the Studios and not at Islands of Adventure. It would be the first time the cinema had officially granted the rights to use the characters in a theme park (though many had tried to bring them to events and parks before). *"We're obviously extremely excited about it. It's going to be a great addition to what is already a great event, we're thrilled!"* Jim Timon, Universal's senior vice president of entertainment had said at the time. Universal promised that they were extremely excited about taking the three characters and exploring where the park's creative minds could take them. And although the properties were shared on both coasts, each coast would utilize the properties differently.

The step change for both events was no longer working on mazes that were 'inspired' or were a continuation of the IP's story. Instead, much like their day attractions, guests would be placed right into their favorite movies. The change was groundbreaking in the industry and although a vast upgrade for Hollywood, it would also be revolutionary in Orlando as they had never really capitalized on IPs. Murdy spoke of this sea change to themeparkinsider, *"I didn't really look back at all. I knew that fans of horror movies just absolutely loved the brands that they were into and I thought that the ultimate wish fulfillment for those fans would be to get to live their favorite horror movies. Having been someone who went to high school in the 80s, certainly with Freddy and Jason and the Texas Chainsaw Massacre movies, even though the first one came out in the 70s, I was real familiar with those properties. They were icons of horror. I wanted to hit all the details that fans of those movies would want to see. We figured if we targeted the uber-fan, that if we got the details right for them, then everyone else would dig it."* And it would be this new manifesto of horror that would see the event continue to grow and grow over the now continuous run of years it has taken place since 2006.

Universal in Hollywood was starting to be a real player in the haunt industry. Whereas locally Knotts had eclipsed anything that Universal had to offer, it would be the first time in a long while that the public now had a hard choice deciding where to spend their evenings in October. (Even Disneyland got in on the act during this time and started offering their own family-friendly Halloween events for the first time.) But unlike Orlando, Hollywood still needed work to reach parity with its east coast counterpart. And as we'll see, many new and exciting attractions were created for 2007's *Horror Nights* in Hollywood but also much was recycled from the previous year. The headline star mazes that promised to be unlike anything you had ever experienced would be *Friday the 13th: Camp Blood, A Nightmare on Elm Street: Freddy's Nightmare* and *The Texas Chainsaw Massacre: Back in Business*.

Local radio stations played regular commercials that invited guests to the horrors that awaited: "*There are some places where evil is born, and others that were born evil. The Bates Motel, Camp Crystal Lake, The Hewitt House, 1428 Elm Street. It's scary enough that Jack Schmidt believed these places were real. What would be even scarier....*" Targeting the horror-aficionado was key to this new strategy, as to make them appreciate and love your event would mean that the rest would follow. And the mazes delivered in spades.

Camp Blood where guests would come face-to-face with Jason would be an interesting induction into his world. The uninspiring façade would lead to a darkened corridor where the classic "chi chi chi, ha ha ha" (or "kil kil kil, her her her" – I'll let you decide) was repeated over and over to build the anticipation with the crowds. Beyond this, the maze delivered a number of honestly recreated reproductions of some of Jason's classic kills (though mostly from the second movie). The recreated versions of Savini's classic horror setups were successfully translated to a live and claustrophobic format that added a whole new dimension to the haunted house. Animated body bags hung from the ceilings, various consistently-huge 'Jasons' would pop out at unsuspecting guests and the classic blood splatter (but really just water) effects were deployed leaving the guests feeling drenched in viscous blood. A recreation of his mother's shrine and a scene involving a camp counselor trying to escape by driving her VW Beetle away were all absolutely spot on in a maze that was as suspenseful as it was terrifying.

Whereas the Jason was similar in context and sets to the Orlando version, Freddy's *A Nightmare on Elm Street: Freddy's Nightmare* would be wholly different to its east coast cousin. This maze would utilize much of the wildly popular *Asylum* maze from last year but it would tie into the 2007's event so perfectly that you wouldn't notice. The reasoning behind the idea was that the icon of this year was Jack the Clown (again, another popular icon borrowed from Orlando but with a slightly different cover story). Jack, as we know from Orlando, is one of a number of icons who by 2006 in Orlando were banding together to present the horror at the Orlando event. In Hollywood, his introduction to the event was very different.

A pair of scareactors working the Camp Blood maze

Hollywood's event website told the story of how The Director in 2006 would live in the backlot following his contract being terminated by the Studio. And it can be said that he was more often spotted during the day lurking at slightly bemused tourists than he was at the actual event in the evenings. Jack apparently had watched the movies of The Director and became violent following them. So at the darkest hour of October 31st he would come to a theater at Universal that was playing one of his 'snuff-movies' and murder the entire audience. Demented and deluded, the clown would eventually be committed to an asylum named Shadybrook. A psychologist that was studying Jack at the facility was told how The Director's films and movies such as *A Nightmare on Elm Street, Friday the 13th,* and *The Texas Chainsaw Massacre,* inspired him to follow in the footsteps of these veritable slasher villains. To him, every day was Halloween, a day to embrace the inner demons of mankind and to unleash terror upon the stars.

Jack would eventually break out of Shadybrook and in his path of destruction sends the Psychologist a number of postcards from horror-inspired addresses that he visited (these would be shown on the event's website). Postcards from the Bates Motel, Camp Crystal Lake, 1428 Elm Street and the Hewitt House were all sent and eventually the psychologist was able to piece together the psychopath's plan: to take guests into these realms and come face to face with these horrific monsters.

Jack supposedly believed that the true home of horror was the Universal backlot and it was his duty to bring 'horror home'. He would make the 2007 event into a Carnival on the "Hacklot" where the horrors he had visited had been recreated for the world to experience. Ringmaster Jack managed to bring his favorite heroes to life, and together they would stand tall among the children of the night as they wreaked devastation on Universal, transforming the studio into *The Carnival of Carnage*.

"*It's scary enough that Jack believed these places were real. What's even scarier... is if he was right.*"

It is this reason why Freddy was based in an *Asylum*, as this was the location of Shadybrook - the facility where Jack planned his marvelous carnival. The story would have been perfect but eagle-eyed fans spotted that the asylum was actually that of Westin Hill Asylum, a key location within the *Freddy* franchise, which has led many to wonder whether Jack went to Westin Hill instead of Shadybrook. Whatever the answer, the west coast Freddy was vastly different from the Orlando version. Whereas the Orlando version was 'testing' a new sleeping drug on east coast guests, this one was taking you right into the action of an asylum being overthrown by its inmates. The classic "One, two, Freddy's coming for you" song hauntingly rang out as guests ended the dark and dank building. Various inmates, either being tortured or being the torturers, were seen in this multifaceted maze. The maze would incorporate far fewer kills from the *Freddy* franchise but relied on purpose-built special effects that created a scary and sinister maze.

The Texas Chainsaw Massacre: Back in Business was presented at the event to lengthy queues of guests. An impressive outdoors-built façade of Leatherface's house was perfectly recreated on the backlot. The guide map read, "*Leatherface and his family of cannibal crazies have taken over the condemned Blair Meats factory, bringing a new level of terror to the heart of Texas.*" Once inside, the classic door slam scene was recreated, and his weird family of freaks were all portrayed with great makeup effects. The sets were vast in this maze; they were highly detailed and stuffed full of props. Every conceivable distraction was portrayed to totally swamp the senses of each guest while Leatherface disemboweled another victim as various others ran for their lives. Water effects to simulate blood were competing with 'burning flesh' smells that left every guest shocked to their respective cores. It truly was a horrific recreation of the infamous movies.

As with the previous year, *Universal's House of Horrors* and *The Terror Tram* both returned. The *House of Horrors* was now a full-time park attraction and would merely be "plused" for Halloween, though essentially it was the same attraction that guests could dare to enter during the daytime. *The Terror Tram* would be different from The Director's version of the previous year but (as with all the future versions of this attraction) it would largely follow the same path as it had every year. This year's version was named *Horror Comes Home* and would be longer and more detailed than the previous year's version. Guest feedback had been very positive about allowing them to get up close and personal with the backlot, enabling history and horror buffs to get different but similar thrills from walking on this hallowed land. Due to this, the attraction was expanded to tell the story of the event and essentially bring the worlds of these horror icons together. The queue video gave guests some clues as to the misfortune that awaited them, with an interview with Jack's psychologist: *"Every day was Halloween for Jack Schmidt. You meet a lot of delusional people in Hollywood. Jack was different. I was his psychologist during his time at Shadybrook. I knew his darkest dreams, his most demented desires. It's quite common for people to associate with characters in horror movies even to the point of imitating their actions. What is less common is when someone becomes a horror movie. People always ask me, 'Does violence in horror movies create someone like Jack?' Well since his escape, I've been asking myself that question. Especially since these started arriving <holding postcards up to the camera>, it's not just that Jack believes these places are real, he wants to take you, like some kind of demented tour guide. They're taking people out to these famous horror movie locations at night. Where do you think Jack is? Where do you think he's going to go? He's already told me where he's going to go!"*

The attraction would tie the event together nicely, providing all the backstory that the website and press releases hinted at. Killer Klowns flooded the areas around Whoville before scaring guests into the Bates Motel area. The famous daytime experience of seeing Norman carrying another victim to his car was replaced with Jack carrying his own victim to the same car and yelling *"Say hello to your dead tour guide people!"*, which was a great gag on the classic Universal spectacle. Whilst Norman posed for photos and his mother berated guests from the window, guests would enter into Camp Crystal Lake where Jason was seen attacking a number of campers in their tents. Next up was Leatherface's kitchen where he used a chainsaw to carve up meat and 'guests' who weren't quite quick enough to escape. The next portion was an interesting sequel to the Freddy maze from the Upper Lot. In the *Asylum* maze, Freddy is seen recruiting an army of insane murderers to finally destroy the town of Springwood. Whereas the maze elsewhere in the event was the recruiter portion of this story, *The Terror Tram* would be the conclusion of this story, with the town was now being destroyed by his new army (using the *War of the Worlds* set). The woodchipper was back, and instead of The Director at the controls, it was now Jack who pushed various victims through it all night long.

Most of the scarezones from the previous year were once again redrafted for action for this year. These included *Zombie Invasion* in the New York Streets but this time they had more military backup. *Deadwood* came back along with *Haunted London* which appeared to have upgraded fog effects. *HellBilly Hoedown* was moved to the Lower Lot but was not as successful due to space demands. Plague victims also returned in *The Black Death* located in the Parisian Courtyard, much the same as the previous year though some guests believed the makeup looked even more gross than last time.

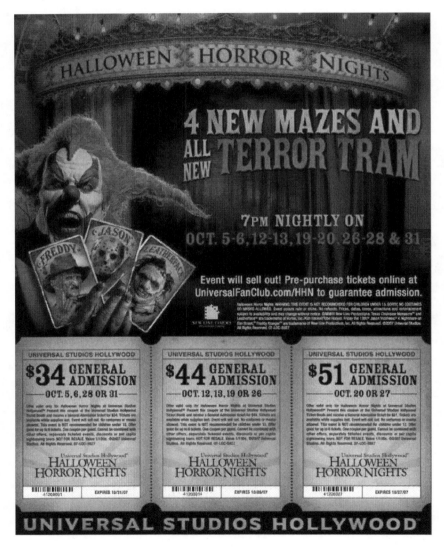

A newspaper advert for the event

Chucky's Insult Emporium and *Slaughter World* both returned in largely the same format as before. *Slaughter World* was slightly different and was marketed as a sequel to the former year's event. Park maps called it: "*A spectacular tidal wave of death-defying stunts, awesome explosions and an ocean of thrills*".

Bill & Ted's Excellent Halloween Adventure made a 'most triumphant' return, thanks to guests demands, as they had been absent the previous year. The usual mixture of pop culture take-downs and satire was played out five times a night to a packed *Fear Factor* auditorium. A much unappreciated magic show was presented in the *Animal Actors Stage* with *Dark Magic and Dirty Tricks*. The show combined a lot of theatrical drama with large visual tricks that seemed very popular at the time. The three rides that were open this year were *Jurassic Park: In the Dark, Revenge of the Mummy: The Ride* and the *Terminator 2: 3D*.

Universal had created an event that was quickly becoming the favorite Halloween destination of Southern Californians. No longer would the argument of whether the event at Hollywood return each year; *Horror Nights* was here to stay.

2008: The Nightmare Tour

"Freddy Krueger the father of all nightmares has invaded Universal's Halloween Horror Nights and turned it and all its attractions into a living nightmare! With Jack gone he runs the show, and dares park guest to take his Nightmare Tour where the world of Horror movies and the Realm of Nightmares collide and for the first time he is loose on the backlot where he dares you to "Live your worst nightmare!"

Guest feedback confirmed that *Horror Nights* 2007 was a huge hit for the Studio. The IP holder was very pleased at how their franchise was used and the ticket sales had reportedly been at near sell-out levels for most nights. This combination of success on all fronts led Universal to work with New Line again and bring the horror icons back to the event. Jack, the icon they had borrowed from Orlando, was dropped and the New Line Cinema *Titans of Terror* became the festival headliners.

It was reported as early as March in *Variety* that Universal's 2007 event had been a major success, so to up their game to the next level they had vastly increased the budget and were about to hire double the amount of scareactors. Murdy told them at the time, *"We keep pushing the limit. As horror movies evolve and change, we feel we have to follow that trend. We're the movie studio that invented horror movies. We have to be more edgy than the horror movies out there."* The mission statement was clear: the event's scope would be enlarged, with more successful use of the IPs that they have secured and with more scares across the board.

The *Titans* were reported to be returning in the summer period of 2008, and by September the official website had been fully updated detailing the horrors that were awaiting. It told the story of how a mentally disturbed Jack had left the backlot, with his army of clowns descending back into their realms and with Jack taking "a bus back to Orlando." It then described how his cacophony of creeps would rise up to stage their own event:

"[Jack] did not count for what would be the fate of the Carnage Killers. One of them, a man in a red and green sweater and a burned visage due to revenge from a lynch mob, had the name of Freddy Krueger. Freddy, like his previous harlequin boss, was a sardonic monster who would lure children with wit, and then brutally take their lives. He was eventually found out and arrested, but due to a legal technicality, he was allowed to walk free, an action which drew forth the decision by the aforementioned lynch mob."

The website recounted how Freddy had raised an army of lunatics from the asylum where he was born. The gang were used to destroy the town of Springwood (as depicted on the *Terror Tram* last year) and eventually his battle was over and Freddy was sent to Hell. Gaining more power within Hell he sought to return to Springwood and bring Hell to Earth via Universal Hollywood. Freddy, as the icon of the event, would bring forth his friends Jason and Leatherface, who together with *The Strangers* would create a living nightmare at *Halloween Horror Nights*.

To show the enlarged scope of the event, Universal decided to vastly increase the number of nights it would be held. These were: October 17-19th, 24-26th, 30-31st, and November 1st. The 'nightmare campaign' as it was named, called on Freddy to star in many of the commercials which for the first time began to air beyond the west coast with more national coverage. A variety of commercials online, on TV and on the radio would advertise the event with Freddy shown gathering his horrors to bring a real nightmare to Southern California. Murdy said of the campaign, *"Every year, if there's a line, we cross it. That's how you touch people. Those things send triggers to your brain."*

The icon's maze that was presented in the Shrek queue would be *A Nightmare on Elm Street: Home Sweet Hell.* The basic premise was that Freddy had been banished to Hell in the previous year, so the residents of Springwood attempt to rebuild their lives and part of that was for them to forget the past and move on. The park maps described the maze: *"When the town of Springwood attempts to sell the dilapidated house at 1428 Elm Street, Freddy Krueger returns to give the beleaguered town a nightmare they'll never forget!"* The façade was a detailed recreation of the house from the infamous movies and once inside guests would see some of Freddy's most famous kills. A stretching room would lead to a room infested with roaches, and beyond that was an electrifying room with dry-ice. Then came a maternity room with a female scareactor giving birth to the spawn of Freddy whilst Freddy acts as the midwife, and finally a lightning effects room would completely swamp the senses of each guest. Throughout each room and most corridors, the flesh-burnt Freddy, complete with iconic razor gloves and striped sweater, was poised to jump out at the conga-line of guests at every available moment; this maze was truly packed with Freddies!

Housed back in the Upper Lot's *Wild Wild West Theater* was *Friday 13th Camp Blood* once more. The maze was an updated version of the previous year's, and included more scareactors and a handful of kills, though it was largely the same as it had been. The park map described it thus: *"After half a century of murder and mayhem, the eternal evil of Jason Voorhees still haunts the ruined remains of Camp Crystal Lake! The grounds are soaked in red at Camp Blood on Crystal Lake, where Jason and his gut-slicing machete are lurking through the woods, waiting to massacre their way through the night. Be careful not to mistake bone fragments for firewood as massacred corpses of previous camp-goers litter the soil. And if you do somehow survive Camp Blood, don't plan on leaving. Because in here, every day is Friday the 13th."*

Another returning maze was *The Texas Chainsaw Massacre: Back in Business* which was an updated version of the previous year's. The maze was slightly extended to feature more of the Blair Meats Factory but by and large it was the same maze. The park map described it further detail, *"Leatherface and his family of cannibal crazies have taken over the condemned Blair Meats Factory, bringing a new level of terror to the heart of Texas. Step inside the #1 rated maze of 2007 and come face-to-face with one of the sickest, most sadistic murderers in the history of film: the one and only Leatherface. His chainsaw will roar as you run for your life through a labyrinth of unspeakable horrors, each more terrifying than the last. You may get out alive, but it could cost you a limb."*

The final maze was also a returner by default but in an updated way. The Universal's House of Horror attraction was still operating full-time in the park and, as with many in future years, it would be slightly re-themed and re-dressed to give exclusive performances to *Horror Nights* attendees. This year it was themed to the recent hit horror movie *The Strangers,* with *Universal's House of Horrors: Meet The Strangers.* Essentially, the maze would be 'cranked-up' by night with all the same scares and scenes but with portions where the masked loons from the hit movie would spring up to scare guests into the next scene. The description read, *"Guess who's knocking on the door? The relentless, masked killers from Universal's latest hit horror film, "The Strangers" have invaded House of Horrors! Come face to face with The Man in the Mask, Pin Up Girl and Doll Face as they stalk the shadowy corridors of a haunted castle, populated by a veritable "who's who" of Universal Horror movie characters, past and present. Terror lurks around every corner, making you wish you'd never walked inside this nightmare. This is one place where you have everything to fear. But they're only movies, right?"*

The tram portion of the event returned with *Terror Tram: The Nightmare Tour.* As promised in the media and on their website, Freddy had taken full control of the backlot and would unleash guests into a seemingly never-ending run of episodic horror-inspired nightmares with each more terrifying than the last. As guests waited in line, clips from some of Freddy's most infamous kills were played on the monitors, the soundtrack to his first movie was played over the speakers and it was announced on loop that *"It is said that if you die in your dreams, you die in real life. You're about to find out. Welcome...to the Nightmare Tour."*

The main areas of the walking portion of the tour were the same as the previous year's, but all were updated and re-themed. *The Grinch* set became a foggy entrance as the guests were dropped off from their trams. The Bates set became a modern slasher movie where a fraternity were being stalked by knife-wielding maniacs. *Friday The 13th: Camp Crystal Lake* was presented on the land behind the *Psycho* House and a small outdoors maze was recreated to house *The Texas Chainsaw Massacre*. *The War of the Worlds* set was repurposed again into a *Nightmare On Elm Street* setup and the pickup (*Mummy* tunnel) had Freddy scaring everyone off from the attraction.

Returning scarezones included *The Black Death, The Dead Shall Rise* (a name change), *Deadwood* and *The Dark Streets of London* – all much the same as they had been in the two previous years. The Chainsaw Drill Team were back and re-costumed as maniacal clowns at the entrance to the park, the zone was called *The Nightmare Begins...* and would act as a teaser for the horrors that awaited. The Lower Lot this year had *Revenge of the Pigs* where, *"Uncle Boarley and his gang of pig-faced maniacs are roaming the lower lot, looking for some fresh meat. Is it true that pigs will eat just about anything? You're about to find out! It's swine time...an experience worse than anything you could ever dream up."* And finally, to really hammer home the cross-promotion, *The Strangers* were free to roam the Upper Lot, posing for photos and generally causing mischief. The shows were all returning and included, *Bill & Ted's Excellent Halloween Adventure, Chucky's Insult Emporium,* and *Slaughter World 3*; each show had been updated from the previous year's versions. *The Freddy Chicks* (as they were known) also debuted this year and were seen dancing on various podiums dotted around the park.

The Eyegore Awards also returned this year and this time included a short-film competition where aspiring film directors could send in their best work for a chance to win a special prize of $1000 and a red-carpet premiere of their feature at the event. The theme was 'where nightmares come alive' and the shortlist of movies was posted on the event's website so that guests could like and share their favorites from the list.

Summing up the event, Murdy told Ventura County's Star, *"We want to keep making the event more extreme to keep up with the horror community at large, and because of a licensing agreement with Warner Bros., we are able to add to this year's lineup. Every year, Horror Nights grows by leaps and bounds. This year, it is twice as long. You get closer to the sets. And there are twice as many sets. The park is surrounded by woods, and we found dusty trails that crisscross in the woods. You will take a trip to Crystal Lake with barely any light to see. The horrors are really around every corner of the park!"* With a combination of returning mazes, revised mazes and the master licensing agreement with New Line Cinema (now owned by *Warner Bros.* as of June 2008), the event had finally returned to its national standing and was yet again ready to deliver the best horrors. It was also not just the fans of the event that were flooding the park but movie executives too. Murdy was seen with a number of different execs, showing them around the park, how the scares worked and the level of detail the event went to in enhancing and protecting the outside IPs they carefully worked with. One such group of these executives was from *Lionsgate,* and their trip on a hot and humid night in October would effectively greenlight one of the most interesting mazes for 2009.

2009: Live or Die

It was following on from the successes of the previous year that Universal began their 2009 haunt season. The change in tempo and the effective stepping up that the event had received had not gone unnoticed. Before long many commentators were observing Universal Hollywood's rise in fortunes to rival Knott's. One such article appeared in the *LA Times*.

'Universal Studios challenges Knott's for Halloween domination', it said, *"The Halloween battle of the theme parks has begun. For decades, Knott's Berry Farm's Halloween Haunt has reigned supreme as Southern California's ultimate theme park for Halloween frights. The Buena Park amusement park started the after-hours tradition more than 30 years ago and is credited with inventing the Halloween mazes duplicated by theme parks nationwide. But this year, officials at Universal Studios Hollywood say they are extending that park's Halloween Horror Nights and relying heavily on its movie connections to knock Knott's from its monster perch."*

To build on the solid reputation they had formed over the last few years, they began by announcing to the press that the event would be extended to 16 nights (up from 13 the previous year) and that various highly-themed IP mazes from a number of special franchises would be presented. They also promised to tie into wider national marketing by having a maze built that would open during HHN as the movie would be hitting theaters, plus a new cell phone app that would help guests with directions, show times and wait lengths.

The movie that was hitting theaters during this time was *SAW VI*. The maze it spawned would be *Saw: Game Over* and it was located in the Mummy queue. The maze would have a twisted description, *"Enter the twisted world of Jigsaw, the demented serial killer from the SAW horror franchise. Someone in your group will not survive this life-altering experience. Will it be you?"* Not only would this maze be the first to tie into the nationwide marketing campaign for the movie, but it was also the first time the franchise had ever appeared in a haunted attraction. Since this maze was devised, the franchise has appeared all over the world in temporary and permanent haunted houses right through to full length attractions such as Thorpe Park in the UK. And although this maze would tease the horrors that were awaiting audiences of *SAW VI*, the maze would effectively be a 'greatest hits' of the scares from the previous five movies. The Lionsgate executives mentioned in the previous chapter were the same people that approved Murdy's (and also Orlando's) use of their SAW franchise at the event. Murdy told bloody-disgusting.com at the time, "*We had to find the greatest hits for all of these movies and bring them to life. We started this in June, Halloween is a year round project. I start during the event thinking about the next year. While we were doing Halloween 2008, filmmakers and Lionsgate were coming down to experience Halloween Horror Nights. They came out saw it last year and saw the level of details. Our target as far as designers is the hardest-core fan in any series. If we hit that demographic, then everyone else will dig it. SAW also plays in the Terror Tram this year, especially Billy. We're actually building Billy, who is animatronic that moves and talks, which you'll see in this attraction. But were using him first for a film shoot that will factor into the Terror Tram, because Billy has a test for everyone on the Terror Tram.*"

Various iconic and gross-out scenes from the franchise were played out within the maze. Starting off with the animatronic puppet as described, the guests were given their instructions as they walked through a decrepit old warehouse. Soon the original bathroom scene from the first movie, complete with blood spraying effects (really just water), would rush guests into faux barbed wired and then into various trap rooms. It was then that a stroke of genius was played out in this impressive house, with 'fake guests' or 'scareactor guests'. It had been rumored for many years that Orlando had placed 'fake guests' within the conga-lines of people to act as not only distractors but for their very loud screams to heighten the tension for the people far behind them in the line of guests. Universal had never admitted this had happened in the past but for this maze this would be the central gimmick. Pulsing through the line in random intervals, Universal would deploy 'Sally' who would tell guests in the line that she was 'on her own' and "do you mind if I cut in here?"; in actuality there would be about three Sally's who would randomly jump into the queue outside the maze but near the entrance. Around a quarter of the way through the maze the now screaming and jumping Sally would be abducted by a Pig Man as guests looked on. Around two scenes later and Sally would be back but not in the line this time but in a trap! Murdy recounted at the time, "*This is the reverse bear trap. Again, you have to pick what part of sequence you want to see. If you remember in the movie poor Shawnee find herself in this bear trap and she has to get the key, which she thinks is in her death cellmate. Right before she takes the scalpel to him, he wakes up. That's the scene we wanna do – with the bear trap, digging in his chest cavity, pulling intestines out, blood spraying all over people!*" Poor Sally. One insider told this author that not one person complained at Guest Services that a female was abducted right in front of them either!

As previously mentioned, Billy the Puppet and the wider SAW franchise were not only the main drivers for the marketing campaigns this year but they also headed this year's *Terror Tram*. The queue would play various scenes from the franchise and run trailers for the upcoming sixth movie. Once on board, the start of the journey was initially very ordinary with the tour guide introduction and a safety warning. But that was until the safety warning's message feed was hijacked and a new video played out... Billy spoke directly to the audience of each tram as it pulled down the hill and into the backlot, it said, *"Hello. I want to play a game. All of you are here tonight for one reason: you want to be scared. You want to know the thrill of being close to death, without ever having to confront it face to face. This is why you watch horror movies. To experience death at a safe distance. Well, tonight all of that is about to change. When this vehicle stops the doors will open and you will get out and walk through a series of test, tests inspired by the very horror movies that you are so obsessed with. Have you ever asked yourself why you watch horror movies? Then let me ask you, Don Roberts: for you and your friends horror movies are an act of rebellion, you're drawn to anything your parents object to. But do your parents know about your other hobbies? The acts of vandalism that you have committed? You'll do anything to leave your mark. But now you are the one who is marked. Tag. You're it. And you, Sherrie Mathews. You say that horror movies give you a rush of adrenaline. But adrenaline is not the only thing coursing through your veins, is it Sherrie? Do your friends know about your secret addiction? Do they know about the things you have stolen from them, to feed those addictions? And what of you, Charles Roebuck? You say horror movies are just an escape. But what are you running from? Could it be the alcoholism that ruined your life? Even now, do you feel the weight of that bottle you've got? Hidden away in your jacket? The one you snuck past security? The day of reckoning has arrived for all of you. But to survive this test, you are going to need help. You see, this is a group test. And to succeed you must survive it together. The game is about to begin. Will your selfish, individual needs trump the safety and wellbeing of the group? Remember: stay together. For even if one of you doesn't make it to the other side, you will all pay the ultimate price. Lose one. lose all. Live or die. The choice is up to you. Let the game begin."* And with that, guests would disembark into their first horrific nightmare.

Despite this initial *SAW* introduction to the Tram, the walking portion of the attraction would be a selection of teaser scares from the various mazes presented (with some extras too!) that would give guests who hadn't attended the other mazes yet some indication of what they might encounter later. Killer Klowns would get guests as they disembarked and they would share with them some show scenes from *My Bloody Valentine*. Next up would be the Bates Motel complete with their inaugural 'Movie Killer Convention'. Unfortunately for

Norman, it turns out he invited real slashers! An outdoors maze of *Halloween* would be next, followed by a zombie containment zone in the *War of the Worlds* set, before more Killer Klowns scared guests back onto their awaiting trams.

2009 would be filled with firsts at Hollywood and another first for them would be the successful inclusive of the Captain James T. Kirk mask-wearing maniac - Michael Myers (I'm not making that mask fact up – google it!). This was located in the Wild Wild West Arena with *Halloween: The Life and Crimes of Michael Myers*. The idea for this maze had its genesis in the previous year, where Murdy hadn't just taken *Lionsgate* executives around the event. Another long-term HHN aficionado and devotee was Rob Zombie, and one evening the pair toured the park together. Eventually, they had seen every maze and zone, and Zombie was heading for the gates. Zombie was alleged to have paused, looked at Murdy and remarked that there was a property that they had never done but actually could be something really big. Murdy recounted to ShockTillYouDrop.com, *"I was walking Rob out and he said, 'Hey, you're missing something'. I said, 'Oh yeah? What am I missing?' And he said Michael Myers. I needed some help on that front so he introduced me to Malek [Akkad]."* What many people didn't know at the time (2008) was that Zombie was in fact making a sequel to the rebooted version of the popular movie madman with Akkad. As soon as the introduction was made, Murdy set to work designing a maze based around the character and within months pitched the maze to the production company. It was greenlit and became this maze.

The maze would another 'greatest hits' maze that would feature scenes and scares from the first three movies (yes even Halloween III!) but would focus on the story of Michael's life from murderous kid to grown psychopath. Murdy told comingsoon.net, *"What's unusual on how this maze is constructed from a design standpoint is we're doing the linear story of Halloween."*

The location would be familiar to park guests from the previous two years as the façade was located right where the *Friday 13th* façade was built. Once inside, the maze began with the murder of Judith Myers. *"Judith's scantily clad body will be laid out on the floor,"* Murdy explains. *"You'll have to walk around it and young Michael, in the clown costume, will pop out to scare you. You'll then get to see something you didn't see in the film. You'll see Michael's room and it's all done in that horrible '70s [vibe] with clown [figurines and paintings]."* After two scenes here, the action moves to a slightly older Michael at Smith's Grove Sanitarium before the murder spree continues in scenes recreated to look like Haddonfield, and that's where *Season of the Witch* comes in (the *Halloween* sequel that didn't have Myers in it). A little-known fact about the movie was that it was released by Universal, so Murdy could hardly pass up an opportunity to have a Universal property in a Universal maze. He said at the time, *"We wanted to embrace a film Universal actually made called Halloween III. The reason why we looked to it is because the movies take place on Halloween night, of course there will be trick 'r* treaters around. So rather than do generic trick 'r treat kids when we're outdoors, we use the pumpkin, skull and witch [masks] from Halloween III for the trick 'r treaters." For which they were deployed to create a great distraction scare!

The attention to detail in the maze was astounding. Murdy supposedly had to commission seven different companies to recreate the iconic mask because each iteration wasn't perfect. Via various Hollywood connections he had obtained many of Carpenter's original notes on the movie. Seeing how meticulous Carpenter had been ensured that every exact detail from the picture was correct, because after all, this maze would be filled with Myers. "For our Michael performers, if you know the movie, every time you see Michael there's a music sting. Those stings John Carpenter wrote. I have access to all of that stuff. So every time Michael appears, that performer has a foot pedal switch that allows him to control his own audio and also control the lighting cue in the room. Behind here <a boo hole>, we'll place a strobe light behind him, so when he busts through that door it's very disorientating. Our guests will be blinded."

Chucky's Funhouse would be up next. It would be a simple layover of Universal's fulltime attraction House of Horrors.

It was billed as, "America's favorite serial killer doll is taking matters into his own, little hands. Chucky has taken over an old, carnival funhouse and is raising an army of Killer Dolls to take his ultimate revenge on humanity!"

Mixing puppets and real-life scareactors dressed as Chucky, the maze would feature a number of gory and jump-scare-type scenes that mixed in with the daytime scares. This wasn't everyone's favorite maze this year but it was cool if not interesting to get different sized Chuckies featuring in a gothic setting which was very unlike anything anyone had seen before.

The final maze would be another newbie to the haunt world, with My Bloody Valentine: Be Mine 4 Ever based on the popular 3D horror movie that had been released in January of that year. Filling the space left by the two previous incarnations of the Freddy maze, the maze would be built inside the Shrek queue. Taking its cue from the movie, the maze would be billed as "Ten years ago, a horrible mine cave in led to the deaths of several miners on Valentine's Day. The mine was shut down and a scape-goat was found. Now, 10 years after the anniversary of the disaster... Harry has returned to take his revenge."

Not only did the maze reuse Freddy's location but some former Freddy props and showpieces were also used and re-dressed into this movie. The reason behind this was a rumor that the maze had originally been planned to be based on the new release of The Wolfman (2010). The rumor said that this decision was later changed so The Wolfman would be an Orlando exclusive and Halloween would be Hollywood's exclusive. Whether this is true or not, it would go some way into explaining why the maze looked as though the same attention to detail that went into building the others had not been wholly matched. One insider told me that, as with the movie, they originally wanted the maze to be in 3D but due to time and scheduling conflicts the idea was pulled. Regardless of how the maze came to be, it was still a faithful interpretation of the popcorn slasher (*or pickaxe slasher!*) movie which was very popular with the crowds.

SAW wasn't just part of a maze and the Tram Tour; it also featured in two scarezones on the Upper and Lower Lots with *Let the Games Begin!*

("Once you step through the turnstiles of Halloween Horror Nights, the game is on! Your first challenge is to make it past Jigsaw's chainsaw wielding, pig-faced minions, but don't get to close... or you may end up a victim yourself")

and *There Will Be Blood!* Hordes of these Pigmen, complete with chainsaws, would wait for guests as they entered and then scare them into the park. Another film franchise that was also presented at the event was the popular British horror-comedy of *Shaun of the Dead*. This maze would have a mere cameo scene in Orlando whereas at Hollywood they had a full zone to play in. The Streets of London area was the base for this fun zone, as characters lovingly recreated from the popular 2004 movie were seen doing battle with zombies down Baker Street. The Upper Lot also had *Welcome to Hell*, where various demons from Hell had been summoned to do battle. The Streets of Paris would be the venue for *Freakz* scarezone, a zone that debuted this year and returned for two more. This year's version featured a ragtag bunch of carny folk who set up shop in Paris, and with a certain amount of misdirection and manhandling, begin to literally consume their customers. Cannibalism was also seen on the *Western Streets* with *Meat Market*, where ghoulish butchers lurked to find unsuspecting victims.

Hollywood HHN would feature two popular shows, with *Bill and Ted's Excellent Halloween Adventure* and *The Rocky Horror Picture Show: A Tribute*. The latter was a new addition to the lineup for 2009. *"A cult phenomenon! Now, Halloween Horror Nights pays tribute to the mad scientist Dr. Frank N. Furter, and all of your favorite Transylvanians in a brand-new production. Sorry no costumes or props allowed."* The last sentence was reinforced to guests in the marketing, as many fans of this show often come dressed as their favorite characters from it, and as we all know, costumes are not allowed!

The festivities of 2009 were very successful. For the first time in a long time, Universal could proclaim to the media and fandom beyond that everything at this year's event was new, never before seen at a haunt attraction and knitted together as though you were in your own horror movie. Fans repaid this hard work by selling out selected nights and thoroughly enjoying the event; many took to social media to let the world know how good the event was. It was also reported in *The Signal* that perhaps for the first time ever, Universal may have outshone their Californian rivals. No matter what the gate numbers were, Universal Hollywood was surely one of the main Halloween haunt players nationwide.

2010: Chucky's Revenge

Building on the success of the last two years, Universal decided to mix up the event and use properties from this past two successful years but with a twist. The tagline for the event would read, "*what fear fears most*", as some of the diabolical cinematic murderers and madmen were assembled for another stellar year of frights. Arguably, the host of this event would be Freddy Krueger who would act as the event's icon and be front and center in most of its marketing. John Murdy, the creative director, was possibly becoming somewhat of an icon for the event as he would be the sole person who seemed to showcase the scores of print, online and television outlets every year. Murdy had quickly become the face of West Coast horror for HHN, with many media outlets and fans alike wanting to know just as much about the horror supremo as they did about the annual event. Murdy took it all in his stride and admitted to one source, "*I have the greatest job in the world.*" The only downside he told the *LA Times* was, "*I can never get the manufactured scent of burning bodies out of my nose!*"

As in previous years, Murdy had been busy as the event was a year-round occupation for him and his ever-expanding team. This year, the staffing quota had grown yet again with 500 scareactors and an additional 250 crew members overseeing makeup, costumes, light, sound, prosthetics, construction and other behind-the-scenes roles. Now planned for 17 nights with the first few weekends selling-out before the event even started, the year promised to be a bumper year filled with some imaginative scares.

The unofficial icon's maze would be first up and it would it be based on the recently released rebooted version of *Nightmare on Elm Street.* Located in the *Shrek* building guests were invited to: "*Return to the town of Springwood, the scene of Freddy's horrific crimes, and take a journey through a living nightmare as Freddy Krueger waits for you in the darkness."* The maze would take guests through the traumatized town of Springwood, including the abandoned ruins of the Badham Pre-School, a spree of carnage at Springwood High and, finally, to a showdown with Freddy himself in his infamous Boiler Room lair. Supposedly, no punches were pulled and this maze was incredibly scary. One of the scariest and perhaps one of the most iconic scenes from the movie was located in the bathroom. The bathtub was replicated in silhouette with the infamous Freddy claw reaching up from beneath the water between Nancy's legs. As guests were transfixed by this moment, another Freddy appeared from the other end of the bath via a bathroom mirror to make guests jump. It was topped by a bigger scare: the mirror Freddy vanishes just as a full-bodied Freddy bursts out of the bathroom wall via a boo-hole with triggered sound effects and lightening changes. It is a credit to Universal's genius that they would take one of the most iconic Freddy scenes and make it the centerpiece for frights within this impressive maze.

Freddy wasn't the only slasher returning for more action, as our favorite hockey mask-wearing weirdo also returned with *Friday the 13th: Kill Jason Kill*. Universal described the maze as, *"The eternal evil that is Jason Voorhees still haunts the ruined remains of Camp Crystal Lake. Now it's your turn to venture into the lair of the infamous killer and come face to face with the man behind the mask. This chilling labyrinth will take you through the cursed woods of Camp Crystal Lake, into the haunted ruins of the Voorhees house and down into Jason's secret underground tunnels. For the first time, Universal had not put an entry showing the queue time at the front of the queue, but instead nearby."*

Located on the Wild Wild West Stage area, the maze would also be a maze based on the rebooted version of this franchise. The *LA Times* was given the opportunity to tour the massive temporary makeup facility named Scare Base that was built in the parking structure every year. On their tour they spoke to a scareactor who worked the maze. She commented on how everyone who works the scares works so hard. Her role within the maze was as one of Jason's kills – a 'grindstone kill', in fact. *"Places on my body get sore that I don't expect,"* she said

"All night long she gets her face ground off by Jason," said Murdy cheerfully, as he watched the makeup artist apply prosthetics that turned her face into roadkill.

Returning for another year of gory torture was the ever-popular SAW franchise with *SAW: Game on*. It was described as, *"Jigsaw's twisted lifework lives on through his demented disciples. However, somewhere along the line, his vision of teaching people the value of life was lost. With his deranged followers running the show, the rules have changed. And that means bad news for you. Get ready to face a new gauntlet of death traps inspired by the most horrific contraptions from the Saw film series."* The maze would effectively be a repeat of the previous year, although some minor tweaks had occurred. *SAW 3D* had been released in theaters towards the end of the haunt's run with the maze acting as a tool to entertain and tease the upcoming feature. The maze was wildly popular yet again, and guests had enjoyed the reliving scares from the previous year. The only changes were that the garage and the blade train from the new movie were added as new scenes at the end of the maze.

Universal's *House of Horrors* was re-dressed yet again with a more female vampire-centric theme, which was a vast improvement on the *Chucky* layover from the previous year. It was described as, *"There is evil living inside Castle Dracul! Deep inside this crumbling, 18th century manor lives an ancient cabal of vampires whose bloodline stretches back to the Dark Ages. Inspired by the vampire origin myths of Old World folklore, Vampyre: Castle of the Undead takes you down into the underworld den of these unnatural beings. It is a shadowy world devoid of light and color, and all you will be able to see is blood."*

The final maze would be *Rob Zombie's House of 1,000 Corpses in 3D ZombieVision!* and it would be featured in the *Terminator* queue building. On first inspection, many diehard HHN fans would be mistaken if they thought this maze was 'just' another 3D maze. It was, but the really interesting thing about this maze was that they used the original sets and props to bring it to life. As you will have read in a previous chapter, the original movie had been built from a maze that was built for HHN on the backlot. So, it was a great surprise to Murdy and his team that when searching the cavernous prop warehouse on the backlot that the company had retained and protected the original set pieces. *"I went through it with people in the movie and the effects supervisor for the film,"* said Rob Zombie at the time. *"They did a build-out using the original props. For all of us, it was a very strange experience because we felt we had gone back in time and were on set."* The vibrant palette of the movie was used by the creatives to inject some nifty misdirection scares courtesy of the cardboard 3D specs that were handed out to guests as they entered the faithful maze. Scenes involving Tiny, Baby, and Otis, using like-for-like costumes and makeup, allowed the scareactors to provide performances that were nearly 100% similar to the movie. The biggest scare of the maze was reserved for Dr. Satan by way of a misdirection that scared guests right out the door. Guests loved this maze. A poll was undertaken at the end of the event's run with *SAW* and this maze apparently came out on top. One guest told this author, *"It was 3D but you didn't need the 3D to enjoy this maze, it was terrifying!"*

You can never keep a killer doll down and that's exactly what happened in 2010 with Chucky taking over the proceedings at the *Terror Tram*. The murderous doll was back but so were many of the scares from last year. And despite attempts to have him hiding in doll form in a variety of windows and displays the tour was very similar to the previous year. The one major change though was that the new daytime attraction portion of the tour *King Kong 360 3-D* was up and running, with guests loving the returning digital ape (the large animatronic had been lost to a serious fire some years previously).

The cavernous Property Department on the Universal Backlot

The scarezones were also increased and bumped up to six, although *Freddy's Fly Girls* were present yet again, dancing and scaring guests in equal measures at the park gates with *Nightmarez*. Perhaps one of the most interesting zones for this year was *La Llorona*. Located in the Western Streets they brought to life this Mexican urban legend to great effect. *"For the first time, cross paths with La Llorona ("The Weeping Woman") who after drowning her children and herself, returns to haunt the living, wailing for her lost children ("Aaaay, mis hijos") and searching for new souls to replace them."*

There had been some speculation that the scarezone was originally to be based on another urban legend, that of Bloody Mary. It seemed that Mary, who was used for the 2008 event in Orlando, had intellectual rights for her likeness on merchandise, therefore it was likely that Universal did not want to tempt fate again and attempt to use the character for the foreseeable future.

On the *London Streets* they had *Lunaticz* which included, *"The notorious White*

Chapel Asylum is home to the most dangerously disturbed inmates in England. Unfortunately, the lunatics have overrun the asylum and slaughtered their caretakers. Finally freed from the cruel confines of the Asylum, these blood-crazed loonies have begun a murderous rampage through the foggy streets of London." Moody and dry ice-filled streets, with Victorian and Jack the Ripper type characters have always worked well in these narrow streets depicting London. Combined with no additional lighting and bright strobe lights, the zone disoriented guests and created some well-deserved and unexpected scares.

Freakz returned for another outing in the Paris Streets, yet again using largely the same props and costumes as before. Pigz was also returning, to the same spot where pig mask-wearing mad people from SAW were waiting at the escalators on the Lower Lot for more victims to chase around. Another interesting zone was Klownz. It was a popular zone with lots of guest interaction and some laughs. The popular zone would be presented in the New York area and would be set to return for forthcoming events based on the positive feedback received from guests. Bill & Ted's Excellent Halloween Adventure returned for another gag and dance routine-filled addition. This time big laughs were held at the expense of the Facebook movie Social Network, Tim Burton's Alice in Wonderland, Prince of Persia flopping badly, Miley Cyrus and a meat-wearing Lady Gaga who proclaimed, "it's okay to wear meat if its organic."

Murdy gave an in-depth interview to the LA Times about his role in the event and how successful it had become for Universal Hollywood. He told them how at the early age of just ten he built his very first haunted house in his parent's garage. He spoke about how horror and the event were a part of his DNA. Following the 'chainsaw chase out', a tradition in Hollywood to ensure the park is empty of event guests at the end of each night, he would always be the last to leave. Closing down the Tram Tour would be next, followed by walking down to the Psycho house to switch the lights off and ensure everything is as it should be. "The last thing I turn off are the lights in the Psycho house, and it's all quiet and everyone's gone," he said. "I'm just still in awe. That's Alfred Hitchcock's Psycho house, one of the most classic horror films of all time."

Sell out nights, strong reviews and excellent guest feedback meant that this year would be a continued success for the theme park, maintaining their well-earned and respected name for providing an excellent Halloween experience.

103

The "Real" Ghosts of Universal Hollywood:

The Psycho Set Haunting

Carl Laemmle opened Universal City on March 14th, 1915. The opening day event would be a huge affair, where Laemmle, ever the showman, would give the performance of a lifetime to open his dream Hollywood film studio. The opening ceremonies for the 15,000 attendees would be spread out amongst the 500-acre lot and include: a cavalcade of Cowboys and Indians, dancing showgirls, flower displays, a gigantic flood (much like the one they still have to this day on the main Studio Tour), car chases, and pilot displays. The festivities would roll into three days' worth of entertainment where the world's media were invited to see this new impressive production facility. But while the merriment and festivities rolled along during this fantastical opening bonanza, it was not all celebrations. For on March 16[th,] a deadly tragedy would strike.

On the morning of the 15[th,] Universal had planned to recreate a war time aviation fight scene. Recreating the scene, Universal got their production crews to come up with a shooting schedule complete with cameras, actors and sets. The centerpiece of the action would be a dogfight in the skies above Universal where a small one-man airplane would fly above a larger dummy plane to seemingly drop a bomb from above. The larger plane would deploy plumes of smoke and then "crash" off property (but would really just land in a nearby landing strip).

Experienced pilot Frank A. Stites was employed to fly the one-man plane and drop the bomb from above. The 33-year-old aviator had an unblemished reputation for flying safely in his 6-year career of flying commercial planes. His reputation and his professionalism were paramount for the Studio, who insisted on finding someone who was competent to undertake the tricky maneuver. He was an unassuming man, he was tall and was reported as having a happy demeanor with a jovial laugh. The process all went to plan on the ground where actors dressed as various military type folk all acted their part. A few minor stunts on the ground were performed including a few special-effects for the gathered crowds. But the finale, with the bombing of the plane scene, did not go according to plan.

An artist rendition of Frank A. Stites and his plane, inspired by actual photographs of the incident

106

The smaller plane or biplane that Stites controlled did not take-off on its first attempt, owing to the fact that the fake bomb attached was too heavy or not properly attached to it. In addition, there were also problems with heavy winds. The resulting delay led the sequence to be rescheduled for the next day (16th) when over 2,000 guests from the press and media gathered to finally see the fixed biplane undertake its daring mission. This time, everything seemed to go to plan. The plane took off and the bomb (which had been changed to a bundle of cloth) seemed to be a suitable alternative bomb for the biplane. The experienced aviator circled three or four times as directed, before heading towards the dummy plane. The problem came when the explosive hidden in the dummy plane went off too quickly. The confusion of the smoke and the now rapidly unwinding cloth bomb ensured that the scene from the ground looked very impressive. But unfortunately, this would not be so safe for Stites. The confusion of the smoke and then the wavering bomb led Stites to lose control of the biplane and while he was around 50 feet up in the air he either fell from his plane, thinking the ground was closer than it really was, or he was flung from it. The gathered audience witnessed the poor man fall and then with great impact he fell head first into the ground where "*his spinal column was driven into the skull*', killing him instantly.

Following the accident, Carl Laemmle himself announced that all further festivities would be cancelled without delay, and the crowds were asked to leave. Stites' death on the last day of the grand opening of the Studio would be reported in the local papers but otherwise no further mention of him would be seen again... that is until some strange occurrences began happening on the backlot late at night during preparations for Horror Nights.

The tales of a ghostly reappearance at Universal began in 2005, around 80 years to the day from when Stites lost his life. John Murdy and his colleague were scouting locations for the Terror Tram when one night around the Bates Motel set, they were pitching ideas to each other and were suddenly disturbed. Knowing that the Studio was shut for the day and that they were the only crew members in this part of the backlot, they were surprised to hear some truly diabolical giggling. Being scared witless, the pair quickly dropped their plans for the evening and swiftly left. Scaring horror fanatic Murdy must have taken some doing, so we can assume that what the pair heard must have been terrifying.

Murdy recounted the whole episode to *Creepy LA* back in 2016. He told how he had run ahead of his colleague Casey before sheepishly returning. The pair picked up their belongings and laughed off the sound. Within a minute or so the laughing started again. This time it sounded closer and even more blood-curdling. The pair ran away from the area and went home for the night. By the next day, the story started to make the rounds that Murdy and Casey had encountered a ghost on the backlot. Within days the whole Studio was talking about the episode but instead of calls of shenanigans or fakery, Murdy would start to receive reports and stories from other Studio workers who had witnessed their own ghostly experiences whilst working late at the backlot.

Murdy made a note of the sighting reports he received from his colleagues. Many were very different and included the Phantom stage, whereas others reported not just a 'terrifying' laugh but also reported seeing a man with a vintage aviator type costume complete with leather helmet, jacket and boots roaming the grounds around the Bates Motel set. What made Murdy's blood run cold was that these experiences took place at the exact same location where he and his colleague Casey witnessed the sinister giggling. He soon dug deep into the archives and discovered the frightful story of Stites on the opening day weekend of 1915. Chillingly, the place where Stites hit the ground is the wooded hill that wraps around from the front of the Bates Motel to the main Bates House in its current location (note that the Bates set has moved location a number of times in the past).

Once Murdy had undertaken this research and found out about this deathly secret from Universal's past he decided to make an effigy of the aviator as a tribute to his sacrifice. Ironically, the set immediately behind the Psycho set is Spielberg's *War of the World* set which features a crashed jumbo-jet. The effigy, if you look carefully the next time you're ever on the *Terror Tram*, is usually located underneath the fuselage, or sometimes in the main cockpit wearing his leather jacket and helmet. Various scareactors have also dressed up as the aviator on select nights. Murdy claims that since the tribute was installed annually for *Horror Nights* the reports of giggling or seeing aviator-dressed men have all but ceased. This author contacted Murdy and asked if the story was true, and his response was, *"It's all true, every word."*

But Stites is not the only ghostly spirit thought to roam the backlot of Universal Hollywood....

The Haunting of Stage 28

It was 1923 when Studio founder Carl Laemmle took a short vacation to Paris. During his time there he met with local author Gaston Leroux who had been working in the burgeoning French film industry. Laemmle remarked to Leroux that whilst on vacation he would be scouting locations for inspiration for another smash hit, following on from his wildly popular release *The Hunchback of Notre Dame*. Laemmle, on one such tour, was shown the Paris Opera House and instantly fell in love with its architecture and grandeur. On recounting this visit to Leroux, Leroux swiftly presented him with a copy of his 1910 novel *The Phantom of the Opera*. Fascinated by the discovery, Laemmle took the book back to his hotel room and read the whole story in one night. He saw that the story would not only be a great follow-up to the *Hunchback* story with its similar unrequited love and gothic showpieces, but that it would also feature the theatre he had so admired. Within weeks on his return to Universal City, he bought the rights from Leroux and set about making the book into his next blockbuster hit.

Production commenced on the backlot at Universal in 1924 where in total some 4,000 cast and crew members would be hired to star in and to build the elaborate sets and showpieces. The movie, for its time, would be the most expensive production ever undertaken at a cost of $1.5 million (a figure unheard of back in the early days of cinema). The centerpiece of the grand auditorium of the Paris Opera House would be constructed exactly like-for-like with only minor changes to facilitate the large camera and lighting equipment. To house this huge set, Laemmle also used the budget to construct Hollywood's first steel and concrete-poured building, such was the confidence in the picture and the studio's ongoing success. Indeed, Laemmle, ever the showman, would show this as a physical sign to the press and stakeholders that he was "*concreting Universal's future and on-going success*" with this picture. That soundstage would be known as 'Stage 28', or later on just as 'The Phantom Stage'.

French artisan Ben Caray, who didn't speak much English, was brought over from France as he worked in and had known the Opera House for many years. It was his job to replicate the Opera House in Hollywood. Caray took onsite detailed drawings and photographs to mirror the building exactly, down to the exact quantity and design of each piece of gilded filigree. The cost of the theatre reproduction alone was around $750,000, which was the highest for any set construction for many decades after its construction. The lifelike theatre would house 3,000 seats (constructed using the same fabric supplier as the real Opera House) and would be ever so slightly altered to enable better film production. This included: putting a slight camber into the stage to enable a better view of the actors upon it; installing miniatures of the sets off camera to plan action scenes; and adding additional rigs and supports to hide lights and to allow camera access.

The production was an unhappy one. According to various reports from the set, Chaney and the rest of the cast and crew did not work well with Rupert Julian (the picture's director). The New Zealand-born director clashed with the cast and crew in equal measure throughout the filming. Tensions got so bad with Chaney, who was playing the title character, that Julian would use his director of photography as a go-between, issuing notes on his performance between takes. Other issues with the crew came to head in December 1924 when during production the technicians and some of the supporting cast grew tired of the shooting conditions. A colder than average spell in December, coupled with the undercroft caves filled with ice-cold water, became a combination for too many to bear. The director laughed off their concerns, even when many workers didn't turn in for work stating they were suffering with colds after being drenched in ice-cold water all day. Their concerns were not taken seriously, as many of the same cast and crew had complained previously that the lightings rigs setup throughout the set made their makeup run and made them sweat into their costumes.

Chaney in his classic makeup

Eventually the bust-ups led to Chaney directing many of his own sequences and for Julian to walk away from the picture towards the end of its production. The first cut of the film was previewed in Los Angeles on January 7th and 26th, 1925.

Three endings were filmed, one as originally written in the book, another as planned by the director and one filmed by Chaney after the director left the company. The ending that was previewed in front of test audiences was the original ending, as per the book. Initially, the test audiences did not like the lovelorn Phantom returning to his lair, and so Universal hired another director to complete a fourth ending which featured the more exciting conclusion of the mob. The movie would be released to great fanfare and would become the blockbuster that Laemmle hopped it would be, cementing Universal's place as the producer of the ultimate 'thrillers' (horror movies would often be referred to as thrillers during this time). The sets and soundstage would be reused for countless productions over the following decades before the Parisian sets would be disassembled and the building totally demolished in 2014. This author was in the backlot in 2014 to witness the disassembles and saw first-hand how the sets were protected and conserved for posterity and possible future use.

The reason for mentioning this classic movie and its infamous soundstage is that for many years it was rumored to be haunted by a tormented soul. For many, that soul was Lon Chaney, the picture's main star and 'the man of a thousand faces'. For years, people working in and around this soundstage would report seeing a 'caped stranger' lurking high above in the catwalks and balconies of the set. The rumor dates back to March 1941 when various workmen dressing the set for use in another production would swear that they were being watched by a stranger in the shadows. As the stories left the Studio and headed for the gossip columns of the local papers, news started to swirl around tinsel town that the strange ghostly visitation was that of Lon Chaney.

As the years wore on and the set became more decrepit and the balconies were definitely out of use, so quite how anyone pulling this potential prank got up there is anyone's guess. Others report that they saw Chaney with his infamous Phantom makeup staring at them from behind a curtain or running down one of the many catwalks to disappear into the shadows. Others, such as John Murdy, say the ghostly appearances are that of an electrician who died during production, falling from said catwalks. This urban legend has been reproduced by many sources over the years but the origin of it is somewhat of a mystery. This author checked the archives and although a few very serious accidents occurred during production, there appears to be no report of said electrician being killed or being injured; perhaps this was struck from the record? Employing a complement of over 4,000 staff would surely have resulted in at least some injuries, particularly in this era long before health and safety restrictions.

However, two serious backlot accidents did occur around the time of production. During production of *The Midnight Sun* (1926) which was shot just after production wrapped for *Phantom*, a number of sets were destroyed in one of the earliest episodes of fires on the backlot. The movie featured a number of actresses who were trampled and some who suffered smoke inhalation. None of these were thought to be fatal but the movie did make use of some of the *Phantom* sets, which were undamaged during this fire. The fire started on a set that was a replica of a Parisian ballet, where lighting equipment got too close to the lumber supports. According to the report, the whole set swiftly caught alight sending the 500 actors and crew running for the doors. The resulting chaos led to the various injuries mentioned and the whole set to burn to the ground, costing Universal some $15,000 in labor and materials to rebuild it. This event was not listed as fatal for the actresses but another accident during the production of *Phantom* had a more serious outcome.

Silent movie actress and British native Kate Lester had starred for Universal in the *Hunchback* movie before being recast in a number of other roles for the company. It was during production of the Phantom movie that she would sadly pass away. Lester, who knew many of the cast and crew of the *Phantom* movie, was said to have been a regular visitor to the set on days when she was not filming on the backlot, or between takes. Sadly for Lester, it would be towards the end of the *Phantom* shoot that she would be killed in an explosion inside her dressing room. Lester, who had retired to her dressing room one afternoon, was re-applying makeup (as many stars of this era all did their own makeup). While she was in there her gas stove, supplied for the cooler months, had been leaking gas into the room. Perhaps it was the smell of the greasepaint or hairspray that rendered her unable to notice the lethal gas entering her room but for whatever reason, when she attempted to light the stove it resulted in the explosion that caused her death. Hearing the explosion inside the room, Studio hands broke the door down and immediately rushed her to the Hollywood Hospital. She had suffered severe burns to her face and torso and arrived unconscious. She passed away shortly after. So as far as this author's investigations have found, this was the only death that occurred during and very near to the production of *Phantom*. So, could the ghostly visitations have been from actress Kate Lester? We shall probably never know, but that didn't stop a few from trying to guess...

By the '80s and '90s, the fact that people reportedly saw ghosts around the backlot was nothing new. It was reported by one insider that security personnel got such a steady trickle of reported sightings that they just didn't bother to check any longer. They remarked that the signage clearly said the set was fragile, so if people wanted to pull pranks they were in the wrong location. However, not everyone shared the security personnels' more tangible concerns, so in late 1998 on Halloween night a team of crack 'ghostbusters' were brought in to investigate the spectral sightings. From 10pm until 4am the team sat all night undertaking a variety of modern tests to finally unmask who the ghost of Stage 28 really was.

The team was headed by Larry Montz a parapsychologist and research society founder of the International Society for Paranormal Research. Within minutes of being inside the creepy theater set, a series of knocks could be heard before a variety of different creaks from the upper balconies were noticed. Listening equipment and a variety of frequency meters were deployed, and initially a harsh and authoritative voice was heard. The voice was bossy and made references to how he/she was in charge and that only instructions from them should be acted upon. It made the team suspect that the ghost might have been a director who wasn't being listened to, much like Rupert Julian during the production of *Phantom*. A Hollywood historian confirms the suspicions of the crew and the case was all but closed until the various readers and recorders started to pick up another voice.

The voice of young and friendly girl started to be heard. She seemed to be about 10 to 12 years old. On site, a physic started to pick up her vibes and could see visions of a young girl of around this age group with long dark hair playing between the soundstages. According to the investigation group, her name was Janet, she had died at some point in the 1970s, and her soul now giggles and plays around the grounds after dark. The only record this author could find of a Janet being anywhere near this soundstage was Janet Leigh in 1959 when Hitchcock's *Psycho* was shot within the building (the Bates House interiors were built at the far end of the soundstage facing the theater). On occasion, production teams had reported seeing children on the backlot but usually these were the kids of the production and cast members who were shooting on the backlot. But what stood out for this investigation team and for this author was the reports of giggling and laughing. Reportedly long after the little girl had left, the final noise that the investigation team heard as they left Stage 28 that night was the faint sound of another person laughing. Instead of phantoms, aged actresses or little girls, could this laughter be that of pilot Frank A. Stites? Surely we will never know but next time you are on the *Terror Tram* and are dodging the scareactors on the various scenes, just have a thought that when these living monsters and ghouls have left for the night, this backlot likely has a few 'real' ghosts roaming forever more.

Or *does* it?

Universal became the home of horror in the following decades and they were keen to play up their monster connections in everything they did. Even during the construction of the *Phantom* Stage, Laemmle paid for all construction vehicles to be emblazoned with the slogans 'Phantom Construction'. The signage would hit the media and act as a tease to the readers for Laemmle's next big picture. So in a way the Studio used this free advertising to better establish the Studio's reputation for horror and now, much later, for Halloween; when people think of Halloween in California or Orlando, for millions of people worldwide, it has to be Universal Studios. There was a real need to use these stories for the betterment of the Studio.

It was with some reluctance that this Author was tipped off about a report that laid bare exactly what the ghost of Stage 28 really was. A longtime Universal insider remembered an article that had appeared in *The Oakland Tribune* on July 17th, 1938. It appears that shortly after Chaney died in 1930, his legacy and back catalogue of horror may have inspired the rumors, but by the end of the decade people started to become obsessed that his ghost was now walking the *Phantom* sets at night. So according to the article, after a good eight years of hearing these rumors, gold medal winning Olympian and actor Buster Crabbe decided he must discover the truth of these spectral reports. The 'Jungle Man' as he was once known following a number of *Tarzan*-like movies he starred in, Crabbe would later become more famous for portraying *Flash Gordon*. It was during the filming of these sequels, in his *Flash Gordon* costume no less, that Crabbe set about searching for the truth within the soundstage.

During filming, the production was using the soundstage for various scenes built to one side of the old theater. As soon as filming began, various 'moans' and 'giggles' could be heard off camera. Swiftly Crabbe quipped to the director and said, "*Old Chaney's ghost is apparently watching us today.*" Actress Frances Robinson who was also on set (and who would eventually be cast in Universal's *Dr Jekyll and Mr Hyde*) started to get uneasy. As the sound continued, she was reported as shrieking very loudly "*there it goes again!*" Crabbe, ever the hero on and off the set, decided now was the time to finally put paid to this legend. Grabbing a nearby rope that hung from one of the catwalks he climbed up and managed to jump onto one of the upper balconies. Carefully walking up to the corner of the balcony in the darkest portion of the stage he followed the 'moans' until they led him to a surprising conclusion.

As Crabbe disappeared from view there was silence and the murmurs of the top balcony ceased. Suddenly and without warning a fight had broken out on the top balcony. Whomever or whatever had been making these ghostly sounds was now in a fight to the death with Flash Gordon (Author's note: *I swear I'm not making this up!*). Within seconds the fight was over and the shouts and cries from the crew gathered below were now silent as they waited with bated breath. A second later Crabbe appeared, cut and bleeding. He grabbed the rope and slowly descended to the ground. The crowd audibly gasped, as his injuries from defending himself from this unknown ghoul could be seen close up. The crowd gathered around Crabbe looking at his bleeding cuts and scratches to his arms and hands. Demanding answers, they looked at him as he suddenly smiled and from his pocket presented a handful of long brown feathers. He said to them, "*It was owls! There is a hole in the corner of the roof. They must have been nesting up there for years!*"

Case closed?

As to why this rumor didn't cease after this discovery is interesting. It is thought perhaps that a good ghost story for the house of horror is better than a flock of aggressive nocturnal birds...

The "ghost" of Alfred Hitchcock

Universal Hollywood is not the only Universal destination to allegedly have "ghosts" within its boundaries, as apparently Universal Orlando also has a ghost or two. The most famous urban legend to come from this East Coast incarnation is that famed movie director Alfred Hitchcock haunts his former attraction. When Universal Orlando originally opened, it housed a fairly popular Hitchcock attraction that was part show and part 3D film presentation. That attraction has long since been refitted as a *Shrek* attraction but according to the legend, Hitchcock has not left the house.

When Hitchcock left this mortal coil in 1980 he had worked with Universal for the final two decades of his life. His production company Shamley, which held the licensing to all his pictures that he produced in the second half of his career, was quickly acquired by Universal to cement his reputation as one of the greatest filmmakers of all time. That's why in the months after his death the idea was floated of adding a celebration-come-attraction to the plans for Universal's own 'Florida Project'.

When Universal Orlando opened in 1990 it featured the *Alfred Hitchcock: The Art of Making Movies*, which was formerly located in the current Shrek soundstage. It was a glorious attraction that mixed show elements with practical sets for guests to explore. It featured a 3D film which included the greatest scares from his back catalogue of movies. Hitchcock wasn't a horror director but he did direct a cacophony of thrillers that featured everything from adventure to spying but mostly murder – the latter of which was the key feature of the show. Birds flying at the screen, slicing knives and rotting corpses ... all were presented in 3D to terrify guests. Added to this was a pre-show that featured Anthony Perkins, the star of *Psycho,* who walked the guests through the process of making the infamous shower scene from his most famous movie. It was all topped-off with re-creations of sets from *Rear Window, Saboteur* and the famous trombone shot tower from *Vertigo* (possibly the greatest movie of all time as voted by modern film critics).

However, it was not to last, as very quietly and without warning the final guests made their way through the Orlando unique attraction on January 3rd, 2003. It later reopened as the attraction that we know today - *Shrek 4D* - some 6 months later.

One ex-team member for Universal (named Kevin) told us, *"I've worked there in 2006. Two co-workers of mine had run ins with Mr. Hitchcock in the first theater. Doors have shut on them on their own accord, lights went off..."* When questioned Kevin said, *"Nah, my co-workers were serious!"*. We also received the following report from a current Universal employee who didn't want to be named: *"Yes, the place is literally haunted by Alfred. His spirit walks that soundstage and he is not happy the ogre replaced his beloved attraction... The weirdest experience I had was one evening we were waving the last group out the door and as I walked back the Pinocchio animatronic started to rapidly kick his legs and then it stopped. The room was deathly silent and then that, it was very strange."*

Another employee posted about this topic online, *"Just wanted to say if any if y'all want an Alfred Hitchcock house just work at Shrek. Believe me he haunts the heck out of that place! Also the second theatre of Shrek has officially closed for the year and team members aren't allowed in so the house construction in there has began! (It also didn't make Alfred too happy.. he broke our first theatre in revenge the first day it went down)."* He continued, *"We have to say hi to Alfred every morning or he gets angry and stuff will go wrong. In the ride throughs in the morning there's quite often a seat in the back row that will go down and when the show finishes it'll go back. All the team members there know it ha."*

Another former *Shrek* staffer told us, *"Lights going out, doors opening unexpectedly, weird bangs and that spooky backrow. Shrek ain't got nothing on Sir Hitchcock!"*

The jury's out on this one – is Alfred Hitchcock haunting the *Shrek* building? We will surely never know. But we do know that an actual fiend was born within these walls, well, in the trailer behind the attraction to be specific. Some of you may not know this interesting *Horror Nights* fun fact, but Jack the Clown, HHN's icon-extraordinaire, was literally born within the Hitchcock attraction at the rear in a production trailer. A fact revealed within the author's *Unofficial Story and Guide to HHN* book, and via James Keaton who plays Jack recounted in an episode of the author's very popular HHN based podcast *ScareZone*. Maybe the spirit of Alfred embiggens the murderous nature of our beloved HHN icon instead...

2011: Scream 4 Your Life

As the Universal creatives got back to work on creating their next fantastic horror event, it was as early as August 3rd when the marketing arm of the company started to tease fans and Southern Californians alike about the horrors that awaited them. In an uncustomary early move by Universal Hollywood standards, they proceeded to tell the world that famous rocker Alice Cooper had been in the designer's chair for the last few months creating his own horror maze.

"Alice has been through the maze a couple of times already," said John Murdy. During the tour of the nightmare labyrinth he was said to have been *"...overjoyed. He was thrilled."* Supposedly, the maze came about with Cooper instigating the idea with Murdy when Murdy took him around the event in 2010. Cooper is said to be a big *Halloween Horror Nights* fan and when the idea was agreed he was said to have been ecstatic at the thought of working on such a unique project.

Universal described it as, *"Enter the gruesomely twisted mind of shock rock legend, Alice Cooper, as he takes the stage in what is sure to be your final performance. Find your way through a labyrinth of razor-sharp guillotines, smell the burning flesh rotting upon electric chairs, and face off against deadly boa constrictors, demonic dolls and more! Lose sight of what's real as you begin your dark, demented journey through the eyes of Alice Cooper. If you didn't believe in nightmares before, you soon will! For even staying awake won't save you!"*

The maze had an incredible level of anticipation. It would prove to be one of the first mazes at USH to truly go beyond the realms of the haunt going public and crossing genres from horror to music and back again. Murdy informed the press that he had been personally told from a variety of sources (but mostly Twitter) that this maze was drawing fans from all over the world, but in particular Norway, Germany and Australia (apparently Cooper has larger fanbases in these countries).

The maze would offer a mixture of storytelling, iconic Cooper set pieces, and scares, all blended together as a maze soundtrack using some of Cooper's most iconic hits. Guests entered into an abandoned home where recurring nightmares of Steven, a semi-autobiographical character from Cooper's songs, guided them through a labyrinth of movie-styled scenes where Steven's nightmare is becoming the guest's reality. One scene featured Cooper's classic 1975 'Welcome to My Nightmare' (which is also the name of the maze).

Built next to the Jurassic Park ride in the Lower Lot, it contained 12 rooms (plus corridors) and was said to hold a steady line of people every single night. Walking inside the haunt, guests came face-to-face with a façade of Steven's decayed home which is in the midst of foreclosure. A lightening effect erupted to reveal the front of house which looked like Cooper's face with the iconic eye makeup splashed around the upper windows. The realtor character selling the property out front was named 'Vincent Furnier', which was a nice Easter egg for guests as that is Cooper's real name. Once inside, guests entered into Steven's bedroom where he is still sleeping. A mirror effect on the wall showed Steven dressed as Alice Cooper and the various toys and posters around all had the eye makeup applied. It all combined to reveal that Steven is becoming Cooper and as guests realized this transformation a scareactor dressed as Cooper would jump from behind a wardrobe manhandling a large chainsaw. Throughout this scene the song 'Years Ago' would be playing. In fact, ever scene would have a specially selected track to reflect the storyline of the maze.

Guests entered into Steven's nightmare via a closet. Inside, disemboweled bodies hung from the ceiling while a musty dust scent was pumped into the scene. Prop skeletons were the big jump scare here, as a female voice, intended to be his mother, calls to Steven asking him to 'come home'. The new scene was the 'Toy Room' which was filled with demonic clowns, possessed dolls and hanging spiders. Scareactors dressed as oversized babies provided the scares (a nod to his 1973 release 'Billion Dollar Babies'), as guests were scared into the next scene. The 'Guillotine Execution' was next up where a surreal French empire scene had been recreated. A number of severed, rotting heads were on display, complete with 'rotting corpse no. 5 scent being pumped in. A stilt-walking executioner wearing French revolution attire (Cooper is a big history buff) held the head of poor Steven by the hair, and as the head prop is thrust at guests it would scare them into the next scene.

'Insane Asylum' was next, where spinning red beacons and the smell of antiseptic would disorientate guests, while another stilt-walking scareactor would scare the guests towards an insane doctor undertaking experiments on a number of inmates. The track 'We're All Crazy' would propel guests into the next scene: 'Electric Chair'. The classic USH scare of the electric chair was back and used to great effect. As scantily-clad nurses and all their distractions shocked inmates from the last scene, all the while 'Nurse Rosetta' would ring out between the large electric sound effects. The now dead inmates are placed into the next scene, 'The Morgue', where their now decaying corpses were coming alive to scare the guests. A great scare of a zombified inmate kissing a 'Sexy Nurse' from the previous scene is seen, guests trying to walk around them are then confronted by a big jump scare that the scareactor zombie isn't kissing the Nurse, he is in fact eating her face! The ironic 'I Love the Dead' rings out as guests get past the horrible zombies.

Within the same scene is the 'Embalming Room' where an obese corpse pumped full of embalming liquid is fit to burst and leaks a green slime from the table. The mad doctor, revealed to be Cooper, is carving him up using a large saw. The next scene was 'Science Classroom', where another stilt-walking scareactor dressed as a school principal but wearing a Medusa snake-like wig is chasing guests in the classroom. Around the room, various tanks and tables display a variety of different faux snakes. Turning the corner guests are confronted with a giant snake puppet bursting through the wall, its 10-inch fangs hissing at the guests as "venom" is sprayed in their general direction. The iconic hit 'School's Out' is played in this fun and frightful scene.

The penultimate scene is the 'Basement Lair' where the nightmare is apparently over for poor Steven (and the guests no less!). Returning to Steven's home for a moment of respite, and assuming the maze is over, guests are suddenly attacked (via lighting effects) with a hoard of spiders, including a giant puppet spider hiding in the corner of the room (which looks like a female human-spider hybrid). Various corpses rotting whilst covered in cobwebs can be seen throughout the scene. 'I am the Spider' is played throughout as guests enter the final scene of 'Black Widow' where a 4-foot tall spider puppet reached out to guests with moving legs as though it wanted to add you to its collection of hanging corpses. Just when you thought it was over, the maze would throw more scares at you until you were as disorientated from the maze as poor Steven likely was.

"There's never just a final scare," Murdy told the *LA Times*. *"There's always a final final scare and then a final, final final scare."*

Cooper said at the time, *"It's like a movie, there's a beginning, a middle and an end. It's so well thought out and it's so ambitious. The designer of the maze is an Alice Cooper fan [Murdy] and usually with something like this you get a two-page description sent over - he sent over 40 pages on this maze and Steven's house and the nightmare, and it was so detailed. When you think you know where the scare is coming from, he has something coming at you from the other side. It's all misdirection. It's amazing with the music. It's a nice thing for Alice Cooper. Alice Cooper is synonymous with Halloween, I'm amazed no one has done it before. We did a haunted house at my restaurant in Phoenix but having Universal do it and do it on this scale, that makes it special."*

Murdy would reveal years later that many of the horrors depicted in this maze had come from real-life nightmares he had experienced when he was a young boy. He told Cooper this during the design stage, and as Cooper's father had been a priest he said he could relate to the images within his dreams. So it was swiftly agreed to make these images a reality and take Murdy's nightmare to the masses.

Combining horror with rock 'n' roll was a huge hit out of the gate. The maze lived up to expectations and drew in the crowds. It would go down in Hollywood history as one of the best mazes they had ever created. Of the development of the maze, Murdy recalled to the *LA Times* and other outlets how the maze conception was like a 'eureka' moment where the joining of Murdy's two favorite worlds of music and horror would finally come together and be realized.

Murdy said at the time, *"I popped them into the player and immediately I was like 'What is this?!' It combined two of my favorite passions – horror with rock 'n' roll. They're very few people who you can truly call 'original' and Alice is in that rare pantheon and you can see how he has inspired so many others down the road. [sic] ...for me, this is a dream come true. There's no way I'd be doing what I'm doing today if it weren't for Alice Cooper. When he left here that day, the last thing I said to him was 'Thank you,' because he had a hugely positive effect on my life. Here I am today, getting to do what I dreamed of doing when I was a kid building these things in my parents' garage. I truly believe without Alice Cooper I would not be doing what I'm doing today."*

Cooper had apparently been drawn to *Halloween Horror Nights* as a fan through the fandom and passion of long-time co-contributor Rob Zombie. Zombie had brought him into the fold and shown Cooper just how amazing this seasonal event really was. Zombie got on board to return another of his unmissable mazes to the event in the same year. Once Cooper knew his friend and touring partner Zombie was 'competing with him' at the same HHN, he ensured no stone was left unturned to ensure his maze was the most frightening for that year.

Cooper revealed, *"At the same time we're like brothers, he's like my little brother. The great thing about him is that he totally gets the idea of rock 'n' roll, horror and comedy all rolled into one. You have to be very clever in how you do these things. You can't play horror against horror. You have to play horror either against romance or comedy. In our case – it's mostly very tongue-deeply-in-cheek comedy. He'd watch my show and go 'Oh brother' and the next night he'd add something to his own show. Then I'd watch his show and say 'Oh, OK, I'll see that and raise you one giant Frankenstein.' By the end of the tour, both of us had added and filled two giant trucks, but that's what makes it fun. Very few people I play with really challenge me and when I get challenged."*

And compete they did as Zombie returned with *Rob Zombie's House of 1000 Corpses: In 3D ZombieVision*. The maze would effectively be a re-run of the same maze from the previous year. Minor tweaks were undertaken to ensure it was not exactly same and most changes were advancements to the scares and scenes. The maze returned because in the previous year it had been found to be wildly popular. It proved that fans of that genre crossover of horror and rock would be well catered-for during the haunt season.

Cooper would not be the only external creator coming to the event for this year. 2011 would also see horror movie director Eli Roth inducted into the tradition with his maze *Hostel: Hunting Season* where guests would descend straight into the torture-laden madness that is *The Hostel* franchise.

"Escape to devilishly hedonistic Bratislava, home to Eastern Europe's most horrifying Hostel where pleasure and pain go hand in hand. Descend to hell's darkest corner as you sample the forbidden fruits of extreme terror. It's hunting season and vulnerable prey is in high demand! Take a sickeningly twisted detour to a torture factory where Americans are sold to the highest bidder and dreams of paradise become nightmares of agony. Enjoy your stay; we look forward to having you!"

The movie was produced and directed by Roth with some script help from Quentin Tarantino. The graphic movie followed 3 backpackers in Europe as they are locked out of a youth hostel and are welcomed into a mysterious man's house who informs them of an inviting hostel elsewhere in Europe that is home to gorgeous women – but that dream soon proves to be a nightmare. The graphic torture scenes and gut-wrenching suspense leads to an unfortunate climax that combines a number of horror ingredients that would be tailored to fit the maze. Murdy teased fans by informing them on Twitter that it would be the *"goriest maze yet!"*. The chainsaw-wielding maniac called the Businessman, complete with a large fresh supply of young victims, were all presented in a variety of scenes from this recently-released movie. Fans appeared to have enjoyed the maze, as it attracted long wait times on most of the event nights.

The *Hostel* maze would also feature the very first use of a new marketing tool that would prove very popular with fans and would ultimately lead to becoming a true *Horror Nights* tradition. This new tradition was the use of a 'password'. Murdy who has part-managed the Twitter account for Universal's Hollywood event has always liked speaking directly to fans, giving them behind-the-scenes news and teasers. It would be via this new social media tool that Murdy would hand out 'passwords' on select nights for this maze. Fans of the event would monitor the Twitter account and then use the password in the maze to obtain a free souvenir (whilst stocks lasted). This year the password would be given to scareactors near the beginning of the maze and the prize would be a business card of the main character from the movies. Over the years these souvenirs have become very collectible and can be very sought after by fans. The process was very popular with the diehard fans and would return periodically in the years that followed at Hollywood.

Another returning maze (sort of!) was *The Wolfman: The Curse of Talbot Hall* which had been presented at Orlando's event in 2009. Unlike the Orlando version, this maze was presented after the movie had been released, as due to post-production delays the house in Orlando would be seen before the movie was released. Despite the house being a very good addition for that that year, it had a mixed response from fans as many of them did not know the story or who the characters were. Hollywood, at least, did not have this problem. The maze would be another creation that was built within the day attraction of *The House of Horrors*. Knowing the fan anticipation for this maze location, Murdy announced to fans via Twitter that "...*this is the best one we have done in that location.*"

The difference this time was that they re-dressed the location almost entirely and hired a different group of scareactors to work the frights. Universal achieved this by appointing veteran and award-winning stage actor Darryl Maximilian Robinson (the Founder of the multiracial chamber theatre, The Excaliber Shakespeare Company of Chicago) as Lawrence Talbot and The Wolfman, and Alexander Peralta as The Wolfen Boy. The pair had worked together for a number of years on a vast number of projects. The duo worked closely with the onsite team to ensure the scares were perfectly timed and would ensure that the vast location would be reimagined as intimate and close, to heighten those scares of every guest. Supposedly using a number of set pieces that had been created for Orlando, the production team worked with original filmmakers to ensure the sets were recreated to match the recent movie.

It was billed as, "*Take a treacherous stroll through Blackmoor's haunting countryside, where the roads run red with blood. Somewhere in the shadows, a truly grotesque creature lies watching, waiting to strike when the moon is full. Explore the decaying Talbot Hall, home to unspeakable horrors and shrouded in mystery, where an indescribable terror has been set free. A beast with an insatiable bloodlust is slaughtering all who cross his path and it just so happens that tonight is a full moon. Feel your heart pound, as you become the hunted. Confront your demons if you dare, for only you can satisfy his hunger.*" Murdy, true to his word, was correct: the maze was a great addition to this year and it did not seem as if it was just another mere reinterpretation of the daytime attraction.

Next up would be *The Thing: Assimilation.* Not to be confused with Orlando's house of the same name from 2007, this maze would be the one and only dual maze for this year, as it featured the property on both coasts. It would be themed to the prequel of the same name that was being released by Universal just before the haunt season commenced. Many guests who crossed the country claimed that the Hollywood version was the superior of the two mazes for this year. Presented in the Upper Lot, the maze would be a good recreation of the movie as an assortment of scareactors and puppets had been worked together to provide a number of authentic scares to the paying public.

Universal described it as, "*Venture on a perilous journey to the isolated outpost of Thule Station. Discover why scientists went missing in the seemingly infinite, frozen reaches of Antarctica. Make the most shocking discovery of your life as you encounter a frightful alien creature that claims its victims without remorse, morphing into anything...or anyone! Feel the paranoia creep over every inch of your body and the icy winds gnaw at your flesh with every step you take. Trust no one as you search for a way out, but be warned, it may already be among you!*"

The final maze for this year would an original, based on traditional folklore that had been adapted from a scarezone from the previous year. Built in the Shrek Queue it would be entitled, *La Llorona: Villa de Almas Perdidas* and would prove to be a very popular addition. Originally the news was leaked to the media that Universal were constructing a non-IP based maze for *Horror Nights*, and for Hollywood it is definitely one of just a small number of non-IP mazes that they have ever built. By late August the maze was confirmed, as construction had started to become more than apparent in the closed queue housing. A large façade rose from behind the tarps to depict a decrepit crypt, which teased the fan community no end. Speculation grew as to what the maze contained before Universal took to the airwaves to give us all a peak at what they were creating. As it transpired, the maze would be non-IP for the event but it still had the unmistakable Hollywood difference in its development, as the team had appointed Diego Luna to work as the haunt's creative consultant. The famous Mexican actor, who most Americans will know best from his lead role in *Rogue One: A Star Wars Story,* was brought in to help develop this haunt. It was designed to cater for all horror tastes but would be specifically targeted and marketed to the Latin community that loves the Halloween haunt season.

He said at the time, "*Story-telling is at the heart of all my work and I'm thrilled to have the chance to help present the great La Llorona legend in a different kind of medium at the Halloween Horror Nights event.*"

The maze told the haunting story of 'La Llorona', who was doomed to wander the earth forever after drowning her children in a desperate attempt to win a lost love. She would then drown herself when this attempt to win her lost love fails. According to the legend, La Llorona's dreadful, wailing cries of "*My children! My Children! Where are my children?*", can be heard eternally piercing the night during the haunt season. La Llorona's frail, drenched body lurking throughout the dead of night will invariably elicit unwavering dread from the helpless village inhabitants or maze guests as her presence signifies impending death to all those that entered. Ancient Mexican folklore which as with all great stories would act as a moral lesson and warning as the tale has been repurposed through the years from anything such as water safety to warning children about not talking to strangers. Its diverse history is as diverse as its catalogue of past additions to popular culture, from comic books to movies, from statues to works of art by Pablo Picasso; there is no doubt that the legend had a longstanding following and could be well deployed by Universal to create an awesome haunt experience.

La Llorona facade

Luna had been brought up by the legend, with him remembering various family members recounting the tale to him from the age of just 12 years old. The maze was described as, "*Explore the chilling legend of pain and anguish as your ears succumb to the petrifying screams of a woman consumed by the dreadful guilt of drowning her children and then herself. Doomed to wander the Earth for eternity, La Llorona will stop at nothing to find the souls of her murdered children. Relive the trauma that has haunted and terrified the hours of dark throughout the*

124

Americas for over 500 years, as you embark on a spine-chilling journey through the rotting remains of a haunted Mexican village. Beware, for those who hear the wails of La Llorona are marked for death!"

The maze would be intense, and for many, too much. Murdy had spent many nights of his childhood in empty churches at night wandering around them and staring at the statues (his mother was a speaker at many). His formative years helped create the ultimate haunt combining religious iconography and the supernatural to create a fantastic haunted house. A series of small caskets within the maze would signify the young dead victims and a number of loud screaming scareactors with great special effects would provide a huge number of great jump scares. The intense nature and the great final twist where the maze would 'fake end' (much like Cooper's) would give the fans something to discuss online. Many took to social media to argue as to whether this maze was in fact the greatest maze that had ever been created out in Hollywood; some agreed and others argued that past mazes were better. Whatever the answer, the maze was very popular and from its Upper Lot location it would attract vast lines every single night of the event.

The Terror Tram was arguably the centerpiece of the event (in at least the marketing) with *Ghostface* from Scream appearing within nearly all their commercials and advertisements. This year's version would be named *Terror Tram: Scream 4 Your Life* where the guise would be more in line with the third movie of the series, where the murderous *Ghostface* is stalking the backlot of Hollywood. Despite this third movie theme, the Tram experience would be tied into their recently released fourth movie in the series, *Scream 4* (*in case you hadn't guessed from the name!*). The movie, which had been released in April of that year, was reasonably successful and proved to be an ideal and intriguing franchise to marry up with the Tram Tour.

Universal were keen to build on the filmic backstory to this post-modern horror enterprise with a fake press release that was released to all media outlets: *"Today Universal announced 4 new horror films are shooting on the backlot, including 'Stab 8' the latest sequel in the popular film series. Eager to capitalize on this publicity bonanza, the theme park has started letting tourists on the Universal Studio Tour visit the production. With thousands of tourists rolling past the set every day, pretty much anyone with a cell phone has been given access to the production. A barrage of unauthorized photos and unsettling rumors about the troubled production have been lighting up blogs and chat rooms across the web. The most damaging of these leaks is a homemade video purporting to show 'Ghostface' attacking and killing tourists on the Universal tram! No one seems to know whether these videos are a clever viral publicity stunt or the real deal... Despite all the negative press, USH is still moving forward with plans to host 'Stab-a-Thon', a Stab movie fan fest on the Universal backlot. 'Stab-a-Thon' will take place during the theme park's popular seasonal event Halloween Horror*

Nights." And 'Stab-a-thon' is exactly where the tour took unsuspecting guests. A mock film set was presented that spread out around the Bates Motel area. It had a variety of injured or scared film crew, and a seemingly never-ending supply of *Ghostfaces* were all seen within the experience. Perhaps the most novel scare came from a casually placed trash can in the exit area of the queue building. Guests thinking their experience had ended were welcomed by a jumping *Ghostface* secretly hiding within the trash – now that was an interesting scare!

There were technically five scarezones this year at the event. The first (at the entrance) had Freddy's go-go dancers from the past few years re-badged as *Ghostface* dancers, to advertise the impending release of *Scream 4* on DVD. Lurking amongst the dancers were a couple of opportunistic *Ghostfaces* who would pop up at unsuspecting moments throughout the night, surprising and posing for photos with guests in equal measures. Following on the theme for the final time from the last two years, the scarezones were nearly all earmarked with 'Z's'. They were: *Freakz, Klownz, and Reapers (with a S and not a Z!)* but there was also a *Zombieville* zone. The latter was presented on the London Streets as some kind of zombie apocalypse set in mainland Britain. *The Reapers* were a horde of *Grim Reapers* and their evil minions (*no not those minions!),* stalking the Lower Lot. *Freakz* was staged for the final time in the Paris Streets, as it had been for the last two years. *Klownz* would also be reused and placed back on the New York Streets. Other than the 'Z' theme each scarezone had at the very least one chainsaw-wielding maniac amongst the lineup, with the exception of the *Scream* zone. The only show this year was the old returning faithful, *Bill & Ted's Excellent Halloween Adventure*, with this year's adventure centered around the usual political and celebrity controversies, *The Pirates of the Caribbean* franchise and the failure of Disney's *Tron* to set the box-office alight; all were done with Universal Hollywood's hilarious and unmistakable take on affairs.

2012: Invaded by The Walking Dead

Debuting in 2010 with over 5 million viewers, AMC's *The Walking Dead* was a very popular TV series. The main story is about a band of survivors in an American post-apocalyptic world as developed by Frank Darabont. The mix of a gritty, survivalist storyline combined with hideous flesh-eating zombies (or Walkers) was becoming more and more popular, and by 2012 the viewership for the show had doubled. The audience was set to rise to over 17 million by 2016, and in 2012 it seemed obvious that this show was going from strength to strength. That is why back in 2011, after the show was recommissioned, Universal began negotiating to bring the popular TV franchise to both coasts for the 2012 season. The talks were successful and making its debut this year on both coasts was *The Walking Dead: Dead Inside*.

Built on the Upper Lot in the *Wild Wild West Show* area guests would, "*Experience a nightmarish maze journey through a post-apocalyptic world where the dead are the predators and the living are their prey. You'll follow in the footsteps of the human survivors as you make your way from a devastated suburban hospital, through the chaotic streets of Atlanta to the remote countryside, where a lone barn holds a terrible secret. Good luck...the world you've entered is overrun with Walkers...they can smell the living...and they need your flesh to survive!*" This however would not be the first haunt to be built around the popular horror franchise. The show had already made its first appearance in a haunt back in the summer of 2012, with *The Walking Dead: Escape* at the *San Diego Comic-Con.* Located at San Diego's Petco Park it combined an obstacle course with scare elements that made the experience a cross between a timed running event and a haunted house. It would mark the beginning of the cross-promotion that the franchise would use in which selected cities around the US would have their own special summer events based around the show, whilst Hollywood and Orlando HHN's would built haunted attractions in the fall. After 2012 the *Comic-Con* 'Walker' event moved to New York before going on an 11-city nationwide tour in 2014. It truly seemed at the time that people could not get enough of this new horror TV show.

Back at Hollywood, the maze went through a variety of designs before the final concept would be built. The mazes would be largely the same on both coasts, with some minor tweaks, but the main purpose was to take guests through elaborately designed sets. These included iconic locations and scenes from the show's first two seasons in linear order and added teasers towards the end of the mazes for Season 3. *"We want people to experience the same terror of the walker-filled reality our characters faced in Seasons 1 and 2 -- and will continue to face in our third season,"* said Greg Nicotero, co-executive producer and special effects makeup artist, at the time. *"Our collaboration with Universal's creative teams is exciting as we work to truly capture the essence of the show."*

John Murdy said at the time, *"With 'The Walking Dead,' we want to make fans of the series feel like they are literally walking in the footsteps of the show's characters, experiencing all of the horrific events from the series just as they experienced them. The goal is to make guests of Halloween Horror Nights feel like they are trapped in the world of 'The Walking Dead,' using all of the attention to detail and movie-quality production values that Halloween Horror Nights has become famous for. You're no longer sitting on a couch, watching a show...you're living it!"*

And despite the fact that the maze did not feature any of the characters from the popular show, they did feature all the iconic scenes such as the hospital, the infamous beating doors and the shopping mall. But *The Walking Dead* wasn't just confined to a maze. The show would also be the main center for the marketing campaigning for the year, it would have an impromptu scarezone and it would also take over the *Terror Tram* experience. All the usual elements were present for this walkthrough attraction, but at every single turn there would be scores of moaning walkers ready to pounce on unsuspecting guests. Guests loved the diverse use of the franchise around the park and the only criticism this year was that there wasn't enough of *The Walking Dead* (such was the popularity of the series at the time!).

Another first for the event this year was that the computer game franchise *Silent Hill* was made into its first haunted house, with *Welcome to Silent Hill*. Located inside *The Mummy* queue, building it promised to take guests into this strange and unique world for an experience that they wouldn't easily forget, *"Cross through the portal of pain from Fog World to Otherworld, where the forsaken town of Silent Hill awaits. Feel your blood freeze as you come face to face with Pyramid Head, the colossal executioner, armed with an enormous jagged blade. Go under the knives of devilishly disfigured nurses, determined to scar you for life. Struggle for your final gasps of air as the Bogeyman smashes everything in his path with his murderous hammer. It's not a game. It's not a movie. This time, the nightmare is real."* The maze would also debut in Orlando with the same name and virtually the same room layout.

The maze would combine the game's main aesthetic of the flashlight look, by creating an elaborate lighting scheme in which guests could only just see their direction of movement but the scareactors were able to use the shadows to jump out with great effect. If anything over the Orlando version, the Hollywood maze would use this effect to their great advantage. The makeup and creature effects were also incredible to see this year. They mimicked the game perfectly and were a mixture of the main villains from the game and some of the lesser known creatures, and were all done extremely well. A towering 9ft tall Pyramid Head was achieved with stilts and scareactors at different heights provided even more scares than usual. After all, a scareactor tumbling around in the dark with not much jump action could be tiresome, so Universal used a set of hidden boo-holes to allow the high placed actor to reach at guests from unsuspecting multiple of directions. Combined with the jittering and faceless Nurses and even Colin the Janitor, the maze was certainly a celebration of the popular gaming franchise. But that was not its sole purpose, as being released during HHN's run was *Silent Hill: Revelation* (a sequel to the first movie from 2006). The movie tie-in would be enacted in the most interesting way, as the use of the fan popular 'passwords' would be used for the second time. This time, a character named Howard Blackwood, the postmaster in a number of *Silent Hill* games, would give out random prizes from the new movie to cross-promote it, the majority of which were posters.

Another returning and dual coast maze was Alice Cooper with his new nightmare maze, *Alice Cooper: Goes to Hell 3D*. Whereas Hollywood's 2011 maze went to Orlando, Cooper would stay in Hollywood and design a brand-new horror for guests to experience, "*Since the dawn of time, there is one place that man has feared above all others; a place of unending darkness, eternal torment and unimaginable horrors...a place called Hell. Now rock/horror icon Alice Cooper is going to take you there! Your journey into the abyss will take you through the mythical levels of Hell, each more terrifying than the last. With mind-blowing 3D visuals, you'll experience the inferno through the eyes of Alice Cooper. This promises to be one nightmare you won't easily wake up from!"* The combination of Cooper, Murdy and Universal combining once again to make another maze based on Cooper's work would be very popular.

The maze would center around the concept of the 'Seven Deadly Sins' and would presented with scareactors and puppets in a fun (yet terrifying!) 3D experience. Located in the Terminator queue building, the maze would also feature infamous songs from Cooper's back catalog, perfectly selected to fit each scene. Notable examples included 'Go to Hell' and 'Eat Some More', the latter being used in the gluttony scene. The colorful settings and use of puppetry would make the maze a fun experience but not as scary as the maze from the previous year. The demonized versions of Cooper and the scantily clad male and female scareactors combined with the prop snakes to make a memorable maze. It may not have lived up to the expectations set by Cooper in the previous year, but it still provided a fun experience.

Another returning maze with a fun and haunting sequel would be *La Llorona: La Cazadora de los Niños* (or *The Child Hunter*). Universal described the maze as "*Immerse yourself in the horrific tale that has tainted the dreams of children for centuries, with new twists and turns, spawning countless excruciating nightmares. Succumb to the bloodcurdling screams of Maria, a mother tortured by the guilt of drowning her children, forced to suffer for an eternity as she wanders the Earth hunting for the souls of her children. Beware, for those who hear her weeping are marked for death! If you think you know how it ends, you're dead wrong!*"

The maze had been an unexpected hit from the previous year, so with the positive feedback received Universal decided to re-run the maze again for a second time. This time, despite the maze being located in the same spot with the same scenes and same façade, it would have all the props, scares and set pieces elevated to heightened new levels to raise the terror factor. The number of scareactors was increased, the make-up was more putrefying, the actors got more into the guests' faces, the lighting effects were altered and more scents were pumped in. The cacophony of darkish delights all combined to make an immersive experience unlike any other maze from this year. The ending was also changed and the number of 'dead' bodies was increased. The queues for the reworked maze were consistently long every night of the event, and feedback from guests showed that it was as popular this year as it had been in the previous year. The maze was certainly one of the most popular for 2012.

Located in the Lower Lot, a new addition to the lineup this year was *The Texas Chain Saw Massacre: The Saw is the Law* based on the popular horror franchise of the same name. The publicity said that "*Some families are sicker than others. Based on the iconic original film that redefined the face of horror, relive one of the most grotesque crimes in all of American history in an all-new maze! Escape from a house of flesh and bone as Leatherface, the infamous human butcher, hunts you for sport. Inhale the nauseating aroma of burnt flesh as you hear the horrific sounds of his blood-soaked chainsaw tearing through victims; ignore their paralyzing screams if you want to make it out alive. Many have entered this slaughterhouse of sadistic terror, leaving no trace behind!*"

Murdy said at the time, "'*Texas Chainsaw Massacre' is one of those films that helped define the horror film genre.*"

The August-issued press release promised fans a gross-out and haunting experience, "*Those who dare to step into the inner workings of a slaughterhouse maze will be gripped with vivid telltale signs of imminent doom. Gruesome and blood-soaked scenes from the controversial classic will terrorize guests as they experience a labyrinth that will captivate all senses and render them defenseless when met with nightmarish images of mutilated bodies on bloody meat hooks; become paralyzed by putrid odors of decomposed corpses; navigate their way through human bones and animal pelts suspended from the ceiling; and run from the unmistakable roaring sound of a chainsaw revving to life when Leatherface lunges from the darkness in search of victims.*"

This was not the first – and was by no means the last - maze in which *Leatherface* would terrify guests. The setting was the original 1974 movie where Universal used their internationally- renowned attention-to-detail talents to faithfully recreate the scenes from this movie. Combining this authentic setting, with a hoard of 6ft-plus tall scareactors, faithfully recreated props, and a whole bunch of disgusting smells ensured that this maze was definitely a step-up from any other previous *Leatherface* installment.

The Upper Lot's House of Horrors was once again re-dressed for the event with *Universal Monsters Remix.* This addition was more or less the daytime house, but with more monsters combining in a disco-like setting, where electronic music and a new lighting design ensured a fun yet mildly scary experience. As with many of the mazes located within this building, it was not the most memorable for this year.

The four scarezones this year would be: *Silent Hill, Toyz, Witchez* and *Klownz.* The last of these would be a rerun of the popular zone in the Upper Lot's New York streets, and was featured for its last time, although the chainsaw wielding clowns would periodically return over the coming years. Paris' Streets would be the setting for *Witchez* where, "*Enter a European fishing village that is haunted by an ancient evil -- a coven of blood-thirsty witches hell-bent on revenge! For centuries, this sleepy seaport was home to witches who practiced their black art under the cover of darkness. One terrible night, the villagers hunted down the witches and burned them at the stake to cleanse the town once and for all of their pagan influence. It is said that some of the condemned swore revenge on the town, right before the flames consumed their flesh. Now, on autumn nights when the fog rolls in, the coven of witches reassembles on the streets of the village to burn the living! Be warned, for if you look into their charred faces, it's already too late!*"

Toyz would be located in the London Streets with, "*Hidden away on the foggy streets of London is a quaint little toy shop. The place looks innocent enough from the outside but don't be fooled, unspeakable horrors are taking place inside the Toy Maker's workshop! For decades, The Toy Maker delighted the children of London with his handmade teddy bears and dolls but times change and toys go out of fashion. Faced with ruin, The Toy Maker snapped and decided to take revenge on the people who turned their backs on him by using his skills to serve a darker calling. Now, anyone who ventures too close to the Toy Shop at night is in danger of being abducted by the Evil Toy Maker and turned into one of his monstrous new creations...human toys!*"

The *Silent Hill* zone was a little disappointing, as it mostly featured the creatures from the maze dotted about around the base of the busy escalators and the maze entrance. Having these characters shoehorned into this busy hub-like space ensured that they acted as great photo-ops and teasers for the maze ahead but they did not provide any great scares.

Bill & Ted's Excellent Halloween Adventure returned for another year and was the only show. The event saw the first appearance of the *Transformers: The Ride 3D,* which had opened in May that year.

2013: Invaded by The Walking Dead (*again*)

In many ways 2013 would be the year that the Creatives took what had worked over the past couple of years and tried to 'plus' this format. They wanted to give fans some familiarity and a guaranteed appearance of their favorite Halloween event, but to also better what they had to offer. *"Once you're inside... there is no way out!"* would be the tagline that rang out on media outlets and websites across the country; a familiar line that was entirely new and the first maze constructed would also follow this winning formula. This maze would be *Black Sabbath: 13-3D* and would not only be co-designed with an infamous rock legend but would also cross-promote the band of the same name's new album: *13*.

Released in June of this year the new album would feature all-new material from a band that had been making music for almost five decades by this point. And in the rock scene no one was more infamous than the legendary Ozzy Osbourne. Ozzy loved horror and he wanted to use the maze to promote his album. What he and the band didn't know, when they signed-up to create this maze, was that the album would go platinum in a very short space of time and end up giving him and the band their very first Number One album in the US. Achieving this long aspired-to milestone and creating their very first Halloween maze would be a big achievement for Osbourne.

He said at the time to *The Signal,* "*It's been a remarkable year because we had our first No. 1 album in America, believe it or not, and now this! I keep thinking I'm going to wake up!*"

The familiarity of 3D maze technology would be deployed yet again and inspired various scenes set to the tracks from this now platinum-selling album. And while all the usual props, UV reactive paint, and boo-holes were deployed, they would all be combined with a new effect that Universal wanted to trial out - the use of video screens. In one such scene, inspired by the song *Electric Funeral*, video screens would be added to the walls of the room. A wind tunnel effect would be added and as the chorus pitches up the screens (made to look like ordinary windows) would run a clip of them shattering with explosive visuals. At a press release Osbourne said, "*I've seen the drawings of what it will look like when it's finished and it looks amazing. I can't wait to walk through it.*" Two weeks later, the maze had been completed. Walking through it with a large assortment of press members and in character as the unmistakable Osbourne, he spotted a bloody, dead mannequin hunched over a church-like altar. Without hesitation, the front man allegedly pounced on the dummy and pretended to eat the dummy's inners via his neck injury; all of which was very reminiscent of the infamous bat-biting saga that occurred many years earlier. Universal described the maze via the event map as, "*Welcome to Black Sabbath: 13-3D, where you'll begin your descent in a demon-filled cathedral and continue on through graveyards, madhouses, corpse-filled battlefields and a nuclear apocalypse with mutated beasts. Listen for the sounds of agony with every chord; your pain is music to their ears!*"

Following in the exact same format of something old (but in a new way) was *El Cucuy: The Boogeyman*, which would be housed in the Parisian Courtyard on the Upper Lot. Based on the Latin American legends, El Cucuy is similar in concept to the European legends of the bogeyman. This maze would be seen as a kind of ghostly sequel to the popular mazes based on the Mexican legend of La Llorona (which in itself had been based on a maze that Orlando did on Bloody Mary). This hearty mixture of popular folklore and urban legend ensured that locals and those they wanted to attract would see some familiarity in Universal's aim to reach out to various communities via their popular event.

Universal said at the time, "*In Mexico, 'the boogeyman' is known as 'El Cucuy', a mythical ghost-monster touting pointed teeth and razor-sharp claws. Some believe it is an evil spirit which lurks in desolate caves and ventures into the pueblos late at night, lying in wait under beds, in closets and on rooftops in search of disobedient children. The legend began as a cautionary tale told by parents warning their children to behave or "El Cucuy" would prey on them. This generations-old myth has haunted children over the years as part of popular Hispanic folklore recited throughout Mexico, Latin America and the United States.*"

And Universal wouldn't be alone in their endeavor to make this Mexican legend a reality, as they had veteran Hollywood actor (and Mexican descendant) Danny Trejo. Trejo would aid in the concept drafting of the maze and then narrate the guests' story as they enter the world of El Cucuy. He said at the time, "*I* remember my mother telling me about 'El Cucuy' as a little kid and it freaked me out. I grew up with it and I told it to my kids, too. I can't wait to check it [the maze] out!"

Trejo's distinctive gravelly, gruff and gripping voice was deftly deployed to narrate the legend through the eyes of the monster as it malevolently morphs into El Cucuy before the guests' very eyes. Maze-goers would follow Trejo's ominous voice as it guided them into disturbingly gruesome sights, ravaged and pillaged by the shape-shifting trickery of the monster. It even included a scene of a child's birthday party gone horribly wrong. Distressing maze chaos continued in sinister scenes which lured guests through a family room, a child's bedroom and a closet. A merciless attack of El Cucuy was witnessed in pools of blood, with lifeless bodies exposed to reveal gaping wounds, and toys, stuffed animals and clothing were scattered about in the struggle. The maze would conclude with guests entering El Cucuy's evil cave, which was a cavernous, macabre horror where muffled cries for help signaled impending torment ahead.

Universal were rightly proud of their faithful recreation of this Mexican legend. *"The 'La Llorona' maze we created last year was extremely well received by our guests and praised for its authenticity, so we're excited to bring another infamous legend from Latino culture to 'Halloween Horror Nights'."* said John Murdy at the time. He continued, *"At its core, this legend is even more horrifying than 'La Llorona' because 'El Cucuy' is known to take on the form of trusted adults like a police officer or your grandmother as a way to approach victims so it's the perfect subject matter for a maze. When I was writing the maze story line, I pictured Danny Trejo as the voice of the monster, so we're thrilled to be working with Mr. Trejo to bring the terrifying legend of 'El Cucuy' to life!".* The maze would be wildly popular this year with guests praising the new content and for taking an urban legend and making it a reality. The maze was a worthy sequel to La Llorona and led to long lines every single night of the run.

Released on April 5th, 2013 *Evil Dead* would be a soft reboot of the cult classic 1981 version. It would also be the perfect material for a haunted house and it was brought to Hollywood and Orlando for this year. Both coasts had very similar mazes, sharing a number of identical scenes.

Universal said at the time, *"Producers Rob Tapert, Sam Raimi and Bruce Campbell– creators of the original 'Evil Dead' film – reunited to present this year's terrifying new vision of the classic horror film. The film follows five 20-something friends who turn a remote cabin in the woods into a blood-soaked chamber of horrors after awakening an ancient demon. Directed by Fede Alvarez, 'Evil Dead' opened No. 1 at the U.S. Box Office, and top 10 for all-time horror remakes. The movie is available July 16 on Blu-ray and DVD with UltraViolet from Sony Pictures Home Entertainment – and now horror fans will get to live it at Halloween Horror Nights."*

The mazes were both faithful recreations of the visceral horror that was depicted on the big screen and sought to 'let guests have it' right from the very first scene. *"I'm thrilled with how popular 'Evil Dead' has become with horror fans, and it's exciting that it's coming to life at Universal's Halloween Horror Nights,"* said Fede Alvarez, director of the rebooted version. *"Just like the film, this haunted maze is going to be over-the-top, in-your-face and completely outrageous – and I can't wait to see it. The Evil Dead series is iconic, and this latest film has set the scare factor to 11,"* said Michael Aiello from Universal Orlando's Entertainment team. *"These haunted mazes will be just as intense and unapologetically terrifying, and I can't wait for my fellow horror fans to venture inside and live the unyielding horror they've seen in the film."*

Universal was able to achieve the difference that their competitors strived for, and were loyally recreating the terror of the big screen and placing guests into immersive world of true horror. Murdy said at the time, *"Watching 'Evil Dead's unrelenting horror unfold in movie theatres was undoubtedly an unnerving experience, but with Halloween Horror Nights, we're taking it one step further. Fans of 'Evil Dead' will feel like they've left the safety of the theatre and stepped through the screen into a living horror movie where the film's demonic characters are coming for them. Our incredibly immersive and highly disturbing maze experience will come to life with the same attention to detail and production value of the film and will be the ultimate thrill for horror movie fans."* All the horror from the movie was presented, from the terrifying surprises in the cabin, to the evil possessions and even the iconic tracking shot through the forest. The maze was a true recreation of that movie and would act as a benchmark for how well a movie can be faithfully developed into a live maze.

Another recent Hollywood movie getting the big maze treatment would be the *Insidious* film with *Insidious: Into the Further*. Presented in the Lower Lot's Jurassic Park queue area, guests were invited to, *"Uncover the horrifying secret that has haunted the Lambert family as you enter Insidious: Into the Further. It's a nightmare journey into the paranormal where the dead crave the one thing they can't possess... your life!"*

The maze would actually be announced via the press junket for the second movie on August 10th (the movie itself was released on 13th September this year). The annual Scare LA convention would be the venue and it would see producer Jason Blum, director James Wan and Universal's John Murdy take center stage to announce that a maze for the popular film series would be presented at 2013's *Horror Nights*. As with the previous maze we have discussed, they promised that the maze would be an authentic, dimensional recreation of the movie where guests would, if they dared to enter, be taken into 'The Further'. Murdy said at the announcement, *"It's an incredible opportunity to partner with filmmakers who share our passion for bringing nightmares of the silver screen to life and who are committed to making every scene and every nuance of the maze as authentic and unsettling as their film."*

The maze would act as a re-creation of the first movie and a teaser (if you hadn't yet seen it) for the second movie, making the maze a two-part design. The terror would begin as guests entered through the door and into the first scene. Scareactors depicting the paranormal investigators 'Tucker' and 'Specs' warned guests to 'turn back now' as the evil that was about to unfold was unlike anything they had ever experienced. Inside, a linear recreation of scenes from both movies played out to show guests just what Universal could do. *"This attraction takes guests through the utter horror of both 'Insidious' and 'Insidious: Chapter 2'. The Lipstick Demon, The Long-Haired Fiend and the victims he murdered – they all come together in a perfect storm within the maze. In fact, I think this maze is the closest you can come to experiencing the kind of fear portrayed in our films, without actually living through it yourself."* said Director James Wan at the time.

Some commentators at the time said the maze 'was the best ever at Hollywood', and their commitment to representing the movie and their attention to every last detail was highly applauded. It also happened to be a very terrifying addition to the event with guests remarking that it was possibly the scariest maze Hollywood had produced in a number of years. One such entrant, who was equally terrified and would agree with those comments was producer, writer and actor in the franchise, Leigh Whannell. Whannell told this author via the ScareZone Podcast that he was absolutely petrified through the maze and was even ejected by security. He said, *"never in all my years had I ever used the 'don't you know who I am?' line in Hollywood but as they pulled me out I said, 'This is my maze! I wrote it!".* Whannell recalled the incident with a tongue-in-cheek attitude and told me that the once security realized their mistake, they apologized and invited him back in for more horror.

The House of Horrors played host to another monster mashup, with *Universal Monsters Remix: Resurrection* which was a near copy of the maze from the previous year. Universal said at the time, *"Universal's infamous legacy of horror is brought to life in a terrifying experience made for the 21st century. Immerse yourself in a modern horror-inspired soundtrack to your merciless slaughter, courtesy of Figure, and follow the trail of entrails through darkened corridors as you enter a crypt of bloodthirsty creatures. There's no escaping the monsters that started it all. Don't worry, it won't hurt...for long!"* The change out would be a combination of new lighting effects and a new soundtrack created by *Figure*, who provided a contemporary dubstep soundtrack to the vying guests.

Another returning franchise that was 'back by popular demand', and would be the center of marketing for both coasts, was *The Walking Dead* with *The Walking Dead: No Safe Haven* (a maze), *The Walking Dead: Dead on Arrival* (scarezone) and *Terror Tram: Invaded by The Walking Dead. The* latter was an updated version from the Tram of the previous year. The maze would be housed in the metro sets on the far backlot, and would depict mostly the second season of the very popular show. Universal described the horror as, *"Follow in the footsteps of the survivors as you journey through the shadowy confines of the West Georgia Correctional Facility. Seemingly abandoned, this prison has been breached by Walkers with an insatiable hunger for human flesh! Then, if you're still alive, make your way into the Walker-infested wilderness that surrounds the prison and into the town of Woodbury, where The Governor is hiding a terrible secret. In a world that belongs to the dead...there is no safe haven."* The scarezone would act as an introduction to the maze and would see almost all of the backlot swallowed up by the franchise. (Orlando would have a similar surprise whereby every single scarezone would be headed by the then vastly popular series.)

The event would also have four other scarezones. Coming from the stage and into a zone, guests would experience *The Curse of Chucky*, based on the sixth installment of the *Child's Play* franchise that was released during the event's run. The scarezone would act as a teaser for the movie and would inject some humor into the event's proceedings. The streets of Paris were yet again home to a ragtag bunch of criminal clowns with *Cirque Du Klownz*, "*Bienvenue! Welcome to the elegant streets of Paris, home to the Grand Guignol. Come see the lively clowns perform right before you. But, beware, they may not be there to entertain you... they may be looking to put you in their next act... the gruesome ending to their horrific show.*"

Meantime, the Lower Lot saw the creation of *Scarecrowz* (they love their 'z' ending scarezones in Hollywood!) A bunch of murderous scarecrows, long thought lost to time, were deployed to frighten guests as they ascended from the mammoth escalators. The final zone right at the front of the park would be called *The Purge: Survive the Night* where guests would see many of the characters from the hit franchise recreate scenes using faux guests. The event would yet again see the first floor of the parking structure taken over for the operations and makeup teams for the event. Now dubbed the 'Scare Base', it would see the media tour the pop-up facility for the first time, in an area where an army of 41 makeup artists would work on the 500+ actors every single night. Every scareactor in the park would have to enter into the line to be dressed and made-up as a monster for the night. Starting at 2pm sharp, actors would go from room to room being applied with makeup, prosthetics, special instructions and costumes before the gates of horror opened at 7pm (just in time to commence the *Purge!*). "*It's basically a giant assembly line of gore,*" said Murdy at the time to the *LA Times*.

Finally, the only show presented this year was yet again Bill & Ted, with their *Excellent Halloween Adventure*. Unfortunately this would be their last outing in Hollywood. 2012's version in Hollywood had been a huge hit, combining the usual assortment of dance, comedy and satire to great effect. Unfortunately, 2013's version was not as well received and the moments of celebrity roasting (which had worked in the previous year), fell flat and seemed somewhat cruel to many commentators. It would be Jamie Lee Curtis Taete via *Vice.com* who would voice the thoughts of many and describe in detail what had gone wrong with the production. The show had always existed precariously with its 'near the knuckle' humor and fleeting use of other people's IPs for the purposes of humor. Many inside the company were apparently unhappy with the show's direction and in a digital world of instant sharing they were not prepared to run this risk any more. So when the negative headlines began to appear about the show, it was swiftly pulled. Announcing on Twitter, Universal said at the time, "*After thoughtful consideration, Universal Studios Hollywood has made the decision to discontinue production of the Halloween Horror Nights' 'Bill & Ted' show for the remainder of its limited run."* Leaving only a handful of nights without a show, the production would not return. The show had originally migrated over from the Orlando site and was seen a comedic respite from the horror, when the event was more of a 'party' in the 1990s. Now in the 2010's there was no space for this show; time had moved on and starting in 2014 it would be replaced with something far more contemporary.

2014: Invaded by The Walking Dead (oh yes!)

In the previous year Universal tested the use of new technologies to scare guests (such as screens and other digital technologies), and for many inside the company it proved to be a successful next step in their mission to provide the best haunted houses in California (or for the whole country?). This year would be the first year where this technology was rolled out to more mazes and deployed in such a way that it would help improve the guest experience and scare them all 'half to death'! And this was good timing too, as 2014 would prove to be one of the biggest experiences Hollywood has ever organized. The first maze announced, which was also a big surprise, was *An American Werewolf in London*. It was a surprise in that this cult classic from 1981 was on no one's radar at the time and being over 30 years old, it was far older than the usual contemporary properties that the event usually worked with. Universal said, "*Cult-favorite 'An American Werewolf in London' is one of the greatest horror films to feature special effects without the aid of CGI, and now, it's coming to life as an all-new, effects-packed maze. There is something evil lurking on the English Moors...an ancient, cursed creature with overpowering strength that prowls the countryside at night, searching for unsuspecting prey. A Four-footed Hound from Hell. Legend has it that those who have been attacked by a werewolf and survive become a werewolf themselves. Now, you must escape the monster's fatal fury, or you'll be next! Beware the moon, stay on the road, keep clear of the Moors...and God help you!*" And it would be Universal's new dedication to special effects and new technologies that would allow this maze to come to life.

The maze's genesis came from a partnership between John Landis (the original movie's director) and Universal Orlando. Orlando debuted their version in the previous year and it was a huge hit, winning 'house of the year'. The Orlando team worked with the director to get the house completed, often using original documents and drawings from the 1981 production. Landis was on hand to help market the house's arrival in Orlando and to take members of the press through. He was equally delighted a few short months later when it was revealed to him that the house would move to Hollywood and be a maze for their 2014 *Horror Nights* lineup.

"The team at Universal Studios Hollywood has gone to great lengths to recreate the mood and details of the movie," Landis said in a statement. *"I want [guests] to really absorb the elaborate sets, makeup and special effects custom-designed for this experience."*

John Murdy said at the time, *"John Landis' iconic horror film and the groundbreaking makeup effects by Academy Award winner Rick Baker have influenced generations of horror filmmakers and fans. Turning such a celebrated film, which has been characterized as one of the greatest films of all time, into a 'living horror movie' can be daunting. As the movie studio that invented the horror film genre, we have the expertise to deliver a realistically compelling experience and are up to the challenge."*

Landis, along with Murdy and Chris Williams, would hold a joint press conference at *Scare LA's* August convention where all the details of every sinew would be discussed at length. Landis recalled at the convention the moment when he was first approached to licence the rights for the event (by Universal Orlando). He described how excited he was to be working with Universal and how thrilled he was to have his movie from all those years ago made into real-life walking nightmare, *"I was so excited I spent days working out ideas of how to scare people"* he said. It was only when he flew out to Orlando for his first meeting with the Creative Team that he was told, *"Mr. Landis, these ideas are all great, but we need to get 4,500 people through this house an hour!"* he laughingly recalled to the convention's audience.

The Hollywood version would differ from the Orlando version in that more scares would be added with more puppetry and more special effects. And whilst the maze would be slightly larger than the Orlando version (with a near two-minute thrill experience) all the same key scenes and set pieces would be added, including the Slaughtered Lamb Pub which was built outside as a full-sized replica to act as the façade for the maze. Taking a cue from Orlando's version, Hollywood was also able to build 'the transformation' scene, a sequence where the film's main character transforms into a hideous werewolf. The scene was achieved using a combination of moving prop body parts which were attached to a real actor. There was an off-set technician who would aid in their movement, with a mixture of terrified screams from the actor and with speakers playing a grisly growing sound (it was supposedly tree branches moving), giving the impression of a transformation. It is worth noting that it was the very scene that

144

secured Rick Baker his Academy Award, so to have it recreated in 'real life' was a hefty achievement for both events.

The new use of technology was also deployed with the use of puppets. The new puppets, almost exactly the same size and design as those from the original movie, were deployed at random times through the maze. The largest puppet with the best scare was located near the end of the maze. Technology was used in three different ways here to make this scare effective. Firstly, the puppet was built on a mechanical arm that cantilevered from a main pivot, enabling any scareactor, regardless of strength, to have the ability to control how far the puppet could move whilst freely being able to control its jaws and sound. Secondly, because the puppet was so large, cameras were installed in the scene to enable the scareactor to know exactly where guests were to allow the actor to time the scare perfectly. And lastly, extra cameras were set up further back near the entrance to the maze, so the pulsing of guests could be controlled to ensure there wasn't a buildup of guests in this pivotal scene, with the aim of giving everyone (or nearly everyone) the best scare yet. The combination of all three techniques made a maze that was incredibly successful in its aims, and incredibly popular.

"We have never done a scene this complicated," Murdy told the *LA Times* at the time.

Another maze that would mix technology and puppetry was *AVP: Aliens vs Predator.* Universal described the new maze as, *"Take on Alien vs. Predator, two of the world's most iconic characters of science fiction and horror, in our most ambitious maze yet with technologically advanced creatures and state-of-the-art special effects! A spaceship belonging to a hunter race known as The Predators has crash-landed in a remote forest. The ship was carrying life form samples of another extraterrestrial species – the cold-blooded Aliens — that use living hosts as incubators, including humans. Now, those life forms have escaped into the countryside, with blood-drenched chestbursters and parasitic facehuggers leaving a deadly trail. But, you haven't confronted the real threat yet. You're caught in the crossfire between these ancient enemies in a relentless battle to the death, and only one will win! One thing is for sure...whoever wins, we lose."*

The maze would be located on both coasts and announced in a dual announcement via social media. *"AVP: Alien vs. Predator is by far the most technically complicated and ambitious maze we've ever created,"* said Murdy. He continued, *"It's a monumental undertaking to re-create these massive, iconic characters for a live event."*

Mike Aiello from Orlando added, *"When attempting to bring two of the most iconic creatures ever put on film to Halloween Horror Nights, you need to rely on everything you've learned up to this point. Puppetry, elaborate costumes and unique environments have all been created in close collaboration with Twentieth Century Fox. Our guests are going to be thrown head-first into this epic battle."* And close collaboration it would be, because as with the last maze, the team at Universal would go right back to the movie's production notes and even liaise with original production staff to ensure the look of the maze was exactly the same in every detail. The mazes' aliens were all created from the original molds as created by Tom Woodruff, Jr. and Alec Gillis when they were commissioned to make them for the 2004 movie. Woodruff had won a Best Visual Effects Oscar for 1992's *Death Becomes Her*, and Gillis also did creature effects for David Fincher's *Alien 3*, for which both were nominated for an Oscar. They also worked together on James Cameron's *Aliens*. They would collaborate with Universal to ensure the creatures were literally like-for-like from the famous film.

What isn't always known is that not only did Universal assemble teams from both coasts to work jointly on this property, but that each coast was separately making their own respective version which was completely different from the other. In Hollywood, guests would find a spaceship carrying the Predators and the Xenomorphs from the *Alien* series doing battle, while in Orlando, the maze would center on a secret *Weyland-Yutani* corporation bio-weapons facility, filled with the belligerent aliens. The mixture of scareactors portraying *Predators* and puppet *Aliens* (which seemed to be popping up all over the place) was a great mix in Hollywood. The combination of a crashed spaceship and then the forest enabled the Hollywood version to have the edge in terms of realism, something that was missing in the Orlando version. The other interesting set piece was the *Queen Alien* that pops up towards the end. Murdy said at the time, "*It's technically one of the hardest scares we've ever attempted but as everyone has seen, it really pays off!*" And pay off it did as the maze competed with *Werewolf* as to which was the best for this year. Regardless of which one won out, the lines for this maze were crazy long every night, with guests often running repeat experiences just in order to absorb every last horrific detail.

The next maze that would use a combination of elaborate sets and makeup designs was *From Dusk Till Dawn*. Based on the recently released TV show (and not the movie), the maze would be located in a remote portion of backlot now named after this maze as the FDTD area. This location for this temporary haunt was set up especially for the maze, because a combination of increased maze numbers, larger visitor numbers and an increase in productions on the backlot meant that this quiet corner of the vast backlot needed space for the temporary increase in haunt locations. Universal described the maze as, "*Experience the twisted world of filmmaker Robert Rodriguez' acclaimed supernatural show From Dusk Till Dawn in a chilling new maze filled with blood lust and darkness on the Universal lot. Step inside The Twister, an exotic nightclub that conceals a terrifying secret. The star attraction is a dancer named Santanico Pandemonium, a mysterious and irresistible siren with a deadly agenda. Hidden beneath the night club is an ancient temple containing a labyrinth of horrors, where "culebras" – snake-like creatures - seek human blood to satisfy their eternal hunger. You'll find the Twister at the place where the dead roads meet. It's open...From Dusk Till Dawn!"*

The larger space meant there was more room to build sets that were sympathetic to the original production. This also enabled more scareactors to be deployed, especially in the club scenes, which gave a sense of confusion with the guests not knowing who might scare them; a concept that would ultimately cause more scares. From distraction scares from the various go-go dancers to the in-your-face scares of the python-like 'culebras', the scareactors did a fantastic job in bringing this TV show to life.

"Universal Studios' Halloween Horror Nights event is the ideal platform to take fans of 'From Dusk Till Dawn' to literally experience the terror of stepping into the show," TV show creator Robert Rodriguez told *Variety. "It has been an incredible opportunity to work closely with the Creative teams at both Universal Studios Hollywood and Universal Orlando Resort to bring this maze to life with such detail and authenticity. This maze will capture the visceral excitement and thrills of the series to great effect."*

Another TV show that would get the dual coast treatment was *Face Off: In the Flesh* (Orlando would make a scarezone out of the property). It was described as, *"Syfy's hit reality/competition series Face Off pits some of the top special effects makeup artists in the business. Now, the most impressive creature designs from the show have gathered here... in the flesh! Step through the imposing castle gates to find yourself facing off against your worst nightmare: a twisted, new dimension crawling with monsters. Vicious human-insect hybrids lie in the dank shadows, while vengeful mummies, knife-wielding villains and a score of horrific creatures await you just around the corner."*

Kicking the *Universal Monsters* out to utilize their *House of Horrors* building, the maze would see a number of mesmerizing and down-right-creepy designs from the hit show deployed to do exactly what they were designed for: to scare people. The premise of the show saw competing makeup artists imagine and create horrific makeup designs, featuring everything from rotting pumpkin heads to demented *Alice in Wonderland* characters. Many of the show's contestants were actually current or past team members for Universal (at both coasts), and many of these creative people returned to the parks to lovingly recreate their designs for their deployment at the event. And whereas Orlando's event would use a scarezone which was mostly a number of highly-themed podiums showcasing their work (not the best idea as every time it rained the models had to be brought inside), Hollywood's would be a more in-your-face traditional haunted house. The maze would see the visions of the show's artist contestants, cherry-picking more than 20 original designs for the experience. Human-insect hybrids, sinister mummies, hideous vampires and a horde of other monstrous mutants inhabited its corridors. The maze also featured sounds from house artist *Figure*, who brought his talents back to the Hollywood event this year having previously designed music for *Universal Monster Remix* maze from last year in this very location.

"'Face Off's' inspiration to create original movie-quality creatures makes for very compelling television," said Murdy at the maze announcement. *"Collaborating with the show's creative team, however, gave us a unique way to extend the life of these exceptional characters that make-up artists have poured blood, sweat*

and tears into creating. We're excited to put these incredible works of art to the test and see just how scared our guests will become when they are face to face with live versions of these nightmarish characters."

Ultimately, it was a fun maze that improved on the past versions of this maze and provided a great guest experience.

Another new maze based on a Universal-owned property was *Dracula Untold: Reign of Blood*. Released on October 17th during the event's run, it would introduce guests to the sadistic Transylvanian ruler Vlad Tepes, known as Vlad the Impaler, who infamously tortured his enemies by impaling them alive with a wooden stake and suspending their bodies for all to see. The forbidding maze would also shed an ominous light on the one-time hero, turned bloodthirsty ruler, who chose to embrace unholy powers in order to defeat his enemies. Shared yet again on both coasts, this maze that was located in the Parisian Courtyard was intended to be the first movie in the now 'status-unknown' *Dark Universe*. With this, Universal was seeking to resurrect their old *Universal Monsters* with fresh, new, interconnecting storylines. The second movie in the lineup was 2017's *The Mummy* which did not meet financial or fan expectations, thus making the new suite of movies move from 'in production' to 'status unknown'. Whatever the current status of the film franchise, the maze would also be received with mixed opinions. The plus points of the maze were that it was very dark and atmospheric. It also offered tons of scares throughout, thanks mostly to a great cast making, but with the use of confined spaces, too, where actors could get up-close and personal with the guests. The main problem with the maze was that the story was hard to fathom as the movie had not been released. Then when the less than stellar critical reviews hit, it may have dented its box-office appeal meaning that fewer people saw the picture.

Taking a lead from the previous few years of working with leading musicians, the event would attract *Horror Nights* fan and legendary guitarist Slash. He would team up with Universal to bring a frightening new sound to an original 3D maze named *Clowns 3D: Music by Slash*. In this, guests experienced a mind-blowing, sensory overload of their darkest fears. A dilapidated roadside attraction was the venue where a once thriving ice cream factory awaited guests. Once through the funhouse doors, guests would quickly realize this establishment was run by a bunch of homicidal and psychotic clowns who had murderous designs on their unsuspecting patrons. It was a kind of Hell-type factory where murder, blood and gore would be mixed with ice-cream and cotton-candy. The maze reused a lot of props from past 3D mazes but with new, vivid and colorful designs. Sweet and sickly smells were pumped in as various demented clowns set about torturing and murdering a number of 'guest appearing' scareactors. The music seemed to be less focused than with the previous musician-based mazes, but it didn't detract from what was a fun and crazy addition to this year's lineup.

As with last year, *The Walking Dead* had a large presence with a maze, a scarezone and the whole of the *Terror Tram*. The maze was *The Walking Dead: End of the Line* and was again based in the Jurassic Park queue building. The difference this time, as announced to the press, was that the maze would feature far more walkers than ever before and would be based around the events of the hit TV a show's fourth season. Lying among the prison debris was a pile of half-eaten rats, a blood-soaked baby car seat and the severed head of a gray-haired man with a pony tail. The fences of the West Georgia Correctional Facility, which had once provided security from the zombie virus, have been destroyed. There's no choice but for guests to take to the road in search of the newly-publicized safe haven: Terminus. On the guests' journey they have to escaped a gauntlet of burned walkers, a dark tunnel of terror, and more biting horrors - all wrapped around the haunting theme music. By most standards it was an interesting addition to the lineup and one that made the best of the events from that season. The scarezone could be reached via the *Terror Tram's Invaded by The Walking Dead* (which was largely the same as the previous year's entry), with the zone eponymously entitled *The Walking Dead: Welcome to Terminus*. The brain-eating walkers weren't the only returning scarezone, as *The Purge* returned with *The Purge: Anarchy* to publicize the new movie to their franchise. Based right at the park gates once more, the felons and freaks of this film series would yet again stalk patrons as they entered into the park.

One of the most successful and applauded scarezones this year was *Dark Christmas* in the London Streets sets. A gothic collection of freaks, all under the direct control of Krampus (aka the Christmas Devil), were on the prowl throughout these tight streets. The zone's character design was incredibly well placed and the large number of scareactors throughout the crowds made for a zone that entertained and scared guests in equal measures. *Skullz* had the short-straw in the Lower Lot, where mostly stilt-walking scareactors made the best of their hurried location, whilst *Mask-a-Raid* was located in the Streets of Paris with their location-specific, pre-revolutionary French Masquerade Balls (but with a cannibalistic twist). And for the first time, no show was presented this year. Any plans that might have been for Bill and Ted to return never occurred Instead, the event focused its efforts on more mazes than ever before, whilst ensuring that the zones in the Upper Lot were like live shows with their theatrical performers aiming to distract fans enough to not notice the absence of the bodacious duo.

2015: Survive The Purge

What had started as a small, humble Halloween party had, by 2015, turned into a national and international phenomenon. Comcast Corp. who had bought the movie studio and all its assets (including all its theme parks) back in 2013, had announced in September of this year that the event had contributed a 30% bump in domestic theme park revenues. The event was now garnering national attention, and its move to create and develop licensed properties into movie-quality experiences had paid off . The event had consistently broken records on attendance and revenues year-on-year for a 10-year run (something that has continued to this day at date of publication). The success kept on coming as by September the longest-ever run of dates for Hollywood's version of the event (as per 2015) was now sold out for a quarter of the dates, with other weekends in the run fast approaching capacity too. Hollywood, which had in the last decade been seen as the smaller sibling of the two domestic events, was now standing firm on their legacy and ensuring another bumper year was upon us all.

As always, a large assembly of properties was gathered and licensed to provide the best haunt experience, and no property was as large as perhaps our first subject for consideration. That first maze would be *Halloween: Michael Myers Comes Home*, located in the Parisian Courtyard area. With the impressive façade of the old Myers place, the maze acted as beacon at the front of the park and would attract huge lines all night. The debut in Hollywood of this maze was big news, as it was announced at Universal's favorite convention, Scare LA. The maze would take guests through the tormented town of Haddonfield, Illinois, where on one fateful Halloween night in 1963, a six-year-old child by the name of Michael Myers inexplicably and brutally stabbed his sister to death with a kitchen knife.

Guests relived the terror that a maniacal Michael Myers inflicted upon the once quiet town after his escape from a psychiatric hospital when he took bloody revenge on new and unsuspecting victims.

"We are extremely excited to team up with Universal Studios Hollywood's fantastic event, 'Halloween Horror Nights," said Malek Akkad, President of Trancas International Films and Compass International Pictures to the gathered crowds. *"The attention to detail that the creative team gives to the Halloween maze creates a realistic and terrifying experience for guests that is truly authentic to the film. This year's maze will be the best yet."*

Directed by renowned horror filmmaker John Carpenter, the maze would be built on the premise that everything in the movie would be scaled into a haunted maze with every last attention to detail. From the shows playing on the TVs in the background to the packets of snacks on the shelf, the maze had every detail locked down. And it wasn't just its attention to detail that was awe-inspiringly shocking but also the sheer number of scareactors deployed as Myers throughout the maze; he was everywhere! And one such guest felt this more than others. Starting her own Halloween tradition, popular TV host Ellen DeGeneres started sending her friends through the mazes and recording their reactions for her popular daytime TV show (produced by Warner Bros, which shows how far-reaching the event was!). One of the most comical and extravagant runs was through this *Halloween* maze with *Modern Family's* Eric Stonestreet. Stonestreet, who portrays the exaggerated character of Cam on the show, played up to his over-the-top image to scream and jump his way through the maze for Degeneres' TV show. Stonestreet, whom this author has met a few times, was so popular on her show that Ellen has since sent him back through these mazes every year following his first successful run; if you haven't done so already, go check this out on YouTube. I asked Stonestreet at the time about this run and he said, *"I loved it, the whole event is just so much fun, that maze was intense!"*

The attention to detail in the maze, as previously mentioned, was staggering and it was something that was highlighted by a number of media outlets. For example, the addition of the dog that Myers kills is present within the maze, *"We thought we would not only show it, we would have you smell it as well, so we pump in the smell of dead animal into this room,"* said John Murdy to IGN. The detail of telling not only the story but also scaring you at the same time was a challenge that the designers had with the maze. The scene in the movie where Lynda is being strangled by Myers (wearing the white sheet as per the movie) is added in not only to tell the story but to create a visual representation of the violence ahead in order to heighten the feelings and emotions of the guests setting foot into the maze. Murdy continued, *"This is purely a scene where it's just a visual. The performers aren't trying to scare you at all but to set a mood."*

Hours of choreography had occurred to get the scene right and ensure the setting appeared very authentic. In the movie she is strangled by a telephone cord around her neck, so to ensure this horror was made for real they had to think outside the box to create the scare, as actually strangling an actor would just not be on the cards. The scare was eventually created by the Lynda actor wearing a 'necklace' made to look like a telephone cord. The actor playing Myers would then tug at two cords lengths attached to a harness on Lynda's back. Add in some specially designed footwork, some perfectly timed emotions, sound effects and action and you create a scene that might be seen for less than a second but in fact had taken weeks to get just right. The maze certainly made the headlines with Halloween event goers loving the use of the property, even though it had been re-presented at the event in 2009.

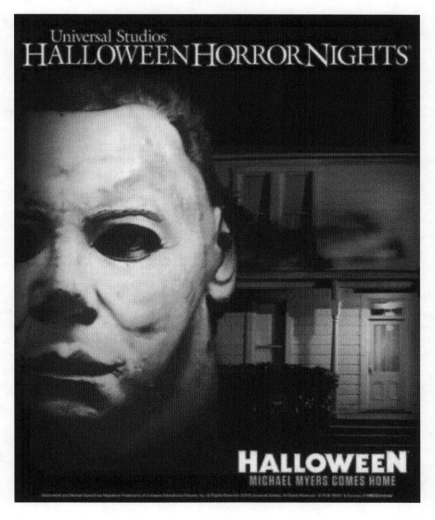

The difference this time would be the attention to every last detail. *"That's why we're doing it again. We kind of always aim for the uber fan. We try to get the set decoration and the props and all that stuff so that we know they'll appreciate those details. And realizing that there could be 90% of the people that will never get it. But we have such an obsessed fan following that we try and nail it for them,"* said Murdy at a press call. He continued, *"It's cool, especially for the generation who might not have seen it,"* Noting that *Halloween* came out in 1978: *"...a long time ago, but those characters have become so iconic over time that people know and love them. But it's also fun to get to show a new generation, that might not be aware of it, 'You should see this!'"*

The next maze would be a repeat of the previous year as it had been very wildly popular. Universal announced at the time, *"Back by popular demand, Alien vs. Predator puts you in the crossfires of battle between two ancient enemies! Using technologically advanced creatures and state-of-the-art special effects, this is the most awe-inspiring maze ever! A spaceship belonging to a hunter race known as The Predators has crash-landed in a remote forest. The ship was carrying life form samples of another extraterrestrial species – the cold-blooded Alien xenomorphs — that use living hosts as incubators, including humans. Now, those life forms have escaped into the countryside, with blood-drenched chestbursters and parasitic facehuggers leaving a deadly trail. But, you haven't confronted the real threat yet. With a relentless battle to the death, one thing is for sure... whoever wins, we lose."* Located in the same 747 Area, it had been agreed with the IP Holder to have the maze run over two years rather than just the standard one, standalone year. The reason behind this move was the vast volume of work that was required to build the maze the first time round. Ensuring the molds were perfect and that the sets were authentic led to the team of Universal wanting to showcase their hard work more than once.

Murdy said at the time to *IGN*, *"This was always intended that we were going to do this twice. We knew this was going to be such a huge, ridiculous endeavor to produce this that we pretty much decided early on, 'We'll do this two years in a row.'"*

From the specially created forest, to the crashed spacecraft, the whole set looked and felt as though it was hot from a movie set. Its location inside a cavernous soundstage on Hollywood's premier backlot also added to this experience. *"Everything you see in here today pretty much comes right off the original molds from the film,"* said Murdy. Such was their dedication to ensuring they got this right, many of the original scareactors were rehired to work this maze. Taking what they had learnt in 2014, they ensured that they worked closely together to make the maze feel as though it was a walking show. Murdy continued by explaining that the maze was using many of the original movie's toys, but instead of remaking the film they were using them to create what he called, *"a new show every 10 seconds."* The layout and scenes were all the same, recreated from last year's blueprint, but some changes had occurred. These included changing up the lighting rigs to create more suspense, adding additional supports for the alien puppets to enable them to jump out into the crowds better, and a whole new soundtrack. Murdy recalled in a press call how he adored the original Alien movie's score over the 'Versus' movies' scores where suspense had essentially been replaced by action and adrenaline. So, moving away from those pieces of music, the team decided to create a new score that would heighten the suspense to enable more scares to occur, *"I wanted something a little bit more atmospheric and spooky,"* Murdy said.

Other aspects of the maze from the previous year that worked really well were left untouched to ensure repeat visitors could see the greatest scares the maze had to offer once more. For example, the room where people were stuck on the walls remained, likewise so did the chestbuster scene and the scene of an alien gutting a teenager via a window. All of which was concluded with a reappearance of the mighty Queen Alien, standing 16-foot tall and filling the room surrounded by her eggs. To this day I still can't remember a scene in Hollywood that has been so impressive to witness and that due to its huge size left every guest utterly astonished with wonder.

Most of the other mazes were brand new and based on recent IPs. The next such maze was *Crimson Peak: Maze of Madness.* Announced at San Diego's Comic Con, it would be located out in the Metro sets on the backlot. Based on the movie of the same name that had been released this year, Universal described it as, *"Some houses retain the evil acts that were committed within their walls. The spirits of the victims of these violent transgressions linger on, long after the dead have been buried, to haunt the living. Such is the case with Allerdale Hall, an ancient, crumbling Gothic mansion in the remote English countryside that has seen its fair share of tragic events. Just below the surface of the house is a dormant clay mine that bubbles up to the surface to stain the snow-covered landscape with patches of blood-red clay. This is why the locals refer to Allerdale Hall as Crimson Peak. Welcome to Crimson Peak: Maze of Madness, a terrifyingly immersive experience inspired by the new motion picture by Guillermo del Toro, the modern master of Horror and Dark Fantasy. Your journey will take you through Allerdale Hall, a creepy and cavernous manor house that's haunted by the vengeful spirits of its past inhabitants and the unspeakable dark secrets of the fractured family that still clings to their cursed ancestral home! Beware of Crimson Peak!"*

The gothic horror movie as directed by Guillermo del Toro would be recreated on the backlot so that guests could experience the ghostly thrills of this very original movie. The maze would also benefit from del Toro's input into its creation and design. In many ways, the star of the movie is the visuals, with the visual recreation of a decaying mansion being its center. That's why for the design of this maze Universal had to ensure that they created the maze to reflect the amazing setting of the movie. From the gothic arches to the watery basement and the blood-red clay, the maze was filled with it all. But ensuring these effects were created accurately gave Murdy and his team real nightmares.

"A piece a cake in a movie, but pretty difficult to do here," Murdy explained to *dailynews.com. "There are a lot of pieces to worry about, like where does the water go? You can't dye the water red because the guests might get too close."*

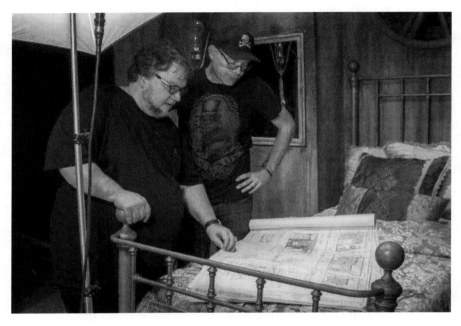

A promotional image released by Universal showing del Toro and Murdy working on the final blueprints

The hard work would eventually pay off, as the maze was visually stunning. Both filmmaker the del Toro and Murdy were justly very proud of their final conception. Murdy recalled that building the maze was made just that more fun as del Toro had taken such an active role in producing the haunt. Apparently, del Toro was huge a *Horror Nights* fan, having attended the event as a guest for years. Within the last four years leading up to this maze he had said to Murdy that he would want to build a haunt but only when the right property came along; lucky for us that the property would be the spectacular *Crimson Peak*.

"When the opportunity presented itself for this one, I thought the house is essentially a maze where Edith is trapped; so this is a perfect journey for a maze," said the horror supremo filmmaker. He continued, *"I love Universal Horror Nights because they orchestrate the mazes like a little story with a beginning, the middle and an end. We were in on the blueprints, and we had gag discussions*

because I'm pretty good with special effects."

The collaboration began three years previously when del Toro mentioned to Murdy about the forthcoming shooting of the movie and how the visuals and story would be perfect for a future addition to *Horror Nights*. Murdy and his team actually set to work right there and then, due to the fact the movie was being produced with Universal but also their partners, *Legendary Entertainment*. Starting with the storyboards (some 38,000 hand-drawn images) and the script, the maze began to take shape in blueprint form from this mightily early stage, making it one of the first mazes to be worked on before the movie was even shot! Del Toro actually worked on the maze and provided notes to Murdy and co. as he was doing the same for the actual picture. The whole *Horror Nights* team had full access to all aspects of the movie's production,

"Guillermo was very passionate about everything and very creatively involved in a lot of specific ideas," said Murdy. One such note that del Toro passed to Murdy was about a specific motive of the movie that had to be implemented into the maze, where black moths are flying out of the mouth of the lead character. Murdy recalled, *"I said, 'Cool, how we going to do that?' He said, 'Don't worry. I'll hook you up with my visual-effects department.'"* The idea would eventually be deployed mixing the Pepper's Ghost technique with digital effects to make it work seamlessly every 25 seconds. State-of-the-art effects such as this were combined with more traditional scares to keep the guests jumping from scene to scene. In the end, the maze was beautiful and incredibly scary. Del Toro was rightly proud of his collaboration with Murdy and his team to create such a fantastic addition to the 2015 lineup. He hinted to the gathered press that, *"I had a really good time... I hope to make more with Universal again some time."*

A returning IP - but in a new fresh way - was *Insidious*, with *Return To The Further* located in the Jurassic Park queue. Universal described the maze as, *"The Further is a world far beyond our own, yet it's all around us - a place without time as we know it. It's a dark realm filled with the tortured souls of the dead. A place not meant for the living... they crave life; the chance to live again. But there are other entities who are malevolent and have a more insidious agenda. A new threat has crossed over from that world into ours, a threat that does not merely seek to possess the souls of the living but to steal the living back to their world of shadows and keep them there for eternity. To face this new threat, we are going to have to confront the demons where they live; we are going to have to Return to The Further! Welcome to Insidious: Return to the Further, a terrifying journey into the paranormal based on all three chapters of the Insidious saga. Keep a steady stride, into The Further you go!"*

This dual coast maze would attract a lot of attention due to the popularity of the movie franchise at this time. Guests would investigate unexplained phenomena in the Lambert family's eerie Victorian home and then find themselves at the ghastly séance that unleashes chaos and horror. They would journey into 'The Further' – a supernatural realm that houses tormented spirits – and face deadly ghosts and demons like the Woman in Black and the Red-Faced Demon who will stop at nothing to infiltrate the world of the living. The mazes on both coasts would be very similar with the Hollywood version edging it with the slightly higher level of scares.

This Is The End 3D would also be presented on the Lower Lot. This adventure-comedy-disaster movie would prove to be an interesting choice for the horror event and would act as a respite from the horror to give some much-needed comedic relief. This made it the first time a comedy-horror (kind of) movie had ever been used as a haunted maze at the event in Hollywood. Universal described it as, *"Today is your lucky day! You have been invited to attend a party at James Franco's house, a once-in-a-lifetime opportunity to hang out with some of Hollywood's biggest and brightest stars! Unfortunately, your timing sucks! "The Apocalypse," the end of the world prophesized in the Book of Revelations, occurs before you can make it to the party! Now you're trapped in a life and death struggle as you're forced to confront not only the Demons of Hell but a bunch of seriously tweaked-out Hollywood A-listers! Will you be saved and raptured up to Heaven or be damned for all time? Based on the 2013 genre-defying blockbuster, This Is The End 3D will combine horror, comedy and mind-altering visuals to create a new kind of Halloween. It will be the party to end all Hollywood celebrity parties... literally!"*

The maze was also remarkable in that a number of the main cast would show up at the maze, giving fans a real meta moment of seeing the actual actors interact with scareactors playing them in the maze. The final maze produced for this bumper year was located right next door to this maze, with *The Walking Dead: Wolves Not Far.* Much of what had gone before had been recycled and refreshed to present the horrors from Season 5 of the then popular show.

Universal's popular dystopia franchise was yet again deployed for two further additions for this lineup, with them taking-over the Terror Tram and then having them on the backlot near the Metro Sets with a scarezone entitled, *The Purge: Urban Nightmare.* The actors on the former were very in-your-face, with their performances replicating the characters from the movie being very authentic. The *Terror Tram* was also made more interesting this year following the opening of the *Fast & Furious: Supercharged* segment into the tour. The Purge wasn't the only returning scarezone, as Dark Christmas once again filled the Streets of London area (much to guests' approval). The front gates, a challenging area where it was hard to scare guests as they ran to their favorite attractions, would see *Exterminatorz* – an assembly of mutant humans doing battle. In addition, Corpz was presented on the Streets of Paris area and saw a ruthless bunch of zombie soldiers do battle every night.

Having missed a show for the previous year following the dudes' departure, Universal was keen to fill that gap with something worthy that could entertain guests away from the scares. The perfect fit came from a dance troupe that developed a show especially for the event. From winning Season One of *America's Best Dance Crew* to headlining their sold-out show *PRISM* in Las Vegas (located at MGM's Grand Las Vegas), the *Jabbawockeez* make their debut at Universal Studios for 2015. The show was all-new and high energy, and it was performed live and created especially for HHN. The original Vegas cast were transported into a new realm of reality through gravity-defying choreography, stunning special effects, heavy-hitting music and their unique brand of humor. The show was selected because the popularity of dance-groups had hit the zeitgeist around the world. The show would be so successful that it stayed at *Horror Nights* during the coming years.

2016: Beyond your wildest screams!

It was early in 2016 that various news outlets (including *HHNUnofficial*) ran stories of how the Hollywood backlot at Universal was supposedly haunted. Stories similar to the ones in this book were distributed around the internet giving the backlot some kind of creepy kudos with a hint of realism that added to the Studio's presence both locally and nationally. This was matched with a phenomenon that had started in late 2015 where people would dress up and scare people as 'killer clowns'. Initially, the trend was confined to just social media or YouTube, but later it spread around the world and was hitting news outlets everywhere. It was this mixture of urban legend and folklore that would be mixed together to create Hollywood's first event icon, that of Hollywood Harry.

The character was created in partnership with Eli Roth who had been invited in for this year to create the *Terror Tram*. Roth would use his production company at *Crypt TV* to document a faux backstory that was presented as an urban legend telling how the maniacal clown had been stalking the backlot of Universal Hollywood for years. To aid in this, promos would run on the station and on social media asking people to share his location, if spotted, and to ask people not approach him because 'he was considered very dangerous'. In actual fact, it was just a very clever marketing ploy. As early as August, Universal started placing an actor dressed as the clown onto the backlot to ensure guests would witness him standing or lurking around the regular tour. It was also at the same time that nightly and evening tours began during the summer period, to tie in with the recently opened *Harry Potter* attractions. Both day and evening tour guides were asked to ignore the character, which only drove fans 'in the know' into more of a frenzy with anticipation of what was to come.

"I'm thrilled to be part of 'Halloween Horror Nights' again," said Eli Roth. *"We wanted to completely fabricate an original story that brings together our absolute freakiest, scariest most disturbing ideas. The 'Halloween Horror Nights' team is the best in the business. Their production and execution is unmatched and I know this 'Terror Tram' experience will blow away all expectations, and haunt guests for the rest of their lives. 'Halloween Horror Nights is the must-see event for any horror movie fan—it's like the Super Bowl for scary movies, and is my favorite event of the year."*

"The goal of 'Halloween Horror Nights' is to create the most intense, most memorable and ultimately, the most terrifying experiences for our guests," added John Murdy, *"and there is no better partner than Eli Roth to deliver unabashed horror that's so real you can feel it. We were fortunate to work with Eli years ago on his original 'Hostel' themed maze, so we can only imagine the terror that he's envisioning."*

The backstory would create a whole legend for the character, and the perfect opportunity to promote this legend was the new program of nightly summer tours. So when Universal began opening the nighttime studio tram tours in the summer of 2016, guests began reporting sightings of a phantom clown, dubbed Hollywood Harry, that was spotted around the backlot. The legend said, *"When they uploaded videos and images on the internet, speculation spread like wildfire. Local Los Angeles residents soon identified the clown as Harold Kappowitz also known as Koodles the Clown. In the late 1950s, the former circus performer hosted a children's variety show that was filmed on the backlot. When Universal Studios Hollywood opened in 1964, Koodles was used as an unofficial mascot for the park. As time went on however, due to sensationalized news stories and unflattering depictions in the media, clowns were no longer viewed as funny, cartoonish characters beloved by children, but as scary monsters. Circus attendance plummeted along with Kappowitz's fortunes. He lost his job and was reduced to becoming an unpaid street performer outside the studio gates. A few years later, he was unceremoniously kicked off the property all together due to his increasingly erratic behavior. Kappowitz vanished into the Hollywood Hills and Koodles the Clown faded into near obscurity. For decades, his presence remained unnoticed despite the disappearing wildlife in the area and the occasional studio tour guide going missing, both of which were merely brushed aside as merely being the company expanding the park and the transient nature of seasonal employees. However, Kappowitz got bolder and got closer to the Universal Studios backlot where he was spotted by multiple guests and became known as Hollywood Harry on the Internet. As the 2016 season went on and as the internet speculation reached a fevered pitch, so-called "clown hunters" decided to go hunting for the phantom clown, only to discover that he was not alone. He employed dozens of other fired and/or disenfranchised circus performers and clowns to join him in his crusade to get back at the people who fired them."*

These characters would band together to create *Eli Roth Presents: Terror Tram* and would be the central theme of the attraction for this year. The main experience was seeing these scores of evil clowns essentially creating carnage and torturing innocent victims at select set pieces around the main *Psycho* and *War of the World* sets. The backstory would heighten the experience, but one common guest complaint was that the backstory wasn't very well publicized beyond the HHN fandom. Universal tried their best to announce this new character either through the media, *Crypt TV*, social media and even on the queue monitors, but for many this was missed. Hollywood's event has always been founded on bringing IP movie properties to Halloween and for many this very first original concept Terror Tram just did not live up to the expectations of its former editions. [Though, author's note: *I thought it was great!*]

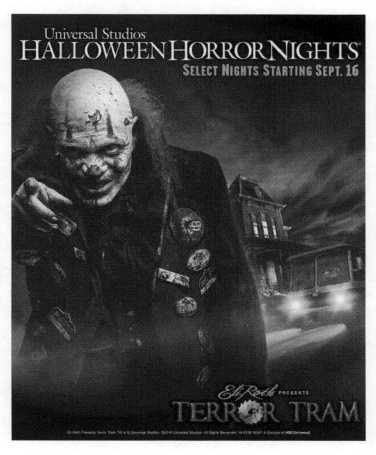

One of the most anticipated mazes for this year, and the one that would to this day be one of the most controversial, was the dual coast maze, *The Exorcist*. The contentious maze, built from the contentious movie of the same name (which is still banned in some countries around the world), would prove to be a real challenge that only Universal was capable of surmounting. When the news broke that Universal was creating mazes based on this infamous horror movie the story was everywhere. Despite the movie being highly controversial at the time (and for many still is) it was a blockbuster for the horror genre making just a few million less than one billion dollars in revenues. The iconic and legendary status that the movie held ensured that Universal had been working to bring it to the event for many years.

As Murdy explained to *Forbes*, "*I have checked off a lot of boxes on that list particularly this year with The Exorcist. I was trying to do that for about a decade but just took a long, long time to get the rights to it. To me, there is no scarier movie ever in the history of cinema than the first one so we wanted to just deal with that which is actually probably one of the most challenging properties because of one of the criteria I mentioned. It does have awareness in spades but when you get to environments, it primarily takes place in the bedroom and when you come to characters, it is primary much a 12-year-old girl that never gets out of bed so when you think about how to make that scary as an experience. There are all those things that happened in the movie but they're all things you watch, her head spins around and she pukes on you, she's levitating and so on - all of those special effects that we're doing are theatrical things across five bedrooms rather than scare-actors jumping out at you. It's very different for us and the audio design alone is terrifying.*"

The movie essentially just occurs in one bedroom, so the challenge for Universal was to tell the story of the movie, but in a maze format that needed room after room, and not just the one bedroom. The test was to ensure that the maze would replicate the scares and visceral moments from the movie in an authentic, practical, and terrifying way, something that Murdy and his team had been planning for years.

He continued, "*It's a balancing act like it is with any production. For example, with The Exorcist this year, that is very effects heavy because we have to do all the stuff with Regan like her head spinning around, puking on people, the spider walk – which we have actually done, you do know that that is a resource essential to that maze so you just learn to balance it out and spread the budget around accordingly.*"

As the maze developed so did the story. Guests would experience the iconic levitating, the terrifying head-spinning, the vomit-wrenching and even the skin-crawling moments from the original film. Playing mostly on the horrific battle between innocence and evil, the maze would assault the guests' senses. Visitors were bombarded with torturous scenes, moist pea soup-laden SIF (stuff-in-face) and even rotten smells. The maze was very scary and it, like the original movie, got 'under people's skin' in a way that perhaps no maze in HHN history had ever done before or since. It would truly be remembered this year as the maze you adored or were so creeped out by that it was your 'one and done'.

Another new edition for this year was *American Horror Story*, located in the FDTD Area of the backlot, which told the stories of seasons one, four and five of the popular horror show. Universal described it as, "*Step inside the twisted world of American Horror Story, the award-winning anthology horror series that's been terrorizing TV viewers since 2011. Your journey begins at MURDER HOUSE, a century old residence on the outskirts of Los Angeles with a tragic past. The unfortunate souls who perished inside are forever trapped within its walls and each room harbors its own horrible secret. Your next stop is the creepy backwater town of Jupiter, Florida where a struggling FREAK SHOW has taken up residence. The human oddities on display inside the big top are nothing compared to the murderous men and women who fight to control this psychotic circus. Finally, you will check in to the HOTEL Cortez, a ruinous relic of a bygone era that conceals a torture chamber of murder and madness! Inside the hotel's haunted hallways lies a host of supernatural characters bent on making you a guest for all eternity.*"

The dual coast maze would be in three stages and represented the TV seasons sequentially inside the maze. So much material would be required to lovingly recreate the seasons that both Hollywood and Orlando had to create the largest (or longest) mazes they had ever developed. Murdy continued, "*The maze is based on three of the seasons which are the first one, posthumously named Murder House, Freak Show and the most recent one, Hotel. Even though you're dividing the attraction into three seasons, you still have to find a thematic thread because each season is environmentally, radically different even though you have the repertory cast. What I latched onto is the fact that they always have a Halloween episode so I thought that would be a cool thread to use. I love the opening title sequences from each season too so I have integrated parts of that throughout the attraction and even outside on huge screens before people even get inside. Even in the queue, there will be a kind of greatest hits reel of some of the characters guests will encounter going through the maze. This is the longest one we have ever done because there are just so many things happening.*"

The maze would be pitched in February, with Murdy outlining his team's ideas for the show to its creator, Ryan Murphy. Almost immediately the idea was approved, and the maze went into full production. Murdy continued, "*When I originally pitched the maze to the show's creator, Ryan Murphy, he had an amazing idea. I mentioned to him that I thought the opening title sequences were super cool and there are often characters that are in there that aren't actually in the show at all. I said to him that I would like to pick one from each season and bring it to life as an easter egg for the fans because the show has a very rabid fan base. So, in the first season, Jessica Lange says her character, Constance, has four kids but we only ever see three. He originally cast someone to play the fourth child, they filmed some stuff for the pilot and it ended up on the editing floor. Fans have been hounding Ryan for years asking about the fourth kid, who it was, what he looked like and it turned into this big thing online. Ryan decided that now was the time to show the fans what this fourth person, her son, looks like and so you get to meet him for the first time ever in the maze."* The maze, based on this award-winning show, was so popular that on most event nights, the line never got below two hours in duration.

Also new this year, as it was new to Hollywood's event, was *Freddy vs. Jason.* The house had been so wildly popular in 2015 at Orlando for their 25th celebrations that it was decided to move to the West Coast. Located on the backlot's metro sets, the maze would be similar in content to the Orlando version but would essentially be missing some of the larger scenes from this addition. Inspired by the 2003 movie of the same name it would see two of the biggest icons in horror history doing battle. Guests were prepared to be thrust into the middle of an epic battle between Freddy Krueger, from *A Nightmare on Elm Street*, and Jason Voorhees, from *Friday the 13th*. It was battle that raged through the twisted landscape of nightmares from the haunted shores of Camp Crystal Lake to the infamous and decrepit house at 1428 Elm Street. Guests would also experience a final showdown amongst the burned-out ruins of an abandoned boiler factory, where Freddy's evil legacy first began. It would see a final fight to the death between the two horror icons to see who had supremacy. In reality, the 'winner' of the maze would alternate, with each 'winner' of the maze appearing at the end carrying the faux head of whichever one had lost the battle that hour.

Another returning creep for the 2016 season was Michael Myers with *Halloween: Hell Comes to Haddonfield.* Located in the Jurassic Park Queue, the maze would see Myers yet again return to do carnage on the streets of Haddonfield. The maze was a terrifying sequel to 2015's *Halloween: Michael Myers Comes Home*, and had been devised as the previous maze had been the highest rated maze in the history of *Halloween Horror Nights Hollywood!* Picking up where the classic film ended, guests experienced the shocking final confrontation between Dr. Loomis and Michael Myers in the Doyle house, only to realize that the real terror is just getting started! As Dr. Loomis well knows, "*You can't kill The Boogeyman.*" This time the streets of Haddonfield to the labyrinth-like hallways of the Haddonfield Memorial Hospital had been recreated in their full, horrific glory to terrify anyone brave enough to enter the maze. As with many this year, the maze would be represented on both coasts and would be a like-for-like recreation of the second movie from this popular horror franchise.

Speaking of dual coast mazes, *Krampus* would another addition to the lineup that was represented on both. Located on the backlot's metro sets it would recreate the story from this new horror classic to great effect. Everyone knows the story of Santa Claus and how he brings toys to good little girls and boys on Christmas Eve, but what is less well known is what happens to the naughty children who don't make Santa's list! Who visits them on Christmas Eve and what terrible "gifts" does he bring them? Well guests would find this out and more in this all-new maze! *Krampus* would be a horrifying twist on the Old-World Christmas legend based on the 2015 hit film by writer/director Michael Dougherty. For centuries, parents in Europe have frightened their children with stories of Krampus, the malevolent version of Saint Nicholas who preys on bad children during the Christmas season. It would be this central story from the movie that would be recreated in this highly detailed maze.

Creating Krampus would prove to be more complex that first thought. The movie featured a number of monsters that would require puppetry and special effects to bring them to life, all of which would combine to make a maze as difficult to create as *The Exorcist* maze from this year. Murdy described the trials and tribulations of creating the maze to Forbes, *"When I saw Krampus, what was so refreshing about it is it was just so different from all the other horror movies coming out. Horror is very cyclical, it goes to these waves and usually, when something hits like Paranormal Activity, all of sudden there are a million paranormal movies and that rides for a while and then trickles off and before that it was probably films like Saw and Hostel, the gore-no movies. So, when I saw Krampus and it's just so refreshing to see a movie that felt like it just had a really cool aesthetic more like an 80s horror movie, that was evocative of movies like Gremlins where it's got a tongue in cheek but still intense and satisfying. [sic] Starting outside there's a van, in the movie, it is a DHL one but we're created our own delivery company. The reason it is there is not just about recreating the movie, it is because of a key character in the experience – a frozen delivery guy."* And this scareactor would have a very important role within the maze...

Another Hollywood tradition would be reinstated inside this maze. Murdy continued, *"On social media since 2011, I run our Twitter account, I've been doing this thing called The Password every night of the event. When we did Hostel with Eli Roth, he was very involved in that maze, and he wanted the girls to pick up the guys at the clubs and then take him to the torture factory and he's like oh we got to have those girls out front but I kept asking what they would actually do. I came up with this idea and pitched him that we have them give out business cards to Elite Hunting if a guest gave them a certain password. It just picked up after that and we've done it every single year. We did in Silent Hill, From Dusk Till Dawn and we did it last year for This Is The End where you got an invitation to James Franco's party. This year I wanted to do Krampus postcards because the original ones from back in the 1800s that featured the creature are really disturbing. They are these weird Victorian illustrations of this demon dragging children off to hell during Christmas which is where the story comes from. When I was talking to the movie's director, Mike Dougherty, and it turns out that every year he does his own Christmas cards with his own designs and so he gave me the files for those and we've recreated them. We're giving away reproductions of the director's own art! It's just for people who follow me on Twitter, around 80,000 people follow me already, and if they give the password to the frozen delivery guy outside the maze he'll reach into his mailbag and give them the artwork from the film or a postcard or something."*

Dougherty, who is actually a huge HHN fan, adored this maze. He said at the time, *"I've been coming to these mazes since I moved to Los Angeles. It's fun because it's a mash-up of my favorite holiday with one of my movies and it also takes me back a little too because as a kid I used to turn my basement into a haunted house for my friends. I still do it now for the neighborhood trick-or-treaters, but this is that to the Nth degree."* And one very rarely-known fact about this maze was that Dougherty would actually work this maze on select nights, if only for a few hours, as a scareactor or as a puppet performer. He said, *"Just for a few hours, but, you know, I scare people 24/7. Whether it's friends or family members or whoever. I still hide under beds at night to scare people. I have a Michael Myers costume in my car right now, just in case."*

Our final maze would be a repeat maze for the event and a dual coaster - *The Texas Chainsaw Massacre: Blood Brothers*. Located in the *Waterworld* queue building, the maze would be a more visceral addition to the franchise's appearances at the event. Using the original movies as their source material, Universal attempted to recreate the crazy and unpredictable world of the Sawyer family. Utilizing all the classic scares from the first original movie, the house was recreated and stuffed full of scareactors with their sole ambition of terrifying every guest who dared to enter.

An additional maze for this year came in the form of everyone's favorite horror TV franchise, *The Walking Dead*. The full-time maze had replaced *The Universal's House of Horror* attraction and would re-open on event nights. This daytime maze, which is pretty scary during the day, was beefed up with more lighting effects and even more scareactors to ensure it was worth experiencing for its differences at night.

The event would feature only one scarezone for this year, but it would be park wide! The franchise picked to head such an audacious move was *The Purge: Election Year*. The idea was a neat concept that aimed to make no areas of the park safe. Similar to Orlando, when they did this in 2013 with *The Walking Dead,* it would result in large patches of the park being completely unoccupied. For the areas that did have scareactors, it would see masked vigilantes go hunting for victims during the government's annually sanctioned killing spree with all the iconic characters from this movie appearing in some guise. Another returning addition from the previous year was the highly successful *Jabbawockeez* with another high-action dance show experience. After performing to sold-out shows and becoming the highest rated attraction at HHN Hollywood in the previous year (*yes it was!*), the *Jabbawockeez* would return from Las Vegas to Hollywood with an all-new, exclusive live show for 2016. It combined gravity-defying choreography, stunning special effects, heavy-hitting music and their unique brand of humor. The show was yet again very popular, and would no doubt see it return for 2017.

2017: The best nightmares never end!

"The Best Nightmares Never End" would be the tagline of this year. It would be a mixture of mostly dual coast mazes but with some new experiences. Based in the Lower Lot's *Mummy* queue building was the first maze that was announced, which was perhaps one of the most anticipated in all of *Horror Nights'* history: *The Shining*. Based on visionary director Stanley Kubrick's horror classic, *The Shining* would let guests experience all the iconic scenes and characters that have made the film a masterpiece of modern horror. The haunting and vast Overlook Hotel, a sprawling, yet isolated, century-old hotel with a tragic history of murder and madness, would be recreated with all its huge detail. The story of the maze would follow central character Jack Torrance, a man with a troubled past, who has agreed to be the caretaker for The Overlook Hotel during the harsh Colorado winter and has moved his family into the shuttered hotel. But as soon as the Torrance family takes up residence in the hotel, Jack begins to undergo a startling change...a descent into madness that would put his family in grave danger. Unbeknownst to Jack, his young son, Danny, is imbued with a dark gift - the ability to see events and people, both past and future, that others can't see. A gift called "The Shining." Danny's nightmarish visions will help to unlock the mysteries of the haunted hotel and allow the horrifying, true nature of The Overlook to reveal itself. It would be this mixture of Danny's visions and the haunting corridors and rooms of the hotel that would be recreated for guests to experience in this maze. Of course, it wouldn't be plain sailing, it would be a challenge that only Universal could possible meet.

"Our job as haunt designers is to interpret his film very literally," Murdy explained to *ew.com* at the time. *"That often means recreating moments from the movie that are purely visual, and resisting the temptation to have Jack Nicholson jump*

out with an axe. We have to balance all of that and, at the same time, scare the living daylights out of our guests. So that's the creative challenge."

The vast empty corridors of the hotel would prove a challenge, though extending out the usual corridors, making them narrower and adding mirrors would help create this effect. Likewise, the blood elevators would also prove a challenge; pumping dyed red water into a circulation system and spraying as the elevator doors open in a controlled environment enabled the effect to work and it also ensured that guests didn't get drenched with red water. Murdy continued, *"The reason we go to such lengths and such detail is because [the fans] know these movies inside and out. The Shining is one of those movies where they're just obsessed about every detail."*

The iconic carpets were made with cutting-edge technology to recreate the intricate pattern. But for many of the props the crew went out of their way when decorating the rest of the hotel either by searching Universal's massive prop warehouse, or by scouring local flea markets to assemble an entire hotel's worth of 1970s furniture, textiles, and props. Even the bathroom scene's sanitaryware was especially procured to match up to the movie's. *"Nowadays, when I go through a modern movie, I'm usually going through 30,000 to 40,000 images from the set to select the images that I'm going to use to give my art department,"* Murdy said to *ew.com*, *"When you're dealing with older movies like The Shining, you can't usually go to an art department at a movie studio and go, 'oh, I need the file,' because they didn't keep that stuff back then. So, the graphics team had only the movie itself to consult."* The painstaking work and attention to detail would really pay off as the maze was amazing and is truly one of the best mazes they had ever created. And one final interesting fact, was that on one single night movie star James Franco, who had been so impressed with the maze *This Is The End 3D* in 2015, came back to the event to work as a scareactor for just one event night. He played an axe wielding Jack Torrance in one scene and was said to have had the time of his life! His co-star from *The True Blood* watching on the monitors told Franco that he was so good that, *"This could be the [their] hiatus job!"*

Located in the Metro Sets, guests would experience *Ash Vs. Evil Dead* - a new maze based on the TV show of the same name. The maze would be referred to this year as the one 'with the laughs', as though each year needs a lighter-styled maze. The maze would begin much like the series where we are introduced to Ash and his new life on the trailer park, and the role at the supermarket. Bruce Campbell would help Universal in the creation of the maze and would provide his voice to scores of pieces of dialogue that were broadcast at various points along the guest's path. Both seasons one and two of the now cancelled show were represented inside this maze.

A new maze for this largest-ever year at Hollywood would be *The Horrors of*

Blumhouse, though admittedly it would feature properties within the maze that had been present at the previous event. Located in the Parisian Courtyard area it would feature three of Blumhouse's popular franchises and would even include one movie that had not been released yet. Universal billed the maze as, *"Get ready for three twisted Blumhouse Productions films in one bone-chilling experience. Come face-to-face with the most iconic and unnerving moments from the blockbuster The Purge franchise, Sinister movies and soon-to-be released Happy Death Day. In The Purge section, you will attempt to survive the night, immersed in the film property's depraved world where all crime is declared legal in the government's annually sanctioned 12-hour cleansing of society. In what can be described as a living trailer for Happy Death Day, you will encounter the deja vu scenario, forced to relive the last day of your lives over and over again, trying to escape a mysterious masked killer. Then, in Sinister, encounter an ancient pagan deity who is determined to trap you for all eternity in the sordid shadow world of the dead."*

The partnership that was created with this maze would be an important one for the future and would see Jason Blum and his teams work with Universal on many other projects. *"It's a privilege to collaborate with Jason Blum and his team at Blumhouse Productions to create 'The Horrors of Blumhouse,'"* said John Murdy at the time. *"The decisive, inventive way in which he interprets underlying issues plaguing today's society into his films provides us with a plethora of content to create truly captivating, one-of-a-kind modern horror experiences for our guests."*

Another maze that Blum would assist on, and one that was returning to Jurassic Park Queue building, was *Insidious: Beyond the Further.* Universal billed the maze as, *"The all-new maze will delve deep into brilliant parapsychologist Dr. Elise Rainer's past, starting with a childhood in which her paranormal abilities emerged... until her mother's untimely death by a demonic entity. Troubled by a lifetime of evil supernatural spirits trapped in the Further-a vacuous netherworld caught between the living and the dead-Elise will take guests on an unsettling journey back in time through a portal into the Further to defy the most depraved and intimidating beings that have tormented her since the 1950s."* The maze would be a bit problematic as it was based on the fourth entry to the series, and when production delays held up release (it didn't open in theatres nationwide to until Friday, January 5th, 2018), the maze's contents didn't make much sense to the visiting public. Murdy said at the time, *"What's unusual about this maze is this movie doesn't come out until January. So in the words of my longtime collaborator on a lot of mazes Jason Blum, this is the ultimate trailer for his movie."*

Another returning franchise with a new release to their repertoire was *SAW* with *SAW: The Games of Jigsaw.* Also based on their new release, *Jigsaw,* for this season, the maze would be located in the 747 area of the backlot. It would be a mixture of the greatest scares from the past movies and have an added section towards the end to tease the forthcoming feature. The maze was possibly the bloodiest of the creations this year where all the classic traps were recreated in this tortuous maze; The Razor Wire Maze, The Reverse Bear Trap, The Automated Scalping Machine, and The Pound of Flesh are just a few of the filmic traps guests saw along the maze. In addition, a few of the traps from the upcoming movie were also present in the form of a 'living preview'.

Murdy told *screenrant.com* at the time, *"Saw: The Games of Jigsaw will encompass the greatest collection of traps featured in all eight Saw movies to bring to life the most twisted Saw maze ever produced, and we can't wait for our fans to relive moments from the films."*

American Horror Story would return this year, following its very successful induct in the previous year, this time with *Roanoke*. Guests would be transported to deep in the backwoods of North Carolina, where an isolated farmhouse that has witnessed centuries of horror is located ready for their exploration. Legend has it that the house was built close to the site of the infamous "Lost Colony of Roanoke", an English settlement that mysteriously vanished back in the late 1500's. Though no one knows for sure what happened to the doomed colonists of Roanoke, the suffering of the residents at the cursed farmhouse has been well documented; a legacy of murder and madness that extends back into the murky past in an unbroken chain of horror. They say that the most dangerous time to visit the farmhouse is during the first moon after the harvest...the Blood Moon! So guess where the public was heading! All to witness scenes of cannibalism, blood-sacrifices and murderous spirits who were still clinging to the cursed land. Located back in the same maze area of the cavernous FDTD area on the backlot, the maze was constructed to ensure that all the significant set pieces from this season of the show were visually recreated. Concentrating mostly on the second half of the popular season, the creatives at Universal wanted to create a maze that was vast in scope but with the unmistakable Universal difference of ensuring every last nightmarish detail was exactly right.

The *Terror Tram* this year was *Titans of Terror Tram: Hosted by Chucky,* and would be a mixture of franchises, containing: *Friday the 13th, A Nightmare on Elm Street, The Texas Chainsaw Massacre* and *Child's Play.* Billed as the *Terror Tram* "plus plus" it would be the longest and most detailed tram to date, something that guests had wanted to revitalize for this Hollywood exclusive attraction. Universal described it as, *" Taking terror to an unspeakable level of bloodcurdling screams, The Titans of Terror Tram Hosted by Chucky will transport guests into a nightmare of carnage pitting you against these four modern horror icons, this time led by infamous serial killer doll Chucky (Child's Play franchise). With his faithful army of degenerate chainsaw-wielding Good Guy Dolls, Chucky will unleash havoc upon guests as they navigate a portion of the world-famous backlot."* The tour would also be complemented by a maze on the Upper Lot that would feature additional scares from the four franchises.

The concept behind the dual tour and maze idea came about due to the vast quantity of available material between the franchises and the realization that they could be 'dovetailed' together to make two excellent experiences. The story is about a young horror fan (probably modelled on Murdy) who builds a crude haunted maze in his own home (something that Murdy did regularly as a child with his family). Unfortunately, the event is cancelled due to the weather and the kid is left alone with an all-night horror movie marathon. It is from this marathon that the nightmares begin, with guests walking through his closet door and directly into his horror-filled dreams. We encounter the puppet scene in *A Nightmare on Elm Street 3: The Dream Warriors* (a prop sent over from Orlando's HHN no less), Jason's underground domain introduced in the reboot of *Friday the 13th*, and the Sawyer homestead of Leatherface and his demented family. To date no maze, ever, has combined these four franchises, in what for many people was one of the best mazes for this year.

Due to the bumper number of mazes this year there were only three scarezones. All three were originals, though: *Hell-O-Ween* at the Front Gates, *Toxic Tunnel* (Backlot Tunnel) and *Urban Inferno* on the backlot. *Hell-O-Ween* was a large and somewhat fun maze that featured witches, ghosts, vampires, werewolves and undead zombie kids. Borrowing heavily from the scarezones of Orlando, this original maze made some good scares and was fairly photogenic. *Toxic Tunnel* featured the classic turning tunnel and would see zombie utility workers of all sizes attempt to attack guests as they fled the area. *Urban Inferno* was also located on the backlot and consisted of various depictions of hell on earth. Guests encountered Burnt Lost Souls, Half-Goat Executioners, Mad Monks, and Blacksmiths forging the chains of Purgatory as Satanic Demons whipped poor unfortunate souls back to damnation; a fun zone to say the least!

Finally, *The Walking Dead* attraction was reopened for event nights with a slightly more beefed-up addition to the lineup. This was also matched by the popular return of *Jabbawockeez* with a new show. The show was described as,
"Originating from the Westside of the galaxy light years away, the Jabbawockeez, have crash-landed on planet Earth and are now stranded in the 1950s. Feeling out of place from outer space, a musical journey ensues as they try to find a way back home. On this fantastic voyage through this strange land, the Jabbawockeez encounter a like-minded and masked character named Alizé-unaware that this being they've just met may hold the key to the Jabbawockeez' homecoming."

In all, the show was yet again another high-octane addition to their catalogue and a good distraction from the horrors and chills from the various mazes and zones.

HHN Europe

The very first international version of *Halloween Horror Nights* would debut at the recently opened Spanish resort destination *PortAventura World* (or just Port Aventura as it was known then). The theme park, the themed entertainment and the subsequent hotels were all originally conceived in the late 1980s by a consortium of international and Spanish companies, headed up by Anheuser-Busch (the Busch Entertainment Corporation). Busch had successfully run a number of themed entertainment companies and theme parks, including the collection of *Sea Worlds* and *Busch Gardens* in the US and some international destinations in partnership with others. However, it would not be plain sailing for the planned Spanish resort, as further on into the negotiations, most of the Spanish organizations pulled their support and their finances from the project. The main ambition of the project was to create a resort in the Catalonia area of Spain that would not just be seasonal but a resort destination that would entice visitors to its gates all year round.

Busch, a US company, tried to reassure investors that the lessons learnt by Disney in its opening of their French resort in cooler climes had been noted. Their view was the warmer climate at this Spanish destination would help negate the issues that Disney had experienced further north. Spanish investors did not agree, and they subsequently pulled their support. Busch looked around for investment elsewhere and although the Spanish authorities were still on board with the project, they still needed a corporate backup to ensure they had the funds they needed to help them complete the project. Some months later it was announced that the British entertainment company Tussauds Group would take up the slack and become full partners in the project. Tussauds, with their global coverage of *Legolands* and *Sea Life Centres* were deemed to be the perfect choice for the newly-formed partnership, and due to this, the project went ahead.

During its conception, Port Aventura's investors researched the market to ensure that their theme park would mirror *Disneyland Paris* (*Euro Disney* at the time), but without the teething troubles. Port Aventura would be located in a sought-after location and would be positioned as a holiday destination rather than as a recreational area or a day trip destination (which is what most theme parks in Europe tend to be). Ensuring these factors would be critical, but it turned out that underestimating the competition would ultimately be their main challenge.

Finally launching in the summer of 1995, the new themed destination was a world class destination to rival any regional theme park, and it was going incredibly well. Not only had they included all the right ingredients but they had also selected a location that benefits from a great climate and high visitor numbers. They created main attractions (aside from the theme park) that they hoped would ensure year-round entertainment for their visitors, including world class golf courses, a convention center and a large shopping mall. However, it wasn't enough and after a fantastic summer of high attendance numbers, visitor numbers dropped off significantly over the winter period.

By this time, Disney's French resort had 14 hotels, numerous golf courses, movie theaters, and it had attracted over 14 million visitors a year with a healthy turnover that exceeded 1.2 billion euros. In the Iberian peninsula where Port Aventura was located there were other theme parks that competed with it. These included *Terra Mitica* in Benidorm, *Warner Bros. Movie World* in Madrid and *Isla Mágica* in Seville, all of which had developed similar business models. None of these, however, had built any hotels or other leisure services (such as spa, golf, convention centers, etc.), thereby limiting their places as full holiday destinations and/or their growth locally. Port Aventura was the only theme park that brought in enough visitors to avoid actual losses, but the competitors nearby certainly ate into their profit margins. Eventually, it was felt that the market was too crowded, and the two founding corporations decided in the fall of 1996 to put the resort up for sale.

Over that winter a deal was done with Universal to buy up the resort and turn it into one of a number of planned international versions of their popular theme parks, Universal Studios. Universal was slowly expanding into the Asian market but wanted a base in Europe to compete once again with Disney. To avoid the delay and cost of building their own park somewhere on this busy continent, they decided to buy up the Port Aventura site, realizing that a retrofit would be a shrewder and more cost-effective move.

In the spring of 1997 the deal was done and the announcement was made: Universal would acquire the majority of the organization's shares and be the main owner of the site. Universal would then set about making the resort more 'Universal' and would take 12 months before the park had achieved this. By 1999 the park had rebranded, and plans were in place to add additional hotels and even a sister park right next to the main park. This would be *Costa Caribe* and it would act as a 'half-day' water park. By 2000, many of these new additions came online and the destination was now known as *Universal Mediterranea*. The park became more successful in the long-term for the new owners, but in 2004 the decision was taken by Universal's new parent company, NBC, to sell the resort and concentrate efforts elsewhere. In 2005 the resort was sold to La Caixa banking group's investment arm, Criteria. They immediately dropped the Universal name and branding, and began rearranging the park. This company still owns the resort to this day.

During Universal's tenure of ownership between 1997 and 2004, the company decided to make the resort more like its successful Orlando and Hollywood operations. And while a number of back office and organizational changes occurred, such as how to monitor guest numbers and feedback, to management changes, new safety features and food quality improvements, the main aim was to infuse the park and hotels with a more recognizable Universal brand. This brand would extend to a number of ride and show additions (mostly using ride manufacturers they had contracted during the construction of *Islands of Adventure*). Similar-layout rides were built here, but themed differently, but they focused on other, smaller cost areas, too. These included the famous Universal walkaround characters, the meet and greets with 'Hollywood'-looking stars and a more general filmic appearance. Woody Woodpecker and his girlfriend Winnie would also act as the official mascots for the park and would appear in most of the resort's marketing.

The main factor that Universal and the previous owners had all tried to ensure was the mission to make this resort have a year-round draw, which was something that theme parks in Europe had always struggled with. And one of the key aspects that Universal implemented to achieve this was to add their very successful Halloween event to the park, to dramatically increase the fortunes of the fall season. It would be the year 2000 that Universal began to test the water with a Halloween event at this resort. A new underwater attraction would be opened in the spring named *Sea Odyssey*, with the ribbon being cut by Bo Derek. This would see the summer months populated with headline-grabbing additions of other famous celebrities coming to and enjoying the park with their families. It was formally announced on the fifth anniversary of the resort that the park would add, for the time ever, *Halloween Horror Nights* to its lineup for that coming fall. And in order to re-create the event for the continent that effectively created the holiday, the company would send a number of their trusted designers from the US over the Spanish resort to work with local designers to recreate the popular event.

In 2000, *Halloween Horror Nights* would take place on select nights from October 16th to November 5th. *The Far West, Mexico* and *Mediterrània* areas of the park would be decorated for the occasion using a number of props and set pieces to give the park an overall haunted appearance. Many of the *Far West* shows would also be modified to have a more Halloween feel, though the shows themselves would effectively be the same. *A Passage of Terror*, the very first

Europe scarezone, would be devised in *Mexico*, in the *El Reposo* area. Additional special nightly events would include a *Vampire Dance* at *La Cantina* on the 21st and a *Horror Movie Night* at the *Gran Teatro Maya* on the 28th, where some of the best Universal Monsters pictures were shown. All activities were included in the price of the same Halloween after-hours park ticket.

The entrance route was covered in cobwebs, pumpkins and skeletons to welcome the new Halloween event and the very first maze was constructed: *The Stable of Terror* – reused in subsequent years but later renamed as *El Establo Maldito*. It was a collection of rooms that basically mimicked a number of horrific folklores and stories that, as the years wore on, would be swopped out for more filmic alterations.

A 2000 advert for the new event

In this early addition, it was the shows that seemed to be the most popular, and one of the biggest draws was in the *La Cantina de Mexico*. There, several times a night, El Diablo (aka the Devil) was presented on stage. The show was based around the concept of discovering how evil a person is capable of becoming in order to become a devil. The show would start off as fairly serious before ratcheting up the tasks, so they would become comical or surreal. For example, some guests pulled on stage by various demons would be tasked with singing karaoke versions of Michael Jackson's *Thriller* or would do comical duets with devilish Drag Queens to the tune of Gloria Gaynor's *I Will Survive*. The shows did exactly what the early shows at the state side version of the event did: they made the party atmosphere. This was key to the event here in Europe and something that the locals and tourists really enjoyed.

The very first mascot for the event would be resort's mascot Woody Woodpecker in a vampire costume, complete with cape and fangs, who would appear around the park for meet and greets but would also feature in all the marketing. A giant statue was also built in the main promenade area, which would be rolled out every Halloween under Universal's tenure, depicting the now vampiric Woodpecker for the ultimate photo opportunity. The main park posters advertising the event around the resort also featured a Boris Karloff-looking Mummy and a figure very reminiscent of Leatherface, scaring guests with a bloody chainsaw. The cover art of the Mummy was also lifted from 1999's *Halloween Horror Nights IX: Last Gasp* from the Orlando event in the previous year.

Other attractions included the premier of *La Selva del Miedo (The Forest of Fear)*, which was an outside tour that ran from *La Plaza de La Cantina* to the *China* areas of the park where a mixture of real forest and faux trees had been dressed as spookily as possible. Tight catastrophic tunnels and small rooms had been built along the path, all stuffed with scareactors to create a version of the popular Terror Tram from the Hollywood version of the event. The tour would finish up with a recreation of a mummy's pyramid, complete with copious amounts of additional scareactors. Elsewhere in the Far West area of the park was a popular band *Los No Muertos de Penitence (The Undead of Penitence)*, a band that played haunting hits inside one of the busy park restaurants. The event would be capped off with *La Parada de los Monsters* as a version of the chainsaw chase-out from both Orlando and Hollywood (though mostly the latter) where a parade of Universal's classic monsters would entertain the crowds before scaring them out the door for park closing. The event would prove to be very successful which ensured its return in the coming year. So in the following year, more plans were undertaken, including sending more designers over from the US. But it wasn't just designers that Universal sent to the park...

2001 would be a bumper year for the fledgling resort. The year started with a Hollywood bang when the *Temple of Fire* opened its doors, with very first riders

183

being Hollywood action star Jean-Claude Van Damme and the model María Pineda. The park also benefited from additional licensing contracts that had been signed by Universal for their opening of *Islands of Adventure* in Orlando, which allowed more walk around characters to appear. These included: Popeye, Olive Oyl, Brutus, Betty Boop, the Pink Panther and the cartoonish Inspector Clouseau (though those last two do not appear in Orlando). Universal Express was added to most rides around the park and the success of *Halloween Horror Nights* at the resort ensured two additional events were planned; these included a New Year Carnival in the spring months and a Christmas celebration in December and January. The additions and pluses that Universal created saw park attendance swell to an all-time high of 3.2 million visitors.

Speaking of not just sending designers over from the US... the very first HHN icon to make it 'across the pond' would be Jack the Clown. The official tagline would be "The Terror Waits For You" and various commercials and posters would display our fearsome clown hiding in a number of bedrooms and houses showing that no place was safe to hide from Jack. The event would be largely the same as the previous year, but guests would see fewer cutesy Woodpeckers and more scareactors dressed as Jack around the park, gnawing on decapitated heads or lunging from the darkness to whispers of "*Terror is your pairing for tonight*".

In 2002 the new additions at the resort had started to pay dividends as the park gate numbers had increased by a further 500,000 in 2002. Additional hotels and the new water park came online, and the marketing was ramped up to draw in guests all year round. A new maze named La Hacienda Encantada (The Enchanted Forest) was constructed to replace *The Forest of Fear* with demonic fairies and wolf-like vampires replacing the zombies and mummies from the former attraction. Not wanting to see the zombies out of a job, they were moved up to the front of the park to their own scarezone.

Another maze was constructed inside one of the ride queue buildings (something that Universal does in the US) where a new *Passage of Terror* was offered. A creepy, haunted mine was designed where the ghosts of dead miners were brought back to life to scare guests inside a re-creation of a failed mine shaft. The *Cursed Stable* maze was also constructed along with the *Jungle of Fear*, all of which had minor theming.

The resort also marketed the Halloween event across Europe for the first time, as in 2002 it was the only theme park resort in continental Europe that had a regular Halloween event, something they were keen to capitalize on. The 'eye-gore' mascot was deployed across all media (a mascot that has been used by both Orlando and Hollywood and is still used to this day as their staff awards for the event). The tagline of their marketing was that "*you will not go back to sleep*" after you dare to enter Europe's *Halloween Horror Nights*.

In 2003 the popular event was expanded once again, and the popular *Woodpecker* was seen in a number of marketing opportunities being decapitated by The Caretaker. He, of course, was an established Orlando icon who himself had debuted in the previous year at Orlando's event. The tongue-in-cheek tagline for the marketing this time was, "*with all security you will lose your head*".

The fourth edition of Europe's version of the event would see the event extended to more nights, with it running from October 9th to November 16th. Not only was the number of nights extended but so were the event's offerings and the event's theming. Strangely, The Caretaker would be known as 'Cortacabezas'.

Spanish celebrity and pop singer Marta Sánchez was on hand this year to open the event and to act as a spokesperson on what terrors awaited guests. One of the first attractions inside the park gates would be a recreation of the guillotine beheadings of the French Revolution. Here, faceless monks would take guests to perform the classic magic trick of the blade passing through their neck without it cutting their head off (you can see the theme this year was losing your head in some way or somehow!). The monks would then be disturbed by their ruler, The Caretaker, would showcase his "tools" to various monks that had been unruly, and the act would be seen as a small show within a scarezone, almost akin to the 'Opening Scaremonies' from Orlando.

For the first time too, the horror was not confined to the theme park, as the hotels were also, weirdly, staffed with a few scareactors. On select nights, a number of made-up zombies would replace some of the hotel staff at the main reception to scare guests as they walked through the respective lobbies. Room Service also offered a number of 'bloody' surprises for anyone brave enough to order from their menu.

Back in the park, the streets' offerings were dramatically increased with more scarezones than before, all of which had a more filmic quality to them. Scareactors depicting Freddy Kruger, haunting ghosts and even a bed being pushed around with characters from *The Exorcist* were all seen (the latter of which used to appear at Orlando in the early days). A new maze of *Psycho's Circus* was presented along with now-returning favorite, *The Forest of Fear*. A hellish bar was devised for *Midnight Saloon* and the Jungle maze also returned with a new theme of *Temple of Fire*. Tarot readers and food vendors selling Halloween-inspired goods were all present, too.

Psycho's Circus was one of the newest and most popular attractions from this year. The story of the attraction is based on a circus (the Wonder Circus), which was owned by a clown named *Psycho*. Weirdly, he had decided to kill all the workers of the circus, and guests got to see all the remains of trapeze artists, clowns, the box office, etc. In the main circus area guests were led through all the rooms that a good circus would have, including the ticket offices, the entrance, the track, the changing rooms, the makeup room, where depictions of their grueling deaths had been reproduced. And in all these rooms, *Psycho* continued to make his own version of the circus, but think replacing juggling balls with human heads (you see the overall theme here) and you get the idea of how the maze played out. The maze was also interesting as it used the 3D technology that many of the US mazes had used over the years and it also featured a version of Orlando's icon, The Rat Lady. They also attempted to change out some of the scares each day. In order to attract the locals it was billed as 'surprises on every visit', something that the US parks don't tend do unless required. The park also experimented with giving hotel guests their own exclusive ticket, bookable only with a room stay, where hotel guests could join a front-of-the-line pass for just one haunted maze. Other than these unique additions, the marketing was ramped up across Europe for the event and the park was given its very own website for the very first time.

2004 would prove to be the final official iteration of the event before Universal eventually sold its interest in the resort. The previous few years had seen Universal invest a great deal at the resort and go all out to make it a global, year-round destination. Over in America, the Universal family of companies would be taken over by NBC, and the new partner company did not want to retain ownership of the Spanish resort. It was subsequently sold with a deal that ensured that Universal would give up management of the resort but would retain a 1.5% benefit from sales of any of their Universal branded products for a period of 10 years. One of these products would be the Halloween events, though this lasted just one year before entirely new themed Halloween events would replace the seasonal use of *Halloween Horror Nights*. 2004's offering was very subdued and would feature the *Asylum Patient* as the event's mascot; this is noteworthy as he would also be the mascot for this year's event in Orlando, making him the first mascot-come-icon that headlined two HHNs around the world (one in the US and one internationally).

A sequel to the very popular maze from the previous year would be the headliner attraction of *Psycho's Circus II: The Revenge*. The maze was largely the same as the previous incarnation, with only a small number of rooms being changed out. As the event ended in November, so would Universal's control of the park end too. Right after this it would revert to the management, making this event the last addition that Universal brought to the park. As the new management found their way, there would be no Halloween offering in 2005 but it did return in 2006. It would bump along as a much smaller affair with the occasional use of Universal-owned or contracted IPs, but used in very small capacities. For example, The Caretaker (Spain seemed to adore him!), Beetlejuice and the Asylum Patient all made cameo appearances in the scarezones for 2009 and 2010.

Two very obvious differences from the result of Universal leaving was how the event's marketing became very muted and how the intensity of the scares rapidly reduced. Whether the new owners reduced the budget or wanted to step away from horror is anyone's guess. However, one slightly ironic difference that did occur the very year after Universal left, was how the competing local parks all started their own Halloween events. *Warner Bros' Park* and the Parque *Atracciones de Madrid*, especially the latter, all managed to make a series of mazes, scarezones and even parades that were all successful to varying degrees. Heck, even *Disneyland Paris* started on the Halloween bandwagon with an adult version of their *Not So Scary Halloween Party* with their *Terrorific Night Halloween Party* in 2009 (yes that actually happened, twice too, in 2009 and 2010!). It can surely be said that the clones of what started with Universal bringing *Halloween Horror Nights* to Port Aventura were spreading throughout the continent and it does make me wonder what effect Universal would have had on the Halloween themed entertainment if only they had retained ownership of this Spanish resort.

Since then, the event has carried on under the new and current management. Today they still present in the regular format they have become accustomed to, but they are sadly lacking any Universal influence or use of their characters (the deal supposedly expired in 2015). The most popular features include the mazes *Horror in Penitence, La Selva del Miedo* and a really fun night time lake show named *Halloween show Horror en el Lago. This last show* appears to be a combination of *Epcot's Illuminations* and the *Opening Scaremonies* with a hint of *Disney's World of Colour* made into a horror genre version!

A promotion image of Disneyland Paris' attempt to corner the horror market!

HHN Singapore

The next international location to open their version of *Halloween Horror Nights* would be at Universal Studios Singapore, which is a theme park located within a wider resort area known as *Resorts World Sentosa* on Sentosa Island, Singapore. The theme park is relatively new, only opening its doors in March 2010. The theme park is relatively small compared to domestic Universal parks at just 20 hectares (49 acres) in size, with the overall island resort being just 49 hectares (120-acres). The theme park has a total of 24 attractions, of which 18 are original or specially adapted for this park. The park consists of seven themed lands which surround a large lagoon. Each land is based on a movie or a television property, featuring attractions, character appearances, dining and shopping opportunities. The park features the world's tallest pair of dueling roller coasters that are based on the rebooted television series, *Battlestar Galactica*. Some of its highest-rated attractions include: a version of Orlando's *Revenge of the Mummy: The Ride* and a meet and greet castle from the world of *Shrek. Monster Rock*, a live musical dance show featuring the Universal Monsters is also incredibly popular. There are around 30 restaurants and food carts, together with 20 retail stores located around the park.

The park would open in March 2010 and by fall they only had a very muted Halloween celebration that consisted of park decorations and some of the more 'scarier' walk around characters. It wouldn't be until the following year that HHN as we know it would officially come to Singapore. It promised to be the "largest Halloween event ever staged in Southeast Asia", despite the fact that the event would have only one house. Using the history of the US parks, the local media outlets were told how the event had started over 20 years ago in the US and how the event had grown and grown at Orlando and Hollywood.

Although Halloween wasn't a new concept to the people of Singapore, the way in which it was celebrated took some induction to the masses. The pagan celebration that was seen by the Singaporeans as 'a Celtic festival' is not unlike the celebrations that many in the country were familiar with. Largely, the celebration here, and for many other countries around the world, is the time of year where the end of summer is marked and the heralding of winter begins. For many who shy away from the frivolity of the celebration and stick to more pagan origins it is also known as the 'Winter Solstice', but for many Singaporeans it is known as the 'Hungry Ghost Festival'. In many Asian cultures but particularly the Chinese culture, the fifteenth day of the seventh month in the lunar calendar is called 'Ghost Day' and the seventh month in general is regarded as the 'Ghost Month'. During this time, ghosts and spirits, and most importantly those of the recently deceased ancestors, come out from the lower realm to be with the living. So although this festival is ingrained in the local culture, the more Americanized version of this festival with its American park would play host to the 'Celtic' (their words) version of the Halloween celebrations. For example, door to door collections for treats, a practice of where children and the poor would collect soul cakes was being anglicized into 'trick or treating'. Universal wanted to honor these traditions but would stick to the formula made so popular in the US and Spain by having the traditional houses/mazes, scarezones and shows that we all know and love.

To build on Universal's US legacy, as this was its inaugural year and had no back catalog yet, Universal would bring one of its own icons over from the US to kick off the start of their new event. The icon chosen by the Singaporean designers as being from the US but with a flair that locals would really get behind was The Director. The icon, although borrowed from the US, would be tweaked to appear more Asian in appearance but still have the main ingredients from this foreboding character. Acting as the 'host' of the film-based theme park's new event, he would welcome 'victims' into the park, both in the various commercials but also literally, with various actors portraying the icon right at the park gates. Once inside, guests would be promised an audition where they would be 'cast for their final cut'. He would be named 'Billy Skorski', another name change to the character, but he would essentially be 'their version' of the beloved event icon. The menacing auteur would sit atop a podium on his director's chair, complete with old-fashioned film camera, pointing and grinning at the guests below. The same makeup and props were used, but to visually signify the difference of their character he would wear a dark green jacket instead of customary jet-black one that we know so well.

Located in a soundstage behind their version of the New York streets was the very first maze, *Vengeance of the Matriarch*. The story told how many years ago a power-hungry Nyonya (a Chinese immigrant to the area) hypnotized the village butcher into brutally murdering her own older sister in their family mansion. Today, the restless spirit of this demented Peranakan (Chinese descendent) matriarch (a type of widow) still resides in this haunted house, inviting guests to enter into her ghostly abode. The maze would be derived from a Southeast Asian Peranakan legend that was told locally as a fairytale. The story was well known and Universal knew that to bring this event to the theme park they would need to bring it in its Americanized form but adapt it. Essentially, they needed it to feel familiar enough to both locals and guests in order to make it successful.

Singapore's version of The Director

The cavernous soundstage would be taken up by this large maze that would feature a decrepit old house filled with sinister spooks; think *Disney's Haunted Mansion* but for grownups! Once inside, guests encountered an entrance hall featuring the title character of 'The Matriarch'. She would be sitting on a rocking chair telling the foreboding tale of how death and destruction had befallen her. After the pep-talk of the horrors that awaited the guests, a series of rooms inside the mansion would be presented. These included: a dining hall where ghosts were feeding on the remains of the living and a library filled with hanging corpse, a walk-in closet literally filled with skeletons and a creepy kitchen where the floors were squishy (some kind of water/gel filled under the vinyl sheet flooring) – but it was enough to distract you as the butcher entered for his next victim! To kickstart their event, the house was incredibly detailed and supposedly contained over 1000 props that had either been manufactured for the event or bought locally from thrift stores. The house was also stuffed with scareactors, with most rooms having around six actors in them, which was enough to ensure the house would take as long as 15 minutes to completely explore. The wizardry of the soundstage setting where the environment, lighting and special-effects could all be controlled together ensured this house was an excellent start to the fledgling event.

The second maze, which was a combination of outside tour (similar to the *Terror Tram*) and traditional haunted house, was *The Pestilence*. Located in their version of Sting Alley, the maze was relatively short but contained some very good scares. The story was that a demonic plague had infected many unfortunate inhabitants in the poverty-stricken docks and alleyways of 19th century America. Their skin peeling, their flesh decaying, their foul, putrid stench overwhelming, this maze was short but very much in-your-face! The makeup alone made the house a must-do, as the scareactors had all kinds of latex and special effects applied to their faces to make them look like rotting, but still living, zombies. Combine excessive amounts of dry-ice and plenty of darkened corners for the scareactors to spring from and you had a pretty good outdoor maze that could rival even the best scarezones that have appeared in Orlando's version.

The rooms inside the maze included: Courtyard, Waiting Room, Portrait Room, Black Hallway (which was long and had a turn in it), Piano Room, Dining Hall, Library (with a slug-like human jumping between the corpses), Occult Artifacts room, Balcony with hanging bodies, Hallway with a flashing red light, Black Hallway with a Pepper's Ghost scare halfway down it, The Matriarch's Bedroom, Her Dressing Room, the Walk-in Wardrobe, unstable floors (squishy and plank floors, crank shaped layout), the Kitchen and the Boiler room, and a final encounter with the Butcher ghost before exiting. The house was a marathon of horror!

As the inaugural year was their way of just testing the waters to see if the event could be popular, only half of the park was actually open (the right-hand side from the park entry). The park is orientated a lot like *Islands of Adventure*. This would mean that only selected rides and attractions would be open, which would mostly consist of the more adult-orientated attractions such as *The Mummy* and *Battlestar Galactica*. It also meant that the event had to cram four smaller scarezones into the remaining walking spaces. The first of these was *Carn-Evil* where guests would 'step right up' to a midway of mayhem, featuring an assortment of freaks, chainsaw handling clowns and gross-out sideshows. Between the mazes in the New York area was *Post-Apocalyptic Rage*. The event designers took the facades in their area and expanded the Sting Alley maze by making it look as though New York had survived some kind of nuclear war. It was made to look as though desperate people who survived the blast, now half mutated, would roam the city as cannibals looking for victims to satisfy their hunger; the zone seemed to work well with the nearby mazes and surroundings.

In the park's Sci-fi Land area they would present *The Void*. The idea here was that in this strange world, a sadistic mad scientist would stalk humans and turns them into mechanical monsters. Screams of pain and anguish ripped through the air as he dismembered and boiled their limbs, then fastened metal prosthetic parts in their place. It was a bit campy but was a twist on the mad scientist and human-cyborg storyline that made for some great photo opportunities. The final scarezone was *The Edge of Darkness* and was the smallest zone presented this year. Located in the *Ancient Egypt* portion of the park it would feature Egyptian-styled stilt walkers, fire eaters and a few mummies who would be assembled to create a 'monster rave party' celebrating the newly discovered 'portal to Hell'; think dance party meets scarezone. Neighboring this scarezone was the one show of the event (if you exclude *The Director's* front of house show *Final Cut*): *44 Sins* would be the show, and it would feature said 'portal to Hell'. A creepy looking judge-come-bouncer/doorman would invite guests into the portal where after a few dramatics and special effects it was revealed to be a dance party themed around soul extraction.

The event would run for seven nights over two main weekends (from October 21st to 23rd and from October 27th to 30th 2011), between 8 pm and 12 midnight each evening. The separate, ticketed event was not included with park admission (something that caused some confusion for the new event), but daytime guests were invited to upgrade their day tickets to stay for the nightly horrors. It was priced at S$60 per guest, and special resort-wide packages were available. The main merchandise consisted of a blood splattered mug, a LED flashing plastic cup and various T-shirts. The event also ran various RIP Tours, though one insider told us that these weren't so popular initially. The medical scrubs-wearing tour guides (just like in Orlando) would give guests the grand tour of around three hours and the pass would also act as an Express Pass (which were also sold separately too) to all other attractions, similar to how Orlando does their RIP tours. The final attraction which had its own long queue of guests was a meet-and-greet with The Director; RIP guests could also spend 15 minutes with the icon at the end of their tour to see how they fared. In all, the event was very popular and guest satisfaction was high, it would cement the event's reputation in the new park and ensure its return for the following year.

2012's event would focus on *The Puppet Master*, the first newly-created icons from the Singaporean event. The event would largely run to the same dates as last year and would be over the weekends of October 19th to 21st and 25th to 28th, from 8pm to 12 midnight each night. The event promised to cater for the people "that missed last year's extraordinary event" but it would also increase the scares for the vying public that had loved the previous year's offerings. This increase in scares would be undertaken by doubling the numbers of scareactors (which was no mean achievement considering how many had been at the previous year!) and by increasing the number of houses.

The backstory of the event was that the evil Puppet Master had taken control of the park and your mission as the guest was to survive the night. Ever since he was a child, the Puppet Master had been an outcast and had been seen as a social pariah who had an obsession with dolls and puppets of all kinds. One dark and stormy night, he decided to try to make the most flawless, human-like dolls that he could. Unfortunately, no matter what he tried, he could not get the dolls to look human enough. So instead he decided to kidnap people locally and turn them into his own slave dolls. He was also not alone in his endeavor to enslave the local population as he had 3 henchmen, The High Priest, Doctor Dementia, and The Undertaker, all of whom would act as sub-icons for the event. Together the rat pack foursome would appear throughout the park appearing for photo-ops and meet-and-greets, while also starring in all of the marketing for the event. Each of them would also head up a particular portion of the event, to showcase both the Puppet Master's control and the overarching theme of the overall event. It can be said that the event borrowed heavily from how the Orlando event has been run, whereby not only the operational logistics of managing the event were mirrored but also the preference for opting for original properties over the licensed ones where they were available.

Of the three mazes, the largest was back in Soundstage 28 with *Dungeon of Damnation*. Universal billed it as, "*Evil resides in the Dungeon of Damnation, lair of The Undertaker who reaps each tortured soul who passes through his cunning hands, all for his own cruel pleasure. Tread carefully through this putrid pit of eternal suffering - even the living are not safe.*" A foul world of gothic dungeons and caves awaited patrons at this house. Ushered in by the sub-icon The Undertaker, the house depicted a Hell-like environment where heated rooms saw scores of scareactors tortured for their souls. Rotating set pieces, ascending spikes and large grinders all gave a kind of *SAW* meets the medieval feel. It was an impressive house that once again made good use of this large soundstage space.

Death Valley was presented in the Sting Alley section of the park. This outdoor maze featured a number of tormented ghosts who came from the bodies of dead people who had got caught up in the cross-fire of a local gangsters' shootout. The third and final maze would be located partly inside the *Waterworld* queue building with *Insanitarium* (mostly built within a 'sprung' tent). Run by sub-icon Doctor Dementia, it would be a mixture of last year's mad scientist scarezone (reusing some of the props) but was presented inside an insane asylum where a number of violent offenders have taken residency. Inside, guests witnessed a number of human experiments as the demented doctor tested out his new 'theories' on scores of hapless victims. One unique feature that appeared in this house was in one room towards the end, where a big scare was undertaken. It used volts of faux electricity to make guests get really jump scared, and then a camera was hidden to flash and capture guests' reaction as the scare occurs. Once at the end of the house, guests could purchase their copy of the photo, much like you can on most daytime attractions in the US parks; making this a unique and nifty souvenir for the paying guests.

Three scarezones were also presented, including the main icon's scarezone of *House of Dolls* in the Hollywood area (more of the park was open for this second year). These human-doll hybrids were seen intermingling with the guests as the main icon controlled them high up from a viewing platform. The scarezone was vast and very much unlike any scarezone we know in the US. Not only was it large but it was also highly themed, containing not only plenty of set pieces of miniature theaters and doll-houses but also a large cast of scareactors. It even included a photo-opportunity where guests could pose as though they were made into one of the human-doll puppets. The other scarezones included *Total Lockdown* in the New York area, which was presented as a large zombie outbreak zone. *Bizarre Bazaar* was located in the Ancient Egypt area, and featured fire eaters and stilt walkers. It was similar to the previous year but this time had a High Priest (sub-icon), with various human-cat-like hybrids prowling the streets, looking for his next victims.

2013 would start where 2012 finished off, by including fairly similar numbers of offerings yet still maintaining that original basis for ideas on how to scare the paying public. This year the *Three Sisters of Evil* were going to reunite at the event to enslave the souls of the local people (do you see a theme here?). The three were the evil Maiden of the Opera haunting in the wings, the Crone of the Forest lurking within the shadows and the Daughter of the Undead haunting amongst tombstones. Together they would be released to unleash their terror over ten full nights of horror in October and November. They would also be introduced to the public by a much larger marketing campaign that started in the late summer and attempted to not only advertise the event but to also educate people as to who this terrible sister threesome was.

The Daughter of the Undead was the youngest of the Sisters of Evil. She was a child-like vampire with a thirst for blood, who raised an army of vampires in a town named Whittemore. She would have her own scarezone, *Attack of the Vampires,* which featured this town which was now infested with hordes of blood-hungry vampires in the New York streets area of the park.

The Crone's scarezone would be located in the Lost World area and entitled *Forbidden Forest* (which was very similar to the zone of the same name from the Spanish version of the event). The storyline was that only fools venture through these woods after sunset. A grand collection of black magic awaits anyone stupid enough to enter, as The Crone eternally prowls the night for unsuspecting souls to whet her voracious appetite for souls. The zone was interesting as it contained actual magicians pulling off a variety of magic tricks, a first for this event and something that is rarely seen at the other parks. The final scarezone was *Convention of Curses* and was again located in the Egypt area, and was not unlike the zones of the past for this area.

The three mazes this year were all, yet again, hyper-detailed and the largest of them was *Adrift.* Universal billed it as, *"A storm-battered ship is found mysteriously adrift, after being lost at sea since 1910. The crew has vanished yet an unexplained presence lingers. On a ship once thought to have disappeared in the dark depths of the ocean, the past is never truly dead".* Not unlike Orlando's *Frightanic* or *Dead Waters,* this house would feature a huge impressive façade of the ship's hull with an assortment of hellish, yet very detailed, rooms for guests to explore. It was almost like what might have happened to James Cameron's *Titanic* if the ship's personnel and guests all became human-hungry-ghosts.

Songs of Death would be presented in a sprung tent over behind the Egypt area of the park. It would also serve as the co-icon The Maiden of the Opera's lair. This theater of death would feature a cast of ghost-like geishas and clowns who are controlled by the icon to extract the souls of the visiting public. Throughout the dilapidated theater a number of cramped rooms were built where scareactors could hide amongst the furniture and jump out where required.

The final maze was *House No. 13 Possessions,* which Universal billed as, *"Some say that the occupants of this crumbling mansion are recluses, but the horrific truth is they are imprisoned here by Evil Spirits. Their dream home is just a memory. Enter if you dare – but brace yourself for a house-viewing like no other as the tables have turned!"*

Located near the *Waterworld* entrance in a sprung tent, the house would act as an experience where you had to survive the scarezone of the *Forbidden Forest* in order to make it to the maze. Before entering, a Realtor gave guests an introduction to the house, the concept being that you are prospective buyers to this mansion, and the ghosts inside do not want you coming in to disrupt their dealings.

The only show presented this year was *Monster Rocks,* where the ghost with the most, Beetlejuice attempted to reanimate the infamous *Universal Classic Monsters* in this rock-n-roll musical; think the Orlando daytime show but with more current hits and you get the general idea.

Their fourth event would use the ingredients that worked well in the previous years and seek to develop these concepts in order to create better storylines and even more scares. One of the most popular aspects was the use of original characters that the guests could identify and want to learn more about.

This year would be no different as the debut of The Minister of Evil would be the headlining icon of the event. Looking like a cross between a character from *Street Fighter* and a creature from the *Lord of the Rings,* he sought to assert his authority on the event by controlling the horrors that awaited guests. Military hero Jonah Goodwill (his name prior to his transformation) had been elected to become the first World Leader, with his opponent, finance titan Walter Bale losing by an electoral landslide. At the world leader's inauguration, many protesters gathered, all of them shouting out Goodwill's name and calling him a tyrant and an evil monster. When he took to the stage, the mob booed and shouted at him, trying to get past riot police squads. Ignoring the crowd and waving to his supporters, Jonah announced, "*Citizens of the world, you were wise to elect me! I hereby stand as the first World Leader! Submit to my rule, and we will rise FOR ETERNITY!*" Suddenly, two protesters broke through and opened fired at the newly elected ruler. Suddenly, the man stood up and revealed his true form: a horned demon with huge, bat-like wings. With a snap of his fingers, he set the two protesters on fire and declared that his rule has begun. And his rule would begin at *Halloween Horror Nights 4.* But he wouldn't be ruling on his own...

Step forward HHN's very own version of *Mickey Mouse,* Jack the Clown. Jack would be brought over to Singapore for the first time to head up his house called *Jack's 3-Dementia* located in the New York area. It would also be the event's very first 3D outing and their very first comical house. The house was very similar in style, content and layout as Jack's house from 2007 (for those that remember it, it was called *Jack's Funhouse in Clown-O-Vision*). It was neon in palette and filled with carnival-styled scares, from mirrored walls to wacky ball-pits filled with putrid mutant rats. Surprise scares from black-suited scareactors making the walls move or decks of cards fly past your face were all complemented by copious appearances of the maniacal clown popping up throughout nearly every room.

The next house would be *Jing's Revenge* and would be built on the idea of Asian-themed haunted house format that had been popular over the last few years at this event. The house's storyline would take place inside a haunted school where a lonely student named Jing would commit suicide and then ten years later return to haunt the school that had let her down. The house was quite contentious due to its content with a few media outlets questioning its appearance at the event. Whereas the Jack house was in-your-face from the moment you stepped in, this house was eerily quiet and demanded some big scares in the moments of reflection to the student who took her own life. Eventually, the eerie atmosphere was replaced with scenes that could have come from *Carrie* where various bullies and evil teachers finally meet their bloody ends.

Mati-Camp would be the icon's house and featured a number of military personnel who had become possessed. There were a large number of water effects and at the very end featured a wholly pitch-black room that was terrifying enough. The final house would be *The L.A.B - Laboratory of Alien Breeding: Now recruiting new test subjects*. The house was like a combination of a horrific *Doctor Who* episode, *Alien* and *Tron*. Unlike anything the US parks have ever done, this house was packed (quite literally) with a huge assortment of weird and wonderful aliens, all with one common theme: they were all blood hungry and dangerous. From exploding alien eggs, 'acid' (really just water) spraying aliens and vast numbers of jump scares, this house was unique in its design and judging by guest reactions it appeared to be vastly popular. And it wasn't just this house that was popular; the whole event by this time appeared to grow from its 'cult like' status, appealing to the locals and Singaporeans and to a wider international audience. So much so, this year would now feature *Frequent Fear Passes* for the first time, to meet the demand of the haunt fans who wanted to come every night of the event.

Four scarezones would be presented this year with Jack not being the sole international delivery package that Orlando passed to Singapore. The other addition straight from Orlando was *Scary Tales*. The theme was easily retrofitted into their popular Forbidden Forest scarezone, where the Asian legends were all sidelined for the more foreboding *Grim Fairy Tales*. The next most popular scarezone and possible the most terrifying they had ever done, seemed to blur the line between house and zone to great effect. That zone was *Bogeyman,* and it was presented in and around the Sting Alley area. It was entered via a series of wardrobes that signaled its start and once inside the free-roaming area, guests would be confronted by a number of childhood nightmares, including: demented dolls, scarecrows and actors portraying 'strangers', all of which combined to find the souls of people who went missing as children. It kind of had a *Shining* vibe but, set in this demented other world where these mini-scarezones combined to create one larger experience, it was very effective.

Demoncracy would be the next zone and it, too, would mix things up. This time, it would mix the scarezone idea with a show, to create a new hybrid entertainment offering. The setting would be the ruins of New York where the Statue of Liberty has been broken up and lay decaying on the ground, with her new torch being lit to herald in a new era of evil. The zone would be the event icon's zone and it would be used to give him a stage show that worked within this area. The show was an elaborate exorcism show that was only ten minutes long but helped add to the scares hidden in this huge zone. The final scarezone was *Canyon of the Cursed* which used many of the sets and props from the vampire zone from last year. It was very similar to Orlando's *Ghost Town* (but in zone form), where the former inhabitants of an old mining town out west have come back to life to wreak havoc on the living.

The one main stage show this year would not be dedicated to our new supreme world leader but to our very own showman, Jack the Clown, with *Jack's Nightmare Circus*. Our popular icon had apparently fled the US to set up his new show in Singapore and it also looked as if he had taken much of the artwork from his 2007 show with him! Setting up here, he hoped to find new stars for his new carnival show. Accompanied by his wicked clown crew (with one female clown looking a lot like *Chance!*), Jack held auditions for three hopeful acts, but instead decides to kill them all. The show was eventful for the risque jokes and language it used, but also because of the number of stunts performed live on stage. It combined an aerial rope act, skating and jumping stunts and a death-defying acrobatic demonstration. Performed four times per night, the show used actual professional stunt performers who did not use any trickery in completing their stunts, thus making them truly death-defying. Ironically, though, they technically weren't *that* death-defying as Jack would slaughter them all, one-by-one, four times every night!

The event this year would be wildly popular with the hotel stays and gate numbers allegedly being very high. The merchandise availability and selection was also increased with a great improvement on what fans could buy, including: shot glasses, more tees, and even jackets.

2015 would roll around and instead of creating their own icon yet again, the designers in Singapore decided to expand on some urban legends to create a buzz for the event. The idea was to expand on the legends and prophesies behind the 'blood moon' of 2015. The blood moon prophecy was a series of apocalyptic beliefs promoted by various Christian ministers and some websites, which stated that a 'tetrad' would appear in 2015. A 'tetrad' is a series of four consecutive lunar eclipses, all apparently coinciding with various Jewish holidays, which, when combined, would make six full moons in between, and no intervening partial lunar eclipses. Various verses in the Bible were cited as backing up this belief, with the finale of this process occurring with a lunar eclipse on September 27–28th, 2015, which was exactly one week before the opening of the event. The idea behind the 'blood moon' was that the world might end, and it would be this doomsday prophecy that the designers would use to great effect at the event.

Singapore had surveyed people over the previous year and found that local Asian-inspired legends and ghost were of much more interest than the traditional western horrors that had been presented in the previous year. *"What we're really finding is that the local and the regional guests love to come and pay and get scared, and spend the night and do everything that you would think you wouldn't want to do,"* said Jason Horkin, Vice President of attractions at Resorts World Sentosa to CNBC. *"The locals don't really get scared from the Western ghost. They like the more Asian stories, so this year, we have very Singapore stories as well as more Asian themes."*

One of the most interesting houses this year would be *True Singapore Ghost Stories - The MRT, which* would headline the event. Designed with some help from local author Russell Lee, who had sold millions of his books to local Singaporeans about native ghost stories, he would be on hand to ensure a nightmare-like experience was had by all. Guests would enter into Lee's latest book, available exclusively at the event, where the main story was about a railway station being developed on a local cemetery. The Blood Moon had awoken an ancient curse set by a village witch doctor, causing the cemetery to re-emerge once again, partly destroying the new station. The house was interesting as it took, yet again, another vernacular twist on an old Hollywood-type story but made it fun and relevant to the local guests. It was also quite interesting in its design, as time would jump between decades and centuries to tell the story. To make this work, guests would walk down tunnels and feel as if they were being transported through time to the next room. The other final twist that this house had to make it very unique was that it was based 'on a true story' as the Bidadari

Station that it recreated for the house was actually built on an ancient cemetery (much to great local frustration) only four years previously. The combination of building a house set within re-creations of real buildings and using legends based on actual local history was very fascinating, and it ensured the house was by far the most popular house of the year.

Siloso Gateway Block 50 would be the zombie house for this year and would be based on a supposed 'virus' that had been released on guests during the event. The house would be built in the enormous Soundstage 28 and would be a series of smaller dwellings resembling a street where infected residents are being removed by the authorities. It was also quite remarkable as it was the first house in their history to feature indoor rain effects, with the concept being that perhaps the virus was not in the water but actually in the rain.

Hell House was up next and it would also be another heavily Asian-orientated house. The idea here was that an offering of your worldly goods had to be made to enable a favorable afterlife, as those that could not or refused would be sent to the *Hell House*. A highly-decorated Asian castle façade hid a labyrinth of rooms where paper dolls had come to life to torture the living in a weird nightmare-styled manor house.

Tunnel People would be next, and it would be located and set in New York. The idea was that a band of mutant folk living in the sewers of New York have been beckoned out by the Blood Moon to take control of New York City. The majority of the house would be set underground and for that it would become Singapore's very first 'dark house' (a house where little to no light exists); Orlando had experimented with this concept a few times but with very little success. The same could be said here, as the combination of Singapore increasing their merchandise offerings by this point to include lots of glowing and flashing goods ensured that hardly any visit was in total darkness.

Three scarezones would be offered this year. *The Invaders* would be a fun scarezone based loosely on their previous house featuring aliens. Guests would be thrust into the middle of firefights between the *UGMF* and *The Horde*, an alien race that is invading Earth under the cover of the lunar eclipse. The sound effects and the set designs made the zone feel like a living video game, and it was said to have been a lot of fun.

ConTERMINATED would be next and it would be a combination yet again of part house, part zone, due to the large, yet confined layout it was created in. Unlike *Bogeyman* from 2014, it was notably larger as *Bogeyman* had experienced queues of people trying to enter (who queues for a scarezone!?). This time that would not happen, as it was large enough for everyone. The story was of the diseased and dying folk who had been moved to a secret location to keep them away from the healthy, living people.

Finally, they presented *Hungry Ghosts,* which was a recreation of a Chinese village that has become possessed by a horde of the dead, who were hell-bent on seeking their revenge on the living. Using the footprint of the *Forbidden Forest,* the designers used the Blood Moon theme to redesign this scarezone with dead Chinese people hiding amongst the trees and shacks in the forest area – it was quite a chilling zone! Due to the increased number of designs and increased number of scareactors, no new shows were developed for 2015.

For 2016 the team at Singapore decided to go back to the drawing board and design their own icon yet again, with that icon being Lady Death. Her design would be inspired by 'Dia de los Muertos' (Day of the Dead) festival held in Mexico. She would feature her own scarezone, *March of the Dead* along with an adjoined procession type show and a nightly *Opening Scaremonies* show, all inspired by the ghostly Mexican festival with a peppering of Hollywood's *La Llorona.*

Bodies of Work house would be presented in the *Waterworld* queue and was billed as, "*Join artist Damien on his trip down memory lane as he unveils his latest exhibition, and witness all the blood, sweat and tears it took to create his final and most complete bodies of work.*" The house would be a twisted take on an art gallery-come-artist's studio, where various people from the artist's life have been mutated and maimed in the name of art. *Hawker Centre Massacre* would be presented in a temporary building behind New York. This would feature a so-called wholesome meal at the Centre, before the banquet becomes a horror feast as food poisoning turns the dinners into savage, flesh-eating monsters; think gross-out styled horror in a supermarket (which is what they call Hawker Centres in Singapore).

Another Asian-inspired house would be up next with *Hu Li's Inn,* described as "*Step inside Hu Li's Inn, set in the swinging 1930s of Old Shanghai. Your fate is in the hands – or should we say, claws? – of these beautiful nocturnal beasts.*" Seductive young hostesses entice guests into this expensive-looking period nightclub, before them transforming in front of your eyes into wickedly devilish looking creatures who wanted to suck the guests' blood. The set design for this house alone was very impressive! *Old Changi Hospital* would be located in a tent behind the *Jurassic Park River Adventure* where visitors would encounter, "*Patients who don't know they are dead. Soldiers who still scour the wards for enemies. Empty morgues that are not really empty. All these and more await at the iconic Old Changi Hospital...*" Very similar in scope to the *MRT* from last year, it would be a series of ghost stories set in a familiar setting. The final house would be *Salem Witch House* located in a sprung tent in the New York area. It promised to be a "*Maison Deux-Six, the witch house of the Defeo Witches in Salem, [which] has stood untouched and abandoned since 1692. But a group of modern-day witchcraft enthusiasts have awakened something within.*" Using many of the fables from *Scary Tales* as its inspiration, it would be a series of room depicting a number of nightmare-like fairytales. One interesting idea here was to have a room which required entry via a door. Once through the door, guests were 'blinded' with bright white light, scaring them with light rather than with the usual darkness, which was an interesting concept.

There would be two scarezones and two shows this year. The first was the previously mentioned *March of the Dead* which was a recreation of the huge Mexican festival, but this time with actual ghosts! The other would be quite contentious, with *Suicide Forest* a new tale on the *Forbidden Forest* from years past. The main show was basically an add-on to the *Day of the Dead* theme but the other show was off-theme, but was back by popular demand. *Jack's Recurring Nightmare Circus* was brought back featuring everyone's favorite clown in a new stage show. It stuck to the previous format of circus acts competing for their lives while Jack acts as ringmaster and judge on their collective fates (he was wearing his 2015 garb from Orlando). Interestingly, the designers were quoted as saying that in the previous edition of the show, the main female clown was in fact Chance, but she was missing from this year's show as she had *"travelled to Orlando to head their event"*, which she actually did in 2016. Another interesting fact for this year was that the RIP tours were extended to include visits to the makeup center to show guests how the performers are made up into the various characters.

Fans yet again thoroughly enjoyed the original characters and stories from which the event derived, so much so that for 2017 the whole process would be incredibly upscaled to meet demand. Revealing in August of that year, the event would be dedicated to the *Seven Deadly Sins*, and this unique idea themed each attraction to one of the sins. These were: Malice, Narcissism, Cruelty, Manipulation, Obsession, Perversion and Deception. Each of the sins also were also represented by one of The 7 Sinisters, who acted as the joint icons of the event: the house *Death Mall* had Malice, the house *Make the Cut* had Narcissism aka the Raven, the *Terrorcota Empress* house was Cruelty with Empress Qing, the *Hex* house was Manipulation with the sinister Midnight Man, *Inside the Mind* house represented Obsession with the Lord Obsession, *Happy Horror Days* was a scarezone with Perversion and Father Time, while scarezone *Pilgrimage of Sin* had all 7 icons within it.

One of 2017's icons for the event

Laboratorium was a show featuring Deception with *Doctor White*, and the *Slice of Life Tour* was a finale show featuring Narcissism and a few characters from *Make the Cut*. *Sting Alley* this year would also feature a scarezone that was by additional charge only, where a futuristic version of *Zombie Laser Tag* had been built. This upcharge zone, though, divided opinion. *"Our teams have put together the latest in technology, science and stagecraft into this year's edition to create truly original scares and the best entertainment for guests,"* said Jason Horkin to Channel News Asia. *"This is the most technologically advanced edition with an all-new zombie laser tag that combines brainwave technology for the most immersive experience. This year's theme is among the most disturbing ones, drawing upon seven new incarnations of deadly sins to reflect the zeitgeist of today's society where people are preoccupied with individualism, beauty and power."*

For 2018 the event would technically have its very first western movie as its central theme and main haunted house, with *Stranger Things*. Apparently, the *Netflix* show is incredibly popular locally, so it will be interesting to see how this house is not only created but how it ties into their usually very original houses and local legends-centric event.

HHN Japan

The next Universal destination to get in on the *Halloween Horror Nights* fun would be *Universal Studios Japan*. The park would be the first theme park under the Universal Studios branding to be built in Asia. Opened in March 2001 (9 years before Universal Singapore) in the Osaka Bay area, the theme park occupies an area of 39 hectares, making it, too, relatively small when once again compared them to the US Parks. It is, however, the most visited amusement park in Japan after *Tokyo Disney Resort*. The park currently has eight sections, including: *Hollywood, New York, San Francisco, Jurassic Park, Waterworld, Amity Village, Wonderland* and *The Wizarding World of Harry Potter*. Guests are able to enjoy many rides, ranging from kid-orientated amusements to more thrilling roller coasters and simulators based on many of the popular movies and franchises which are represented in other Universal parks. USJ is also interesting in that it has the last and final working version of the *Jaws* ride (excluding the jumping carrot-toothed Bruce at Hollywood's Tram Tour).

Originally, the Osaka Universal Planning Inc. was formed to create, design and build the Japanese theme park with a master licensing agreement agreed in the 1990s with MCA, the former owners of Universal Studios. Various buy-outs and sell-offs, including a short period with Goldman Sachs as a significant shareholder, would eventually lead to ComCast (Universal's current parent firm) buying the remaining shares in 2017. This enabled the park and surrounding investments to all be run under the same company as the US parks.

Halloween events would begin at the park not long after construction. The yearly events would mostly be child-centric and would focus their activities on trick or treating, which would be a departure for a nation that does not usually follow this 'western' tradition. The main attraction in these early Halloween events was the "*Sorcière Show*" (or Witch/Magic show) where a cast of 90 performers from London would be drafted in to create a circus show- come-audience experience. The show featured stage performers and walkaround characters including:

witches, jack o'lanterns, buffalos (yep?), black swallowtails, lizards, crows, owls, bats, butterflies and even spiders, which would perform acrobatics and illusions to entertain the crowds. This tradition would continue until 2007, so here we shall consider only the new additions to the event each year, as many of the houses and zones are repeats with just minimal alterations.

Despite what the records online say, the very first event to use the HHN branding would be held in 2011. It would be a fusion of Universal's *Mardi Gras Celebration* and *Halloween Horror Nights* to create a fun event that would appeal to all ages. The typical Mardi Gras parade would be held through select areas of the park and the rest of the park would see one giant scarezone of brain-hungry zombies freely roaming around (exactly 100 scareactors were employed for each night). Other attractions included a *Masquerade Ball* in Venice where vivid and colorful floats appeared. Strangely, the masks used in the masquerade ball as their motif featured *Hello Kitty* (yep?). A costume party was held with host Woody Woodpecker, and a carnival inspired by the South American Rio carnivals was another popular attraction. This also featured Elmo, the Cookie Monster and other *Sesame Street* characters wearing gorgeous costumes, all set to rhythmic Latin-inspired music.

It would be 2012 when the first true edition of *Halloween Horror Nights* was announced. This followed hot on the heels of a huge announcement that a certain boy wizard would be opening with a new land and attraction, making his Asian park debut in 2014. The event would be announced as *Universal Surprise Halloween* and would take place on selected nights from September 14th to November 11th (which is an incredibly long run when compared with other sister parks). The reason behind the different name was that this seasonal event would be parkwide and aimed at all guests. During the day, daytime guests would be offered trick or treating, *Parade De Carnivale* (their version of the Mardi Gras parade) and other seasonal activities. Then at night, the park would be adapted and fitted out to become *Halloween Horror Nights*. USJ has used the same 'umbrella' term for their fall festivities and nightly setup regime for most of their past Halloween events since.

Despite the program of events running to the above setup, there would be some crossover and many of the haunted houses would (and some still do) open as early as 10am. The Mardi Gras parade would be held every 40 minutes and would be located between the Hollywood and New York areas. The trick or treating would also be located in the *Wonderland* area (these areas were deemed as the areas for 'persons with nervous dispositions') and the rest of the park would be dedicated to *Halloween Horror Nights*.

The press release read, *"As night falls, an "Halloween Horror Night" begins, the normally bright and lively Studios transforms into a place of screams and horror. We present three horror events, including "Resident Evil", "Jason" from* the world - shaking and unbelievably popular *"Friday the 13th"*, and *"The Mummy Museum II"*, themed on the film series *"The Mummy"*. These 'events' would be houses and they would be located around the park in areas not considered to be for the 'faint at heart'.

High resolution projectors, audio and lighting, and special effects transformed the Gramercy Park area of the theme park into a large scarezone, all themed to the popular video game franchise (and not film franchise) of *Resident Evil*. All the popular monsters from the games were represented, and even puppets were deployed to create versions of the virus-infected dogs. The other unique addition that this zone brought was using trained Parkour specialists (the urban discipline of scaling walls and free running). These were made up as zombies to scale the walls of the event and it added another dimension of terror to see these fast moving 'zombies' climbing walls and jumping overhead.

Camp Crystal Lake would be presented as the main haunted house for this year and would feature scares from the *Friday 13th* movie of 2009. Recreations of many of the sets and various iconic scenes from the movie were played out inside one of the large soundstages. The second and final haunted house this year was a beefed-up version of *The Mummy Museum*. This was an attraction opening in the spring of that year as a form of walk-through Mummy exhibit with scareactors, to celebrate Universal's centenary. The attraction was very similar in scope as Hollywood's *House of Horror* but contained a mixture of film props and some real-life exhibits based on Ancient Egypt. Given the themed merchandise, special nightly 'haunted' menus, specially created cocktails (including one with eyeballs floating in it) and re-dressings of some of the rides (they put some scareactors into Jaws, RIP the Shark in the Dark!), the event would be a huge success.

In 2013 the event was largely the same with the addition of a house based on *The Rings* film series entitled *Sadako,* which would reappear for two further editions of the event. In 2014, the same houses would appear but swopping out *The Mummy Museum* guests would get their first comedic house with *Chucky's Horror Factory. The* event was admittedly a more muted affair due to the opening this year of their version of *The Wizarding World,* however, the event would return in style in 2015.

HHN Japan's scarezones can be very intense with scares!

For 2015, four houses would be presented including: *Sadako* (a repeat), A *Nightmare on Elm Street, Chucky's Horror Factory 2* and *Alien vs. Predator* (which had appeared in previous years in the US parks).

The press release for the latter reminded us that, "*Alien vs. Predator, a popular*

Hollywood film, was released in 2004 and featured a showdown between two species of creatures. Now, they appear at the Park for the first time. In a laboratory that has become an Alien den, guests are drawn into a battle between the cruel, inhuman Aliens and the ferocious, elusive Predators. During this fierce battle, the targets are transformed into hunters that are thoroughly focused on taking the guests' lives! This chilling attraction, which reproduces the movie at a stunning quality and scale, will allow guests to experience the despair of trying to escape and having nowhere to run."

For those that attended, the house was designed around the plans drawn up for the Orlando event, so if you attended Orlando that year you have some idea as to what this house was like. It mixed scareactors with puppets in confined laboratory-type spaces to create some genuinely terrifying scares. *The Nightmare on Elm Street* house was a particular fan favorite for this year. Loosely based on the original movie from 1984, it would have an interesting layout that was, for most of the house, completely in darkness. Instead, guests would be pulsed through (not in a conga line) and would need to hold onto guide ropes to enable them to find their way. Once inside, various scenes from the movie were recreated, though most of the best scares came from rooms that did the opposite. And strangely, most of the actors portraying Freddy in this house were allowed to speak (and shout), all of which was done in English.

Two interesting shows were performed this year, making way for the carnival and circus styled shows of the past. These two shows were incredibly terrifying! *Gakkō no Kaidan* (or Haunted School) was performed in the park's cinema where this famous Japanese horror series appeared as a 4D experience. Guests witnessed familiar stories unravel from the world of Gakkō no Kaidan, including Hanako, a young girl who haunts school bathrooms, and Kuchisake-onna, a malicious spirit with a slit mouth. The video and seats were linked, with special effects to create an eerie phenomenon with an astonishing sense of realism that left some guests petrified. The other show was *Trauma: The Experimental Hospital Ward of Horror*, which was advertised as a 10/10 on the horror scale. It was presented inside Soundstage 18 from midday onwards, and would feature a historical psychologist conducting experiments to see how much fear humans can withstand. Here, guests would witness many gut-wrenching experiments and were forced to follow erratic instructions from the guards. This attraction was a new type of "forced" interactive show-come-maze experience, where guests who accepted the possibility of experiencing mental trauma would be allowed to participate. They were also required to sign a waiver and purchase this experience at a separate cost; no park on any continent has ever produced such a terrifying experience for any HHNs! The show/maze was a mixture of both, and was designed for groups of six people at a time only. They would work together to navigate a large dark maze (complete with flashlights) and were 'forced' to do various sickening tasks such as searching through real animal entrails or having live insects put on their faces. Disturbing images, and allowing the scareactors to 'touch' and manhandle the guests, were also a part of this unique experience. Apparently, other Halloween events nearby also do similar 'extreme houses' so Universal were supposedly compelled to add this experience to compete with the other attractions locally. The experience would also return for 2016 where portions of the maze were replaced with VR elements and the show would begin with everyone in each team being strapped to an operating table!

Other additions for the 2016 season would be the house *Tatari*. Translated loosely as the 'cursed area', the house would be themed on the Shinto (a traditional religion of Japan) belief of how malevolent spirits walk the earth to seek objects they can inhabit. The idea of this house was that the *Tatari* would be a possessed doll that, if looked directly in the eye, could cause the victim to be cursed for life. Utilizing this central premise, the house would be stuffed full of scareactors portraying the doll with their soul ambition to get into the eye-line of all guests entering the attraction. In addition to the high cast numbers, the house used digital mapping, display screens to mimic scenes and windows, and puppets and animatronics, to ensure every single guest got a good view of a doll at least once! The other big house this year was *The Exorcist* (as it was in Orlando and Hollywood too). Opening daily at midday, the house would be a weird take on the movie, in that the house from the movie would be upscaled into a full manor house. It had various rooms depicting the possession of different people, but mostly children, and the house would utilize scenes from the movie but with increased grossness (oh yes!) and with other, additional scenes. It was advertised widely on social media and on local media outlets as an

11 on the scale of 1 to 10 for how scary the attraction would be.

One of the biggest shows from this year, and something that made all Harry Potter fans feel very envious, was *Death Eater Attack* that was held in the newly-opened *Wizarding World of Harry Potter*. When night fell, this peaceful, cheerful world of magic would transform into a feared land of dark magic with the *Death Eaters* appearing throughout *Hogsmeade*. Wearing black hoods and masks, the devilish gang of wicked wizards would perform a mini show and mingle with the crowds. The area would also receive a new themed dessert party with *Hallowe'en Dessert Feast*, where a selection of the desserts inspired by *Harry Potter and the Philosopher's Stone* would make an appearance. These included: a mountain-shaped chocolate ganache treat, carrot cake, traditional English custard creams (a form of cream filled cookie), and a selection of various Japanese candies. Savory dishes would also be sold including a juicy pork rib platter with a pumpkin au gratin.

Horror and fun are mixed to new levels in Japan!

2017 would roll around and the event would be expanded to its largest yet. Seven houses would be presented with returning, yet refurbished, favorites such as: *Cult of Chucky* (themed on the new movie), *A Nightmare on Elm Street 3* (but not themed to the first movie), *The Exorcist* as this was by far the most popular attraction of 2016, *Trauma 3* (the upcharge extreme house that this year featured guests getting lost in a torturous haunted prison) and *Sadako* (The Rings inspired house). The two new houses were *Deadman's Forest* and *Gakkou no Kaidan*.

Deadman's Forest, which was inspired by the part-house, part-scarezone from Singapore would utilize the same footprint but in a slightly more extreme way. Situated half outdoors and half inside the *Backdraft* attraction building, it would feature a zombie outbreak (yes, more zombies, which considering every year to date has so far had a huge zombie scarezone, the Japanese must love some zombie action!). The initial pre-show would feature various military personnel giving a debriefing on the spread of a zombie-like virus, before it gets interrupted and the soldiers are 'devoured' in front of guests. Guests would then enter the attraction where their mission was to avoid a fate similar to the army generals. The maze was very well done as they specially planted and built a mini-forest for guests to explore, which was well-themed and staffed generously with great scareactors.

Gakkou no Kaidan would be next and it would be themed on the movie of the same name. Literally meaning 'stories from the haunted school', the premise was again inspired by popular houses from Singapore. 'Breaking-in' to the school after dark, guests would experience the various scenes from the popular movie that would feature various nightmarish situations as inspired by the school kids of the picture. Pre-entry screens reminded guests of the central plot, that there were rumors that the school was haunted, and that strange things occurred around 4:44am. Clocks that read this time were pictured as guests entered. Once inside a number of dark rooms showcasing the spirits of the 'missing children' and demonic teachers were all featured.

The 2017 event was yet again heralded as a huge success because of its mixture of popular returning houses, both new western and local IP use, and scares for everyone within their wider fall festival.

About The Author

Christopher Ripley was born in the UK but has been traveling to and living in the US for many years. He has been attending both Universal Studios Florida and Hollywood for over 20 years. He authored his first book in 2015, *Halloween Horror Nights: The Unofficial Story & Guide*, which went on to become a bestseller. Since then he has set up the wildly popular HHN Blog hhnunofficial.com, become a co-presenter of the *ScareZone Podcast* (a dedicated HHN podcast) and *Dis After Dark* (the Europe/UK's number one downloaded Florida theme parks podcast). He has also ghost written a number of books and articles and has a further four books in the pipeline all related to Universal Studios coming soon.

And remember, as his pal Logan always says *"keep your eyes closed and your ears open – we'll see you at Finnegan's!"*

Other Books By The Author

Made in United States
Orlando, FL
09 December 2024